LIBERALISM AND ITS DISCONTENTS

Liberalism and Its Discontents

Patrick Neal
Associate Professor of Political Science
University of Vermont, Burlington

NEW YORK UNIVERSITY PRESS
Washington Square, New York

© Patrick Neal 1997

First published in the U.S.A. in 1997 by
NEW YORK UNIVERSITY PRESS
Washington Square
New York, N.Y. 10003

This book is printed on paper suitable for recycling and
made from fully managed and sustained forest sources.

Library of Congress Cataloging-in-Publication Data
Neal, Patrick, 1955–
Liberalism and its discontents / Patrick Neal.
p. cm.
Includes index.
ISBN 0–8147–5796–0
1. Liberalism. I. Title. ̄
JC574.N4 1997
320.51—dc21   97–8084
                                                        CIP

Printed in Great Britain

For Granny, Mom and Diane
Three Extraordinary Women

Contents

Acknowledgments

With good luck, there will be other books to write, but I'm not taking any chances. So I shall not pass up this opportunity to publicly acknowledge and express my thanks to the friends, teachers, colleagues and students who have helped in various ways to teach me how to think and write about the matters discussed herein. Robert DiClerico and William S. Haymond, at West Virginia University, made me love the study of ideas. Ed Andrew, Christian Bay, Asher Horowitz, Ron Replogle, Joe Fletcher and Brad Adams at the University of Toronto, helped me learn how to study them. David Paris and Ted Eismeier, at Hamilton College, taught me the appropriate way to treat ideas, by helping me learn the art of teaching. Alan Wertheimer and Bob Pepperman Taylor, my friends and colleagues in political theory at the University of Vermont for the past eight years, have been not only intellectual instructors but also, and perhaps more vitally, sources of constant support and encouragement. I also wish to acknowledge the help and support of Candace Smith, Fritz Gaenslen, Tom Rice, John Burke, Richard Alway and Charley Bockway. I am grateful as well to the students I have known in a decade of teaching; they have been my companions in thinking through the ideas and issues raised in this book, and have been more than liberal in their willingness to bear my inadequacies.

The essays comprising this book were written over nearly a decade, a time during which I quite literally grew up, at least to the degree I am likely to. I have no way to fully express my gratitude to my wife Diane and my children Brendan, Derek and Laura, my teachers in life's ways and wonders.

I am grateful to the following journals for their permission to reprint the essays which appear here. My thanks to *Polity*, for chapters 2 and 6; *Canadian Journal of Philosophy* and the University of Calgary Press for Chapter 3; *Review of Politics* for Chapter 4; *Political Theory* and Sage Publications for Chapters 5 and 9; *Social Theory and Practice* for Chapter 7, and *Legal Theory* for Chapter 8. I am also grateful to the Graduate College of the University of Vermont for financial support which aided in the preparation of this material.

"Liberalism and Neutrality," *Polity*, vol. 17, no. 4 (Summer, 1985), pp. 664–84.
"A Liberal Theory of the Good?," *Canadian Journal of Philosophy*, vol. 17, no. 3 (September, 1987), pp. 567–82.
"In the Shadow of the General Will: Rawls, Kant and Rousseau on the Problem of Political Right," *Review of Politics*, vol. 49, no. 3 (Summer, 1987), pp. 389–409.

"Justice as Fairness: Political or Metaphysical?," *Political Theory*, vol. 18, no. 1 (February, 1990), pp. 24–50.

"Does He Mean What He Says? (Mis)Understanding Rawls' Practical Turn," *Polity*, vol. 27, no. 1 (Fall, 1994), pp. 77–112.

"Perfectionism with a Liberal Face? Nervous Liberals and Raz's Political Theory," *Social Theory and Practice*, vol. 20, no. 1 (Spring, 1994), pp. 25–58.

"Dworkin on the Foundations of Liberal Equality," *Legal Theory*, vol. I, no. 2 (Summer, 1995), pp. 205–26.

"Vulgar Liberalism," *Political Theory*, vol. 21, no. 4 (November, 1993), pp. 665–90.

Part I

Neutrality and the Good
in Liberal Theory

1 Introduction

Nearly half a century ago, Lionel Trilling wrote, "It has for some time seemed to me that a criticism which has at heart the interests of liberalism might find its most useful work not in confirming liberalism in its sense of general rightness but rather in putting under some degree of pressure the liberal ideas and assumptions of the present time."[1] This book is an attempt to enact a version of Trilling's program. Many of the reigning ideas of liberal political theory are challenged and criticized, though for the most part the spirit animating these criticisms is itself liberal.

Trilling referred to the "primal imagination" of liberalism as comprised of "an essential imagination of variousness and possibility, which implies the awareness of complexity and difficulty." With a prescience which stands out in retrospect, he remarked with some foreboding upon the inevitable discrepancy between this "essence" and its "particular manifestations," noting especially the "impulse to organization" which has come to characterize the manifestation of liberalism as the orthodoxy of rule in the modern bureaucratic state. This impulse, he said, "did not suit well" with the "lively sense of contingency and possibility, and of those exceptions to the rule which may be the beginning of the end of the rule" he took to bespeak the essence of the liberal spirit.

Trilling was still enough of a modernist to say "did not suit well" rather than "betrays," and the difference between the verbs marks the difference between a still hopeful, if chastened, liberalism and a more cynical rejection of it, which has come to be known under the label of post-modernism. I am not sure which perspective is the more defensible, though I believe the issue between them is of vital significance to us. Trying to think clearly about the question of, as it were, whether the letter betrays the spirit, has led me to think about things other than liberalism, and these other things now seem to me to cast a shadow on the place of liberal ideas within a more comprehensive order of reflection. But this perspective and concern is largely absent, at least consciously, from the chapters which follow. Herein, I set out to think critically about the reasons offered by leading liberal thinkers in support of the political morality they affirm, and would have us affirm. When I began to think and write about these matters I had a somewhat inchoate notion that their "completion" would be marked by some sort of decision or judgment, one which would answer with finality the question "Liberalism – Yes or No?" This turns out not to be so, though I hope that a reader moved by the desire to advance toward such an end will find sustenance here to help him or her along the way.

The chapters in the remainder of Part I take up the issue of neutrality (regarding the good) in liberal theory. This issue was made the subject of attention for liberals and their critics in an important essay, "Liberalism," written by Ronald Dworkin in 1978.[2] Dworkin's essay has probably been subjected to as much if not more critical commentary as any written by an academic political theorist in the last twenty years. Its brilliance lay not necessarily in being correct (or incorrect), but in formulating an idea of liberalism bold and sharp enough to at once both reinterpret the history of liberal thinking in a fresh and illuminating way while provoking the minds of contemporary social and political thinkers. While even Dworkin himself has now come to revise certain of the views expressed in this piece, the stimulus to reflective thought it provided continues to make it worth reading.[3]

Dworkin's distinctive idea was that liberalism could be best understood as the view that the state treated its citizens as equals just insofar as it aimed at and practiced neutrality with regard to the question of what constitutes the good life. The implicit contrast is with views that maintain that the purpose of the state is to affirm and aid its citizens in seeking the realization of some idea of the good. Such illiberal political moralities would be seen, from the liberal's point of view, as failing to treat each and every citizen with equal concern and respect, because they would allow some particular conception of the good to be embodied in the laws and institutions of the state which apply to all citizens, including of course those who might reject the view of the good affirmed by the state. Liberalism was understood by Dworkin as the rejection of such a "perfectionist" view of the state. Liberals would prefer instead to restrict the state to the task of insuring that each citizen be treated in such a way that he or she be free to pursue his or her own conception of the good, subject to the constraint that such freedom be extended to each and every individual equally.

This is a very powerful idea, and in our time and place a very entrancing one. It is, in a sense, the high theoretical expression of a common attitude in our culture – that which insists that we shouldn't "impose" our "values" on one another, but should rather "respect" the freedom of each to live as he or she pleases. Failure to embody this attitude is often taken as tantamount to being a "fanatic" who would be so pretentious as to tell others how to live. What could be more illiberal than that?

The idea is also very powerful because it appears to show that liberalism as political morality is of a different, and more deeply reflective, epistemic order than are non-liberal political moralities. From the perspective generated by the neutralist account of liberalism, liberal principles of right stand as the ordering principles for diverse and conflicting views of the good. These principles of right are treated as insulated from the ravages of intractable controversy taken to plague disagreements about the good. They are taken to form, as it were, a fair and neutral meta-perspective from which ethical disagreement might be judged and ordered in a non-partisan way. To take this view of liberalism is to take liberalism to be not "merely" one ethico-political view amongst many, all competing at the same practical and epistemic level, but rather as a meta-view "above" other views and hence capable of judging and ordering these others.

I believe that this self-understanding of liberalism is at once false, arrogant and practically dangerous. The remaining chapters in Part I are exercises in defense of these judgments. "Liberalism and Neutrality" attempts to demonstrate that no state, including a liberal state, can practice neutrality with regard to the competing conceptions of the good existent within its domain of power. My claim is not simply that states fail to achieve neutrality, but that neutrality is by its nature an unachievable goal for states. It does not follow from this that liberal political morality is wrong (or that it is right); but neutrality regarding the good cannot be the warrant for an affirmation of liberalism.

The sense of neutrality criticized in "Liberalism and Neutrality" is what has come to be labelled "neutrality of impact" in recent discussion. It is the strongest and most robust sense of neutrality at play in discussions of liberalism. A decidedly weaker, but perhaps more plausible, sense of neutrality has come to be defended by some liberals who have abandoned the idea of neutrality as impact and argue instead in support of "neutrality of reasons." Here, it is acknowledged that state action (and inaction) cannot but have a differential impact upon various conceptions of the good and the social groups pursuing them, and hence cannot but depart from neutrality of impact. As Jeremy Waldron describes this view in its original Lockean incarnation, it maintains that "the government and its officials are required to be neutral only in the reasons for which they take political actions.... They need pay no attention to the evenness of the impact of their actions on those with whom they are dealing."[4]

"Liberalism and Neutrality" criticizes neutrality of impact theories, but leaves untouched neutrality of reasons theories. "A Liberal Theory of the Good?" aims to fill this gap. A neutrality of reasons makes epistemic matters central to liberal politics. The idea requires the identification of an epistemically privileged class of reasons for political action which, it is claimed, is available to all civic actors on terms which are just and fair, without respect to the differing views of the good maintained by those actors. The specification of this class of reasons is a matter of difficulty and dispute, even among those professing faith in the general project. Some have tried to draw the line of distinction substantively, distinguishing, for example, "secular" from "religious" reasons.[5] Others have appealed to the (allegedly) non-substantive distinction between "public" and "private" reasons to define the privileged class of considerations. "A Liberal Theory of the Good?" attempts to demonstrate that such attempts to rationally ground a political ethic of what might be labelled "epistemic correctness" are misguided. My claim is that there is nothing epistemically special or superior about liberal principles, and that attempts to argue in support of the political ethic of liberalism by means of an appeal to epistemic neutrality are both flawed and distorting.[6]

The idea of autonomy plays an important role in these chapters on neutrality, as indeed it does in all the chapters in this book. But that role has changed significantly. In Part I, I more or less casually assume that the ideal of individual autonomy is one worthy of human striving and an appropriate object of political endeavor. Indeed, my view in the chapters here may be summarized as maintaining that autonomy is in fact the good to which contemporary liberalism is fundamentally committed and that liberalism would benefit from openly affirming this rather than continuing to cloak it, even if unwittingly, under the illusory guise of neutrality. The focus of the critique being upon the hiddenness of the ideal, I did not directly take up the worthiness of the ideal itself. The chapters in Parts II and III manifest an increasing amount of attention upon that ideal, and a growing sense of uneasiness about affirming its fundamental value. Asking liberals to, as it were, bring autonomy out of the closet, I imagined that the unveiling would be a cause for celebration. However, seeing autonomy openly and directly defended as the fundamental good to which liberalism is committed allowed me to begin to see, as it seems to me, some of its rougher edges and darker dimensions. This is latent, for example, throughout the first chapter in Part II, "In the Shadow of the General Will," and explicit in its conclusion. The question posed there has gripped me ever since.

The chapters in Part II turn to consider the work of the leading liberal thinker of our time, John Rawls. The first deals with Rawls' views as expressed in his famous *A Theory of Justice*. The second and third chapters concentrate upon his writings since then, writings recently collected and revised as *Political Liberalism*. The three chapters deal primarily with critically understanding the structure, form and grounds of Rawls' understanding of politics; I have little to say about the substantive political proposals (the two principles of justice) Rawls defends. I have little quarrel with the social-democratic nature of those substantive principles, though I do agree with Michael Sandel that they implicitly invoke an ontology of common fellowship as their ground which is not overtly redeemed, and may not be capable of being redeemed, within the explicit confines of Rawls' liberal theory.[7]

"In the Shadow of the General Will" concentrates upon the Kantian dimensions of Rawls' theory of justice. I argue that these dimensions are ultimately both more important for understanding Rawls' project and more plausible as grounds for it than the dimensions which point in the direction of seeing the theory (as many originally did) as an account of rational choice under conditions of uncertainty. A recent account which emphasizes this Kantian view most forcefully is Brian Barry's interpretation of Rawls as a theorist of "justice as impartiality."[8] However, I also argue that it is important to understand the precise ways in which Rawls departs from Kant on issues of political right, and to see that these departures incline him in the direction of Rousseau's account of political right given in *The Social Contract*. The chapter tries to reveal the sense in which Rawls' theory lies uneasily and unsteadily between what might be called the Kantian and Rousseauean voices of the discourse of modern autonomy and political right. The political expression of that tension is between liberalism as a reformist and a revolutionary idea.

When Rawls' theory is read through the lens of its Kantian elements, it can be seen to appear as a theory of justice invoking claims of universal scope and foundational metaphysical commitment, especially in respect to the idea of the autonomous person. There continues to be disagreement about the degree to which these descriptions are appropriate to the theory as originally advanced. However, what is perfectly clear is that in his writings since *A Theory of Justice*, Rawls overtly denies that his theory is to be understood as invoking such claims. As he puts it, the theory is now to be understood as "political not metaphysical."

The final two chapters in Part II are devoted to explicating and critically analyzing this "practical turn" in Rawls' thinking about liberalism and justice. In "Justice as Fairness: Political or Metaphysical?," I examine the precise meaning(s) of Rawls' idea of a "political" account of justice. Rawls distinguishes his idea of a political account of justice from two alternatives: a metaphysical account on the one hand and a "merely prudential" account that is "political in the wrong way" on the other. This tripartite typology of possible descriptions of his theory later becomes generalized into a typology of possible understandings of liberalism itself. On this scale, Rawls' "political" liberalism is distinguished from an account of liberalism premised upon a "comprehensive moral view" and also from "mere modus vivendi" accounts of liberalism. Rawls has tended to emphasize the contrast between his theory and metaphysical/comprehensive accounts, leaving the "prudential" or modus vivendi possibility as a relatively neglected option. This division of labor is reflected in the scholarly discussion of Rawls' work, where the predominant line of discussion is concerned with the question of whether Rawls has in fact "retreated" from the larger, metaphysical, ambitions of his original theory and the question of whether, assuming he did, he ought to have done so. Such questions are addressed in Part II, but I also try to bring into a more prominent light the virtues of what both Rawls and his more comprehensively-minded liberal critics tend to dismiss as the "mere" modus vivendi account of liberalism.

The theoretical ground which Rawls wishes to claim and occupy does not, in my view, exist. I think that Rawls' theory of political liberalism hovers unsteadily, rather than securely, between the comprehensive and modus vivendi alternatives. I attempt to show that the dominant inclination in his writings is in the direction of the comprehensive form of liberalism which he wishes to avoid. What finally keeps Rawls from fully affirming that form is, I think, an admirable concern to confront and affirm the pluralism of ways of thinking and being which increasingly characterize the modern world. Thus as I see it, this dominant inclination toward, but stopping short of, the scylla of comprehensiveness coexists with an inclination to avoid the charybdis of seeing political justice as a modus vivendi. The pull of the modus vivendi view lies precisely in its acceptance of robust diversity; justice comes to be seen on this view as a matter of pragmatically working out some common political practices amongst divergent ideas of the good and the groups who embody them. But Rawls, for numerous reasons which are taken up in Part II, refuses this conceptualization. I try to show that there is no secure theoretical resting point between the two, and hence that Rawls' conception of a "political" conception of justice is unstable. Perfectionist liberals who see their political views as part and parcel of a more comprehensive moral view tend to agree with this analytical judgment. Where I differ from them is in thinking that the modus vivendi view is preferable to the comprehensive one. They think Rawls (or liberals generally) should abandon the pretense of being neutral or merely political and go ahead and affirm comprehensive liberalism. I have come to think that Rawls (or liberals generally) should abandon the pretense of being neutral or merely political and learn to live with the chastened and minimalist politics of the modus vivendi model, a model which, as I see it, most honestly and openly faces up to the fact that not every reasonable and decent person is, or is going to be, or for that matter should be, a liberal.

The chapters in Part III turn to consider types of liberal theory which constitute alternatives to the "neutralist" and "political" liberalisms considered in Parts I and II. "Perfectionism With a Liberal Face?" analyzes the perfectionist liberal theory of Joseph Raz. Raz rejects neutralist liberalism, and develops instead a philosophically sophisticated version of liberal theory with the value of personal autonomy at its foundation. Together with his innovative account of moral pluralism, Raz's affirmation of the role of the liberal state in supporting the good makes his liberalism at once distinctive and provocative. Though I offer a number of criticisms of Raz's positions in this chapter, I admire the forthrightness with which he articulates and advances them. One great virtue of this aspect of his theory is that it provides one with a clear account of what commitments are entailed in defending and affirming a perfectionist version of liberalism. This chapter argues against such an affirmation.

The second chapter considers the theory of liberalism recently advanced by Ronald Dworkin in his Tanner Lectures.[9] Dworkin's views in these lectures are in many significant ways different from those expressed in the essay "Liberalism" referred to above, and though the subject of much less discussion (at least, so far) than the views expressed in that famous essay, I think them ultimately of greater importance and theoretical depth.

On one hand, Dworkin articulates a vision of liberalism which is at once perfectionist (rather than neutralist) and comprehensive (rather than political). To a degree greater than any other contemporary liberal thinker, Dworkin, in these lectures, boldly argues for a connection between the ethical idea of a good life and the political virtue of justice. On the other hand, a lingering neutralism infects and undermines the consistency of these claims. For even as Dworkin insists that liberalism must affirm an intimate connection between an ideal of the good and a political doctrine of justice, he attempts to articulate this ideal of the good in terms of its formal properties rather than its moral substance. His claim is that the "challenge model" of ethics is superior to the "impact model," and that liberal justice is at once connected to this account of the good (hence implying perfectionism and comprehensiveness) even as the model itself, because it is formal, does not prohibit any "significant" substantive accounts of the good (hence implying neutrality). This chapter aims at demonstrating that these dual claims cannot ultimately be made good.

Dworkin's lingering neutralism not only generates a theoretical inconsistency but leads him to distort the positions of non-liberal views in ways that inhibit rather than contribute to serious discussion of the differences at play here. The comparison with Raz is, I think, instructive. Having more decisively abandoned than Dworkin has the (as I see it, vain) aim of showing liberalism to be *the* political morality that a reasonable person will hold if she thinks about it long enough and clearly enough, Raz is not compelled to cloak his liberal commitments in the dress of neutral and universal categories. Perhaps the greatest, though not the only, virtue of this approach is that Raz does not wind up having to treat people who do not agree with him as if they were inferior in insight and intellect. Dworkin, like Rawls in his latest writings on public reason, is tempted by the thought that to reject the foundational commitments of liberal justice is to depart from reasonableness. I think this is false; I think that it is simply to depart from liberalism.

The final chapter in this part speaks in defense of a "vulgar" liberalism, a view closest to the idea of a "modus vivendi" account of political justice in Rawls' typology, and in important ways to certain aspects of Hobbes' political theory.[10] It is not by chance that affection for vulgar liberalism is expressed only after the lengthy consideration of perfectionist and neutralist types of liberalism. A sparse and desolate beachfront has little to recommend it in and of itself, but appears in a somewhat different light seen from the wreckage of a ship at sea. The virtues of a Hobbesian, modus vivendi account of liberalism are best appreciated when seen against the background of the vices arising from perfectionist and neutralist versions. Modus vivendi liberalism certainly does not constitute a political theory capable of speaking to the deepest needs of the human soul; indeed as I understand it, it openly eschews the attempt to do so and acknowledges (at least ideally) both its modest reach and its limited aspirations. The essence of the idea is that political justice is to be understood as the agreement upon terms of political procedure which can be worked out amongst the actually existent groups embodying differing accounts of the good in a given set of circumstances. The agreement is provisional and always subject to change, and is understood to be so by those who have agreed to abide by it.

Many criticisms might be levelled at this idea. I want to speak briefly to two that I take to be worthy of response by anyone who would endorse the idea of a modus vivendi account of political justice. Rawls presses the first, the claim that such an approach must fail to secure stable social unity. The key idea in this criticism is that the political agreement conceived only as a modus vivendi rather than as the "overlapping consensus" Rawls advocates will last only as long as the fortuitous balance of power making it possible in the first place persists. Rawls imagines each group in effect working to subvert the agreement by hoping to strengthen its relative power position so as to renegotiate or rewrite the terms of the political contract. In the chapters in Part II, I criticize Rawls' arguments which purport to show that his idea of an overlapping consensus escapes this problem. Still, even if I am right about that, the problem remains as one confronting the modus vivendi account.

There is a certain sense in which the criticism cannot be denied or met. I can think of no principles or account of justice which is immune from the corruption which results when such principles are utilized as means to the ends of those who seek power over others. But the critic will insist that nevertheless the modus vivendi view is especially subject to such corruption, for it appears to openly acknowledge and even legitimize this sort of behavior. However, I do not think that is the best way to understand the modus vivendi idea. If it is, that is to say, if the modus vivendi idea ultimately results in the view that might makes right and justice is whatever the powerful say it is, then I would wish to reject it as well. But I do not see why it is best understood in that way. The difference between the Rawlsian idea of overlapping consensus and the idea of a modus vivendi is *not* that the former presumes a motivating desire to seek and live by principles of justice whereas the latter does not, but that the overlapping consensus restricts the bounds of political community in a way that the modus vivendi idea does not. In the overlapping consensus idea, conceptions of the good and the groups embodying them which reject the liberal principle of political legitimacy are defined as outside the sphere of full political legitimacy. I think this is too narrow a view of pluralism to adequately capture and express what is best about the essential spirit of liberalism, that "imagination of variousness and possibility" of which Trilling spoke.

But then the critic may ask, in what sense is justice on the modus vivendi model necessarily a *liberal* brand of justice? Does not the modus vivendi idea leave open the possibility that in a pluralistic setting where liberalism is not dominant, the terms of political justice will not themselves be liberal, or at least fully liberal? It certainly does leave open that possibility, up to a point (see below). I see no reason to regret this. Perhaps that is because I see no reason to conclude that the idea of justice is fully expressed and embodied in its particular liberal formulations. But it is also because I think the spirit of liberalism itself counsels a greater willingness to risk contact, contagion and common dialogue with non-liberal modes of life than is countenanced by the idea of the overlapping consensus. In this sense, I think that the modus vivendi idea better (though certainly not perfectly) gives voice to the sense in which the spirit of liberalism points beyond the boundaries constructed whenever liberalism receives institutional expression or theoretical expression in the form of rules and principles.

I imagine that many liberals will have disagreed with my characterizations before this point, but if there be those who continue to agree, they will surely ask now that I define "the point" referred to above. For even if it be allowed that the liberal be open to meeting the non-liberal on a risky border ground where the liberal principle of political legitimacy is not presupposed as a foundational safeguard, surely, it will be said to me, you do not propose that the liberal *never* draw a line in the sand and refuse to negotiate the terms of common life, insofar as it is within his or her power to so refuse? Even liberals sympathetic to my claim that the move from overlapping consensus to modus vivendi as the self-understanding of liberalism is an appropriate one will want to know whether I am counselling unilateral disarmament, as it were, on behalf of liberals in all cases of pluralistic political difference and conflict.

As it happens, I do believe there are powerful things to be said on behalf of such a view, but I cannot say them. Thus I do not counsel unilateral disarmament, and I acknowledge that in my view there are circumstances where compromise is wrong. The class of those circumstances constitutes the point at which a modus vivendi liberal will draw a line excluding some non-liberal other from treatment as an equal except in accordance with what is mandated by his or her own liberal understanding of equal treatment, an understanding which will fail to gain the assent of the excluded. I think we should resist the temptation to tell ourselves that in so acting we act in accordance with a principle which is neutral or universally available to all "reasonable" persons, that is, we should resist the temptation to wash our hands through appeals to justification. And while the act may be understood as a necessity, I would wish to insist upon saying that justification through appeal to necessity ought never to be uncoupled from the hope, and the consciousness of hope, to be delivered from our necessities.[11]

I do not believe it is possible to specify the class of such circumstances (defining the point of exclusion) according to their formal or rational properties, and thus I acknowledge that I am unable to specify, even in principle, the boundary line beyond which I think liberals ought not go in their endeavor to be open to those unlike themselves. Perfectionist and political liberals, who espouse in different ways a clear line of demarcation in this respect, may well count this a deficiency of the modus vivendi view. In the face of such complaint, it is tempting to utilize historical examples which implicitly appeal to a shared contemporary consensus of judgment with regard to practices judged to be beyond the pale of even minimal justice in order to build up the appearance of developing one's own principled line of demarcation. The temptation is fed by the desire to avoid being labelled a nihilist. The candidates for such an enterprise (which I believe to be essentially ad hoc) are well known to all of us: slavery and Nazism top the list of evils available for construction. But I think it best to avoid this way out, and to acknowledge instead the intractable nature of the problem of identifying that which is to be denied and resisted. In regard to evil, it is moral vision of the thing itself of which we stand in need, not a theory of morality.

The critic may at this point remark that it is surely a peculiar liberalism which is unwilling to say a clear and decisive "No" to slavery or Nazism, but I think it must also be remembered that nothing is easier and cheaper than to speak such a "No" now. Some liberals, like some other human beings, did not say "No" then. And to what do we say "No" now, right now? Can a theory answer that for us? And can a theory, and the practice of such theorizing, which takes it aim to be answering that question for "us", even begin to prepare us to confront a prior question, the latent question buried beneath our righteous concern to legitimize the exercise of power – suppose "we" are the evil ones? Or should we think that unthinkable?

Modus vivendi liberalism will not be liberal enough for liberals who insist upon a doctrine yielding a clear distinction between us and them. But for those, like me, who have come to think that being a good liberal may require one to be more than a good liberal, it will be a liberalism sufficient unto the day. Whether that day is nearer dusk or dawn is not easy to say.

NOTES

1. Lionel Trilling, *The Liberal Imagination* (Garden City, N.Y.: Doubleday, 1953), p. 6.
2. Ronald Dworkin, "Liberalism," in Stuart Hampshire, ed., *Public and Private Morality* (Cambridge: Cambridge University Press, 1978), pp. 113–43.
3. This is not to say that there were not other important works articulating the idea of neutrality. Dworkin's essay gave crystallized expression to a view which may also be found most powerfully expressed in Bruce Ackerman, *Social Justice and the Liberal State* (New Haven, CT: Yale University Press, 1980); Charles Larmore, *Patterns of Moral Complexity* (Cambridge: Cambridge University Press, 1987); and John Rawls, *A Theory of Justice* (Cambridge, Mass.: Harvard University Press, 1971).
4. Jeremy Waldron, "Locke, Toleration and the Rationality of Persecution," in *Liberal Rights* (Cambridge: Cambridge University Press, 1993), p. 106.
5. See, for example, Robert Audi, "The Separation of Church and State and the Obligations of Citizenship," *Philosophy and Public Affairs*, vol. 18, no. 3 (Summer, 1989), pp. 259–96.
6. See also in this regard Larry Alexander, "Liberalism, Religion and the Unity of Epistemology," *San Diego Law Review*, vol. 30, no. 4 (Fall, 1993), pp. 763–99.
7. Michael Sandel, *Liberalism and the Limits of Justice* (Cambridge: Cambridge University Press, 1981), pp. 142–7.
8. Brian Barry, *A Treatise on Social Justice: Volume I, Theories of Justice* (Berkeley: University of California Press, 1989).
9. Ronald Dworkin, "Foundations of Liberal Equality," in Grethe B. Peterson, ed., *The Tanner Lectures on Human Values*, vol. 11 (Salt Lake City: University of Utah Press, 1990), pp. 1–119.
10. A more elaborate account of my understanding of Hobbes is in "Hobbes and Rational Choice Theory," *Western Political Quarterly*, vol. 41, no. 4 (September, 1988), pp. 635–52; a reading of Hobbes to which I am both sympathetic and

indebted is in Richard Flathman, *Thomas Hobbes: Skepticism, Individuality and Chastened Politics* (Newbury Park, Ca.: Sage Publications, 1993).
11. See St. Augustine, *The City of God* (New York: Penguin Books, 1984), Bk. 19, ch. 6, pp. 859–61.

2   Liberalism and Neutrality

One of the most attractive recent defenses of liberal politics is based upon the idea of the state acting as a neutral authority to fairly order the terms of interaction between the competing interests, both moral and material, of the various groups and individuals in society. This chapter aims to reveal the inadequacies of this idea through a critical analysis of Ronald Dworkin's articulation of it.

In a series of recent works, Ronald Dworkin has defended a coherent and powerful version of what he terms the "liberal political morality."[1] He takes a certain conception of equality to be the constitutive principle of liberalism. He argues that governments are liberal when they aim to treat citizens as equals, as distinguished from treating them equally. The core of this conception is that "government must be neutral on what might be called the question of the good life."[2] Let us refer to this principle as the neutrality thesis.

Dworkin argues that two positions widely thought to be constitutive of liberalism, a commitment to economic growth and a commitment to capitalist economic relations, are in fact derivative liberal positions, not constitutive ones. As a matter of historical fact, liberals have often endorsed both economic growth and capitalism (often in the same breath); Dworkin argues that there was, and is, no necessary reason why they must do so. In light of circumstance, liberals might (and of course do) endorse capitalism and economic growth as the chosen means to maintain and secure the more fundamental value of liberalism, treating citizens as equals by maintaining neutrality on the question of the good life. Many self-defined liberals would likely object to this account, especially those who see capitalist economic relations and liberal political freedoms as necessarily dependent upon one another (libertarians) and those who see the maximization of utility as the end of political society (utilitarians). Nevertheless, I leave the problem of descriptive adequacy aside here because I think Dworkin's conception of liberalism is potentially a more powerful and interesting one than these others.

I also consider it to be potentially more powerful than the recent attempt by Bruce Ackerman to defend liberalism upon the basis of a principle of neutrality.[3] In order that Dworkin's neutrality thesis not be confused with Ackerman's, I shall briefly explain the differences between these two notions before analyzing Dworkin's argument in detail.

Dworkin himself has devoted some effort toward distinguishing his conception of neutrality from that of Ackerman.[4] The essential difference is this: where Ackerman bases his defense of liberalism upon the principle of "neutral dialogue," Dworkin takes a certain conception of equality to be the constitutive value of liberalism, and recognizes that this value needs not only specification, but philosophical defense. In providing this specification, he is led to defend the "neutrality thesis." Note, however, that according to Dworkin neutrality is not the constitutive value of liberalism, but is rather derived from the more fundamental value of equality. For Ackerman, it is the other way around; a commitment to neutral dialogue is the constitutive value of liberalism, and any legitimate principle of equality must meet the conditions imposed by neutral dialogue. So while Dworkin's neutrality thesis is limited to the question of proper governmental responses to the question of the good life, Ackerman's principle of neutral dialogue has a much wider scope: it extends not only to governmental action in response to this question, but also to philosophical inquiry into the question itself.[5] However, it is extended in a most peculiar way, for by its very nature it rules out philosophical inquiry into the question of the good life. While Dworkin at least sees the necessity of providing a philosophical defense of liberalism as equality, Ackerman's conception of liberalism as neutral dialogue makes it impossible to provide a philosophical defense of the liberalism he values. Dworkin in effect criticizes Ackerman for articulating a conception of liberalism that presupposes moral skepticism; he describes liberalism in such a way that a defense of it is made impossible, for no defense of anything can result from skepticism.

Ackerman holds that we can reasonably accept his conception of liberalism as neutral dialogue about the struggle for power on the basis of neutral dialogue itself.

> There is a perfect parallelism, then, between the role of political conversation *within* a liberal state, and the role of philosophical conversation *in defense* of a liberal state.[6]

In this neutral dialogue, no one can claim that his conception of the good is superior to that of another, or that he is intrinsically superior to another.[7] Now if the practice in which we are engaged is the distribution of scarce resources,[8] this may not be a bad principle to follow. However, if we are to engage in the practice of philosophy, and ask *why* this is a principle worth following, it would be both absurd and circular to follow Ackerman in imposing constraints of neutral dialogue upon the practice of philosophy. Circular, because neutral dialogue needs to be defended, not presupposed. Absurd, because we cannot prove that there is no good common to all persons as such by preventing anyone from raising the question of whether there might be in the first place.[9] This is ordinarily called coercion, not argument. If we do not allow the question to be raised, liberalism as neutral dialogue wins a hollow victory; neutral dialogue legitimates neutral dialogue. If we allow the question to be asked (that is to say, if we do not suppress philosophy in the name of a liberal politics which could thereby have no philosophical defense), then liberalism must be defended. By ruling out the question at the level of philosophy, Ackerman rules out philosophy, and thereby rules out a philosophical defense of the liberalism he values. There is a world of difference between the practice of philosophy and the practice of seeking political power; between seeking knowledge and claiming power over others. To my mind, Ackerman does not fully appreciate this difference. In extending the scope of neutral dialogue and its requisite constraints from politics to philosophy, he suppresses this difference, and along with it philosophy. Ackerman is not so much a philosophical skeptic as he is a skeptic about philosophy, and it is his politics that makes him so. But how then will he defend his liberal politics to those reasonable persons who are not liberals? Or are we to suppose that all reasonable persons are liberals, or at least would be if they thought about it, as is implied in those passages where Ackerman speaks as if the alternative to liberalism were some form of authoritarianism?[10] And is that a neutral description of the alternatives?

Dworkin would thus seem to be correct in his assessment of Ackerman, and the promising character of Dworkin's work, in my view, arises from his refusal to suppose that philosophical skepticism can provide any basis for preferring liberalism to any other political morality. He sees, if somewhat darkly, that liberalism as a political morality is just that: a political morality, not its *transcendence*. Liberalism thus stands in need of a positive philosophical defense, to replace "pseudo-defenses" based upon skepticism. In the bulk of this chapter, I shall attempt to demonstrate that Dworkin does not provide such a defense, and that he and other liberals who rightly reject skepticism cannot provide such a defense so long as they understand the neutrality thesis in the way he proposes. Dworkin's defense of liberalism fails to fulfill its promise because he implicitly adopts a form of the "pseudo-defense" which he rightly criticizes Ackerman for adopting.

I shall argue that Dworkin's conception of liberalism is ultimately indefensible because it is logically and existentially impossible for governments to be neutral on the question of the good life. After critically examining Dworkin's arguments, I shall attempt to explain what would be necessary for a successful philosophical defense of the liberal political morality, and how this task might be accomplished.

THE NEUTRALITY THESIS EXPLAINED

Twentieth-century liberals and conservatives are often characterized as valuing liberty and equality differentially: conservatives emphasizing individual liberties; liberals, social equality. Radical egalitarians are thus conceived as those who value equality (to the detriment of liberty) even more than liberals, leaving liberals to occupy the happy mean. The stage is thus set for a defense of liberalism on the familiar grounds of moderation and prudence.

Dworkin rejects both this conception of liberalism and the defense implicit within. He argues that it is a particular conception of equality that forms the core of liberal political morality rather than a balance between the values of liberty and equality.[11] This conception of equality requires that government treat its citizens as equals, that is, as "entitled to its equal concern and respect."[12] It is to be distinguished from that which holds that government ought to treat citizens equally in the distribution of resources.[13] The first conception of equality, he argues, is the constitutive value of liberalism; the second may form the rationale for particular actions in a liberal polity, but only as a derivative strategy or means toward the realization of the more fundamental end of treating citizens as equals. Treating citizens as equals will not necessarily entail treating them absolutely equally in the distribution of resources. The point here is as old as Aristotle: treating unequals equally may be an unjust policy.[14]

The principle of treating citizens as entitled to equal concern and respect is open to various interpretations. Dworkin argues that it may be interpreted in two fundamentally different ways:

> The first supposes that government must be neutral on what might be called the question of the good life. The second supposes that government cannot be neutral on that question, because it cannot treat its citizens as equal human beings without a theory of what human beings ought to be.[15]

Dworkin then argues that the first interpretation (the neutrality thesis) is that which accords best with the liberal political morality. He proceeds to present an ingenious, if controversial, argument designed to show how the actual history of liberalism can be accommodated within his conceptual framework. I shall assume for the sake of argument that his account is descriptively adequate. Let us concentrate instead upon the neutrality thesis to see what may be said for and against it and, by implication, for and against Dworkin's conception of liberalism.

We must first note an important feature of the conception of treating citizens as equals which Dworkin rejects. This alternative conception, according to Dworkin, holds that "government cannot be neutral on that question (the good life), because it cannot treat its citizens as equal human beings without a theory of what human beings ought to be."[16] The verb "cannot," used twice in this passage, may be understood in either a moral or a logical sense. In the moral sense, "cannot" is another way of saying "ought not" (he cannot justifiably do X, because X is wrong), while in the logical sense it denotes impossibility (he cannot do X, because it is logically impossible to do X). Dworkin clearly uses it in the moral sense; the government ought not to be neutral on the question of the good life, because to do so would not be to treat citizens as equals, on this conception of equality. It is just this disagreement over what the government *ought* to do in regard to the question of the good life which sets liberalism apart from alternative political moralities. There is no question of logical impossibility here; if "cannot" were used in the logical sense in the passage above, Dworkin's neutrality thesis would be ruled out by his own criteria. For his conception of liberal equality to be defensible, it must be logically possible for government to be neutral on the question of the good life; otherwise, it would be otiose to raise the question of whether it ought to be neutral.

I want to argue that it is logically impossible for any government, whether liberal or not, to act in such a neutral manner. Thus I shall defend the position which Dworkin sets out as an alternative to his neutrality thesis, with this important difference: I shall take "cannot" in the logical, rather than the moral, sense. Thus to Dworkin's alternatives, I add a third.

Table 2.1: Alternative Interpretations of the Principle of
Treating Citizens as Equals

(1) NEUTRALITY THESIS	(2) MORAL NON-NEUTRALITY	(3) LOGICAL NON-NEUTRALITY
Government should be neutral on the question of the good life.	Government should not be neutral on the question of the good life.	Government cannot be neutral on the question of the good life.

The first step in my argument is an attempt to demonstrate the validity of this third position. But that in itself is not enough. As we shall see, the argument is rather straightforward and uncontroversial to the degree that Dworkin recognizes some of the same points which I shall make in support of my position. A second step is therefore necessary, and this is to demonstrate the *significance* of this third alternative for the adequacy of the neutrality thesis. Plainly, Dworkin must hold that the argument in support of alternative

3, though valid, does not undermine his neutrality thesis, for he both
recognizes the position I shall shortly explicate (alternative 3) and defends
the neutrality thesis (alternative 1). Thus the second step of my argument is
an attempt to show that the considerations raised under alternative 3 do, in
fact, undermine the neutrality thesis, to the point that there is a logical
incompatibility in holding both positions at once. We shall then be able to
see both the inadequacies of Dworkin's conception of liberalism and what
would be required to construct a more adequate defense of the liberal
political morality.

THE NEUTRALITY THESIS CRITICIZED

Why cannot government be neutral on the question of the good life? Because
governments are not merely passive receptacles which respond to autonomous
demands, interests, and preferences arising from society by coordinating and
reconciling these "inputs" and generating "outputs" in the form of public
policy. Governments play quite a significant role in shaping both the form
and content of those demands, interests, and preferences. We need not
attribute any devious or sinister motives to particular governments or
governors to account for this phenomenon. Any particular society is
constituted by specific patterns of behavior and belief (institutions) that are
maintained over time, patterns often referred to as the "social fabric." It is
the specific content of these institutions that constitutes the society as a
particular, and not some other, one. These institutions are maintained and
reproduced through socialization processes, and government, through both
its action and inaction, is perhaps the primary (though of course not the only)
agent in the process of maintaining this social fabric.

   These mundane facts are familiar enough, and Dworkin does not ignore
them, though he does seem to underestimate their significance:

   tastes as to which people differ, are, by and large, not afflictions, like
   diseases, but are rather cultivated, in accordance with each person's theory
   of what his life should be like.[17]

What needs to be added here is the recognition that the ground upon which
individual preferences are "cultivated" is the collective social fabric. A
person's theory of what his life should be like, his hopes, dreams and fears,
do not arise out of thin air. A person's conception of alternative life
possibilities is never an infinite set; it is constrained by the social context,
the form of collective life, of which he is part and from which he draws a
conception of himself and his future.

Governments play a role in maintaining forms of social life, and in doing so they necessarily inhibit the development of alternative forms. This is why government cannot, in the logical sense, be neutral on the question of the good life. Specifically, governments play a role in shaping popular perceptions of the good life through mechanisms of the socialization process. In a deeper and more general sense, they necessarily maintain some forms of life at the expense of others. In saying this, I do not wish to be understood to have collapsed "government" into "society." I should think it evident that no society can be neutral on the question of how to live, for societies *are* ways of living. One might agree and yet maintain that we should not confuse government with society, and wish thereby to rescue the neutrality thesis. However, to suppose government and society to be entirely separate is no better than to suppose them to be entirely indistinguishable. I do not maintain that government *is* the social fabric, only that it is an important part of it, and thus partakes of and sustains the particular character of that fabric. In contributing to the sustenance of one form of life, governments necessarily inhibit the development of others.

These sociological truisms would seem to call into question the neutrality thesis. Assuming the weak condition that "ought implies can," it seems peculiar to demand that governments be neutral on the question of the good life if by their very nature they cannot be. Let us examine Dworkin's reply to this line of criticism, which I quote here in full.

It is sometimes said that liberalism must be wrong because it assumes that the opinions people have about the sort of lives they want are self-generated, whereas these opinions are in fact the products of the economic system or other aspects of the society in which they live. That would be an objection to liberalism if liberalism were based on some form of preference-utilitarianism which argued that justice in distribution consists in maximizing the extent to which people have what they happen to want. It is useful to point out, against that preference-utilitarianism, that since the preferences people have are formed by the system of distribution already in place, these preferences will tend to support that system, which is both circular and unfair. But liberalism, as I have described it, does not make the content of preferences the test of fairness in distribution. On the contrary, it is anxious to protect individuals whose needs are special or whose ambitions are eccentric from the fact that more popular preferences are institutionally and socially reinforced, for this is the effect and justification of the liberal's scheme of economic and political rights. *Liberalism responds to the claim, that preferences are caused by systems of distribution, with the sensible answer that in that case it is all the more important that distribution be fair in itself, not as tested by the preferences it produces.*[18]

There are a number of important aspects to this response. First, Dworkin assumes that the thrust of the criticism to which he is responding is that "preferences are caused by systems of distribution." However, this overlooks the point that preferences ("the opinions people have about the sort of lives they want") are also, perhaps even more so, a function of systems of *production* and the relations that obtain therein. Whether or not a scheme of distribution is fair is not the whole of justice; one can also raise the prior question of whether the means used to generate the resources to be distributed, that is, the system of production and productive relations, is fair. One need not be a Marxist to appreciate the force of this point.[19] A moment's reflection suggests that what people do, and not simply what they get, is a relevant consideration in any discussion of justice. I shall have more to say about the consequences of reducing the problem of justice to its distributive aspect presently.

The essence of Dworkin's reply is contained in the concluding sentence of the quoted passage. There he both accepts a narrow version of the logical non-neutrality thesis ("preferences are caused by systems of distribution"; narrow because he reduces the sociological framework to its distributive aspect) and maintains the neutrality thesis, arguing that in light of the validity of the former it is all the more sensible to maintain the latter. What is the logic behind this position? I suggest that Dworkin's position here is tenable only if we accept an unduly narrow conception of the concept of "preferences." The concept could be understood in either of two ways in this passage, and in outlining them I hope to show why the first is unduly narrow.

(1) We take as given that in society X persons have different preferences (P) regarding the sort of life they wish to lead (G); let us say these preferences regarding the good life (PG) range from PG_M to PG_N, where the distance between M and N is inclusive of every individual preference in society X. The neutrality thesis can then be couched in the following terms: the government acts in a neutral manner insofar as through its policies and procedures it does not (or at least attempts not to) discriminate in favor of, or against, any of these particular preferences, PG_M to PG_N. In principle, the preferences of each citizen in X are subject to empirical verification; the sum total of these various preferences is constrained within the distance from M to N.

(2) Suppose, however, we focus not upon those actually existing preferences PG_M to PG_N, but rather upon those preferences which by definition do not exist in X because they fall outside the parameters M and N. These preferences

are not, of course, subject to empirical verification, because they do not exist. If they did, society X would be some different society, Y. Now one of the reasons society X is not some other society Y is because of the particular institutional patterns of which it is composed, and one of the socializing factors maintaining these patterns is the government. Thus, although the government in X may in a sense be neutral amongst the preferences PG_M to PG_N, it cannot be said to be neutral amongst the whole range of possible preferences regarding the good life (let us say PG_A to PG_Z) because it is one of the institutions defining and sustaining the particular character of X, and it thus contributes to the constraint of preferences within parameters M and N.

A simple example may help illustrate the point. Suppose society X is modern America. My conception of the good life centers around becoming a doctor, yours around becoming a lawyer. The government may or may not be neutral toward our preferences through its distribution of opportunities and resources. But what about Ralph, who wishes to lead a virtuous life but feels he cannot do so in an industrialized nation-state of two hundred million people; his preference is for a small, socially homogeneous polis in a preindustrial setting, for only in such a setting does he think it possible to develop moral virtues. Does it make any sense to say that the actions of the American government, each of which takes place within the context of and in response to the demands of modern industrial life, are neutral in regard to these three preferences? I take it as evident that it does not. Ralph can *express* his preference, but he cannot *live* it. Nor should we say liberalism allows him to pursue his conception of the good privately, because his conception of the good entails an alternative understanding of the nature of "private" and "public" to that of the liberal. Ralph's conception of the good cannot be translated into a liberal language of private preferences without losing its essential character, which is to call into question such translations. In order to respond to Ralph the liberal needs a defense of this translating activity and a defense of the form of life that results thereby, not an invocation of neutrality.

Dworkin can both maintain the neutrality thesis and admit the thesis of logical non-neutrality only by interpreting the non-neutrality thesis in a narrow and weak sense. Thus, although granting that preferences do not, as a matter of fact, arise out of thin air, he wants to treat them for theoretical purposes *as if they do*. In the terms employed here, his statement can be rendered as: "liberalism responds to the logical non-neutrality thesis with the answer that in this case it is all the more important that distribution be fair in itself, not as tested by the preferences M to N that it produces." The point however, is that although a liberal government might be neutral amongst preferences M to N, it cannot be neutral in a strong sense, for it acts to produce preferences *M* to *N* and not some other set. Since liberal governments, like all governments, play a role in producing a particular set of preferences, how are we to evaluate liberalism in relation to alternative political moralities if not in terms of the substantive preferences it produces? Admitting that preferences are functions of forms of social life, but treating them for theoretical purposes as if they were not, does not provide a very stable ground for the neutrality thesis.

Two other lines of defense might be pursued by a defender of the neutrality thesis. One would be to reject the proposition that preferences in a particular society are constrained within theoretically definable parameters, and argue instead that the range *M* to *N* is equivalent to the full range *A* to *Z*. However, such a move flies in the face of the most elementary facts of sociology.[20] A second approach would be to argue that sociology is, for all intents and purposes, irrelevant to philosophy. A weaker version of this second strategy, that philosophy cannot be collapsed or reduced to sociology, is a much more defensible one. But the defender of the neutrality thesis cannot rely on this weaker version, for he cannot allow his conception of autonomous preferences to be contaminated by *any* sociological (or historical or psychological) propositions that imply that the range of these preferences is constrained. He must maintain that sociology (or more generally, the empirical study of human behavior) is irrelevant to philosophical discourse. However, one would then have to wonder how he could develop theoretical conceptions of "human beings," "preferences," and so forth. At the very least, these conceptions will have to be developed within the context of language, which is itself part and parcel of a social form of life. My conclusion is that anyone who grants the thesis of logical non-neutrality can then maintain the neutrality thesis only on pain of logical inconsistency, for to grant the thesis of logical non-neutrality is to undermine the thesis that government can be neutral on the question of the good life. Perhaps this is why some liberals have traditionally, in various ways, denied the logical non-neutrality thesis, preferring instead to treat individuals as asocial and self-contained atoms while treating society as the derivative set of instrumental relations that result from their bargains. Here, however, logical consistency is attained at the price of an untenable account of "individuals," "society" and the relation between them, as other liberals (not to mention both conservative and radical critics) from Hume to Rawls have rightly recognized.

DEFENDING LIBERALISM

Are we then left to conclude, as do so many critics of the theory, that liberalism is plagued with inherent inconsistencies? Not necessarily. Suppose we grant that a coherent defense of the liberal political morality cannot be based upon an atomistic account of individuals and an instrumental account of social relations, for such a defense contradicts the fact that individuals and their preferences are partly functions of the social relations within which they are situated and within which they come to define themselves as particular selves. We also eschew the attempt to defend liberalism in terms of Dworkin's neutrality thesis, for the reasons stated. What, then, are the theoretical strategies left for the defender of liberalism to pursue? Three seem open, and I shall attempt here to explain why the third seems to me to be the most promising and, in general terms, what would be entailed in pursuing it.

(1) A defense of liberalism might be based upon an essentialist and substantive definition of human nature. This is not the same as basing it on *formal* propositions regarding the theoretical construction of the concepts of "individuals" (atomism) and "society" (instrumentalism), though the two are often conjoined. For example, psychological egoism (an essentialist and substantive conception of human nature) should not be confused with logical atomism and instrumentalism (which provide a formal structure for articulating concepts). The essentialist strategy has been a favorite of those liberals who have understood the essence of human nature to be that set of basic desires and passions which Macpherson has summarily described as "possessive individualism."[21] Either these desires are raised to a moral status and made the ground of natural rights (Hobbes, Locke), or this moral structure of rights is razed and government defended directly in terms of the protection and sustenance it affords these desires (Hume, Bentham). Strategy 1 is also pursued by all those who attempt to ground a political morality in some conception of basic human needs, including those whose conception is a non-possessive individualist one.

In either case, the defense stands or falls on the basis of two factors: (a) the validity of the universal substantive conception of human nature from which it is derived, and (b) the validity of the proposition that moral imperatives can be deduced from empirical propositions regarding human nature. Although this strategy continues to find adherents, its weaknesses are evident. Concerning (a), contemporary epistemology does not support the expectation that empirical science can yield timeless and universal descriptions of "human nature," while (b) is based upon an attempt to reduce morality to a science, and is open to all the familiar objections which have been brought to bear on such attempts, many by liberal political theorists themselves.

(2) A defense of liberalism might also be based upon a version of philosophical skepticism, constructed upon the principle that competing conceptions of the good are equally arbitrary and/or ultimately the subjective

expressions of individual wants, desires or tastes. Lacking any defensible conception of the good, we either assign rights to everyone (by default, as it were), or set out to maximize the degree to which everyone has whatever s/he happens to want. One great attraction of this strategy for liberals is that it renders commensurable two key concepts that were traditionally thought by most liberals to be incompatible: individual rights and social utility.[22] This strategy provides the underlying rationale for the pre-eminent contemporary form of utilitarianism, public choice theory, and if we detach Hobbes' material propositions regarding human psychology from his formal propositions regarding the structure of rational agency, we are left with what remains the most powerful articulation of this line of defense of liberalism.

We might call this the negative defense of liberalism: with no generally accepted or objective criteria of public virtue or the common good in terms of which to define the basic political duties, we assign basic rights to all persons and let them create their own duties through a voluntary process of mutual exchange. The alternative, as Hobbes so clearly put it, is to fight to the death. Seemingly, tolerance becomes a virtue in a virtueless world.

The problem is that this negative defense is actually no defense at all, but rather a pseudo-defense. One can always ask, "Why not just fight about it?" And, as we know from painful experience, the answer to that question is not self-evident. Not everyone agrees that tolerance, peace and survival are irreducible components of the good. Nor is it enough to argue that any rational man would agree to these criteria, unless one wishes to maintain that most of those who lived prior to the seventeenth century, including Socrates, Christ, Aristotle and Aquinas, were irrational. That would be modern hubris with a vengeance, but even were one willing to maintain this view (I count it as part of Hobbes' greatness as compared to his contemporary descendants that he both recognizes this implication and does not turn away from it) it would not be enough. Survival and peace understood as the good would still be a conclusion in search of an argument, and as soon as one began to provide such an argument one would thereby have denied the proposition that conceptions of the good are equally arbitrary. But what if such an argument were presented? Besides the fact that this would no longer be a negative defense of liberalism, I must say that I cannot imagine, nor do I know of, anyone who has ever attempted to directly defend the proposition that survival is the ultimate moral good. Many (including Hobbes) have indeed attempted to show that survival is useful, or that it is an innate human desire. Neither of these positions, however, tells us anything about the moral status of survival, unless one goes on to attempt either to redefine morality in terms of prudence or to redefine morality as a natural science. Now many people have attempted such reductions, but no one to my knowledge has, in the absence of such a reduction, explicitly argued that mere survival is of greater moral value than a morally good life. And with good reason, since such an argument would be internally inconsistent. If there is a moral standard of the good common to all persons, it follows tautologically that a morally good life is of greater moral value than merely life itself. Doing what is morally right may conflict with doing what is necessary to stay alive, and one's moral duty is to do what is right. Thus those who would grant that the negative defense of liberalism is no defense at all, but would then attempt to defend the proposition that survival *is* the good, must adopt one of two untenable positions. They must treat morality either as a natural science or as prudence, projects that fly in the face of our ordinary moral experience, where we face conflicts between the demands of doing what is right and doing what will satisfy our natural desires.

(3) A third strategy for defending liberalism is what I shall call the positive strategy, and although Dworkin does not provide such a defense, he clearly intends to. He argues, in accord with what has just been said here, that

...liberalism cannot be based on skepticism. Its constitutive morality provides that human beings must be treated as equals by their government, not because there is no right and wrong in political morality, but because that is what is right.[23]

The defender of liberalism must address two questions here: (i) Why is it right to treat persons as equals?; (ii) What does it mean to treat persons as equals? I have attempted to show that Dworkin's answer to the latter question, the neutrality thesis, is inadequate. In proposing that answer, he implicitly ignores what he explicitly recognizes at other points: that individual preferences are not randomly self-generated, but are rather constrained within the boundaries of a form of social life. He notes that "since the preferences people have are produced by the system of distribution already in place, these preferences will tend to support that system, which is both circular and unfair."[24] It is wrong, it seems to me, to say that this condition is "unfair." Rather, I would characterize it as a necessary, unavoidable and constitutive condition of human social existence. To say that it is unfair is to say that the human condition is unfair, a proposition that I suspect is more meaningful to gods than to men. Be that as it may, it is clear that the liberal value of treating persons as equals cannot be interpreted by falling back upon the neutrality thesis. What is needed instead is an interpretation of this value grounded by reference to some deeper value that would allow us both to take account of the fact of casual non-neutrality and construct a positive defense of the particular form of social life that the liberal political morality encourages and sustains. The positive defense of liberalism cannot be that it is neutral amongst preferences; it must be a defense of the *kind* of preferences liberalism produces.

Having rejected the neutrality thesis as a plausible answer to question (ii), we find that we cannot answer that question without first addressing question (i). In other words, we can construct a specific interpretation of "treating people as equals" only in light of the value underlying the assertion that it is morally right to treat people as equals. Employing the neutrality thesis as an answer to question (ii) is to fall back upon a version of the negative strategy of defense, not to offer a positive defense of the liberal political morality and the form of social life with which it is connected.

Dworkin is not alone amongst contemporary liberals in seeing that liberalism cannot viably be based upon skepticism and yet failing to provide the necessary defense. I shall make no attempt here to provide such a defense; I shall, however, argue that there are two areas of discourse in which liberals will have to engage (which they have traditionally been hesitant to engage in) if they wish to construct a plausible positive defense of the liberal political morality. Dworkin's work is instructive in this regard, for although he does not successfully satisfy the two requirements I shall outline, he does provide some of the conceptual and theoretical revisions necessary to the task.

At the risk of oversimplification, I shall call these two areas of discourse the metaphysical and the social. I shall briefly discuss the former, reserving most of my remarks for the latter, because I suspect that the problems arising from the social area of discourse are likely to be the most intractable for the defender of liberalism.

By metaphysical, I mean to refer to the need for liberals to provide an answer to question (i) above: Why is it right to treat persons as equals? A positive defense of liberalism cannot at this point say simply, "because liberals by definition believe in equality." That answer may descriptively distinguish liberals from those who do not believe in equality, but it is surely no defense of liberalism, or the belief in equality for that matter. There is a region of political thought, most ably represented by Plato and Aristotle, that not only "believes" in natural inequality, but also provides a philosophical defense of that conclusion by articulating a metaphysic (a total understanding of man, nature, the cosmos and their relations) within which that conclusion appears not as absurd, but as obvious. Yet liberals rarely make the effort to take this argument seriously; "arguments" for natural inequality are put into the mouths of straw men and then summarily rejected, if they are considered at all.[25] If liberal political philosophy is to be positively defended, classical political philosophy cannot be simply brushed aside, on the ground that it must be wrong because it sanctions inequality or because it contains a teleological understanding of nature. The liberal needs an alternative metaphysic to set against the classical one, an alternative that is not only coherent and comprehensive in its own right, but also able to reveal the inadequacies and resolve the anomalies of the classical metaphysic.

Liberals have long been reluctant to enter this area of discourse because liberal political theory has often been conjoined with a philosophical tradition of empiricism that has avoided metaphysics like the plague. Yet this area of discourse is likely less of a problem for the liberal than the social area because the components of such an alternative metaphysic that would provide the basis for a liberal political morality may be found, I suspect, in the work of Kant.[26]

This may partly explain the increasing attention Kant has recently received from liberal theorists, including Dworkin and especially Rawls. Though I suspect that this attention is rightly directed and that Kant's work may serve as the basis for a viable liberal metaphysis, two rather large qualifications temper this suspicion. First, it is nothing more than a suspicion at this point, and appeals to Kant are just that: appeals, not arguments. It is not enough for the liberal to assert that Kantian metaphysics provides a viable alternative to classical metaphysics; this has to be demonstrated. Second, there is the problem of determining just which way the Kantian knife cuts; theorists as different in their political views as Nozick and Rawls, and even Habermas in some respects, claim an affinity with Kant.

The element in Kant's metaphysics that accounts for much of his appeal to contemporary theorists is his articulation and defense of the concept of autonomy: freedom understood as obedience to a law one gives to oneself. The autonomous person is not Hobbes' isolated natural man; autonomy is expressed through obedience to the moral law, not by the absence of law or other constraints upon desires. The autonomous will is endowed with a rational and moral quality; it is not merely a desire put into action. The concept of man as autonomous, as a morally free being rather than a naturally free being, is part of Kant's attempt to reconcile freedom with authority on a moral basis rather than that of prudential interest. This is indeed a promising project. However, the divergent uses that are made of the concept of autonomy by contemporary political theorists are themselves a reflection of the lack of attention paid to the fact that Kant's concept of autonomy is not stillborn, but is the conclusion of a controversial argument at the level of metaphysics. That argument entails a separation between reason and nature sharper than contemporary theorists might want to accept.

The confusion surrounding the concept of autonomy may be glimpsed in Dworkin's concept of "equal concern and respect." If he were to turn from the task of specifying this concept to that of defending it at the metaphysical level of discourse, I suspect it would be tied to the Kantian conception of autonomy.[27] There are, however, difficulties here. "Concern" and "respect" are not the same thing; it would seem possible to respect others without having concern for them ("you stay out of my way, I'll stay out of yours") and vice versa; indeed, genuine concern might lead to a paternalism not entirely consistent with a "mere" respect for the rights of others. Perhaps these potential difficulties are resolvable and perhaps Kant is even the source of such a resolution. If this is so, however, it is by no means self-evident.

Let us assume for the moment that liberals can provide a viable answer to question (i) based upon the Kantian value of autonomy. We are still left with question (ii): What does it mean to treat persons as equals, as autonomous rational beings? Here liberals will have to engage more directly than they traditionally have in what I have termed the social area of discourse. Just as classical political philosophy has a much deeper metaphysical dimension than liberalism, the other great alternative to liberal political thought, Marxism, has had a much deeper appreciation of the social dimension of political philosophy. I can best explain my point here by reference to the specifics of Dworkin's argument.

We have seen that the neutrality thesis fails as an answer to question (ii), and this conclusion holds even when we stipulate an answer to question (i) in terms of the Kantian value of autonomy. However, even with this stipulation, we need an idea of what it would mean for a form of social life to nurture the development of autonomous persons. We need to know what the social conditions of autonomy are, for if treating persons as equals means respecting and encouraging their autonomy, we need to know (a) what sorts of preferences are consistent or inconsistent with this moral conception of the person and (b) what patterns of social life are consistent or inconsistent with the end of nurturing autonomous persons. In evaluating institutions in light of these ends, we have to assess them not only in terms of their outcomes, but also in terms of the processes from which these result. We have to assess not only how institutions affect what people get, but also how they affect what people do, what they think, how they define themselves and their fellows, and how they come to be some persons and not others.

One institution that liberals have tended not to assess from this broad point of view is the market. The market is not simply a mechanism of distribution; it is also a particular way of organizing production, a particular way of relating individuals to one another as they engage in one of the activities of their common life. As a result, a social structure based upon market relations leads to the development of a particular type of individual character. Critics of liberalism have long pointed this out. They have also, of course, assessed that character type in negative terms. My aim here, however, is not to claim that liberals must adopt this negative assessment. My point is simply that they must, at the very least, assess the social, personality producing role of the market in light of their commitment to the autonomous personality. If it is not self-evident that a market society nourishes a nasty and brutish character type, as so many critics of liberalism hold, neither is it self-evident that a market society nourishes the free and autonomous person, as so many liberals assume. The merit of Dworkin's conception of liberalism lies in its analytical separation of the constitutive values of liberalism (equality, autonomy) from the instrumental strategies (market) that might be used as a means of embodying these values in the social world. This conceptual move leaves a theoretical space for evaluating the market as a means to the ends of equality and autonomy, rather than assuming that the two are synonymous by conceptualizing freedom as market freedom.

However, when Dworkin turns to the task of actually assessing the value of the market in light of these ends, he treats it as wholly a mechanism of distribution.[28] A positive defense of liberalism must assess the market not only in terms of how well it satisfies (given) preferences, but also in terms of what preferences it gives. Only then can we determine how well it embodies and encourages the development of autonomy. I suggested earlier that problems of this sort, arising from the social area of discourse, were likely to prove more difficult for the liberal than those arising from the metaphysical area because I suspect that it is easier to provide an argument in defense of Kantian metaphysics than it is to provide an argument in support of the proposition that a market-based social structure nourishes the development of autonomous persons. If I am right, it does not necessarily follow that the market has no place in a just society; it would follow, however, that it cannot be the basis of such a society.

I have attempted to show here that the neutrality thesis cannot form the basis of a successful defense of liberalism, and I have attempted to outline what would be necessary to such a defense. Liberals need a philosophical defense of the value of autonomy and a conception of the social conditions of autonomy. The neutrality thesis, and any other thesis that ignores the implications of the logical non-neutrality thesis, can satisfy neither condition. Such answers are in essence versions of the negative strategy that provides only a pseudo-defense of liberalism. I have tried to show why a successful defense of liberalism requires a closer encounter on the part of liberals with Plato and Aristotle on the one (metaphysical) hand, and with Rousseau and Marx on the other (social) hand. The conception of liberalism that might emerge from such encounters would not likely be the one to which we are accustomed: it would, however, likely be much more defensible than those that stand behind the Maginot Line of neutrality.

NOTES

1. Ronald Dworkin, "Liberalism," in S. Hampshire, ed., *Public and Private Morality* (Cambridge: Cambridge University Press, 1978), pp. 113–43. Other relevant works by Dworkin include "What Is Equality? Part 1: Equality of Welfare," *Philosophy and Public Affairs*, vol. 10, no. 3 (Summer, 1981), pp. 185–246; "What Is Equality? Part 2: Equality of Resources," *Philosophy and Public Affairs*, vol. 10, no. 4 (Fall, 1981), pp. 283–345; *Taking Rights Seriously* (Cambridge, Mass.: Harvard University Press, 1977), especially Chapters 6, 7, 11.
2. Dworkin, "Liberalism," p. 127.
3. Bruce Ackerman, *Social Justice and the Liberal State* (New Haven, CT: Yale University Press, 1980). Ackerman's argument is criticized by various authors in *Ethics*, vol. 93, no. 1 (January 1983), pp. 330–71.
4. Ronald Dworkin, "What Liberalism Is Not," *New York Review of Books*, January 20, 1983, pp. 47–9; see also his "Why Liberals Should Believe in Equality," *New York Review of Books*, February 3, 1983, pp. 32–4.
5. Dworkin, "What Liberalism Is Not," p. 48.
6. Ackerman, *Social Justice and the Liberal State*, p. 359.
7. *Ibid.*, p. 11.
8. Ackerman considers this practice to be that of politics. This is, however, a contentious issue. It is Hobbes whom Ackerman is unwittingly following here; see Bernard Williams, "Space Talk: The Conversation Continued," *Ethics*, vol. 93, no. 1 (January, 1983), pp. 367–71.
9. Ackerman seems to think that a philosopher who rejects skepticism and inquires into the question of *the* good life must also wish to impose some conception of the good upon others. Philosophy and tyranny, however, are not the same thing.
10. Ackerman, *Social Justice and the Liberal State*, pp. 14, 16, 363–5, 367.
11. Dworkin, "Liberalism," p. 126.
12. *Ibid.*, p. 125.
13. *Ibid.*, p. 126. In "What Is Equality? Part 1: Equality of Welfare," and "What Is Equality? Part 2: Equality of Resources," Dworkin has provided a further specification of his preferred conception of equality, arguing that equality of resources rather than of welfare accords best with his understanding of the basic value of equal concern and respect.
14. Dworkin, "Liberalism," p. 126.
15. Dworkin, "Liberalism," p. 127.
16. *Ibid.*
17. *Ibid.*, p. 129.
18. *Ibid.*, p. 143; emphasis added.
19. See, for example, Robert Nozick, *Anarchy, State and Utopia* (New York: Basic Books, 1974), pp. 198–228.
20. In terms artfully elaborated by Jon Elster, this strategy fails to distinguish the "feasible set" from the "possible set" of choices open to an agent within a social context. See his *Ulysses and the Sirens* (Cambridge: Cambridge University Press, 1979), pp. 112–13.
21. C.B. Macpherson, *The Political Theory of Possessive Individualism* (Oxford: Oxford University Press, 1962).

2. See Douglas Rae, "An Altimeter for Mr. Escher's Stairway: A Comment on William Riker's 'Implications from the Disequilibrium of Majority Rule for the Study of Institutions,'" *American Political Science Review*, vol. 74, no. 2 (June, 1980), pp. 451–5.
23. Dworkin, "Liberalism," p. 142.
24. *Ibid.*, p. 143. In *Taking Rights Seriously*, pp. 234–6, Dworkin distinguishes personal from external preferences, and it might be supposed that this distinction could be employed in defense of the neutrality thesis. However, that distinction refers to the formal objects of one's preferences, not to their substantive content, which is at issue here.
25. In Ackerman, it is "Nazi" who puts the case for natural inequality; *Social Justice and the Liberal State*, pp. 76–7. Dworkin has "Amartya," a Hindu, put the case. Each makes the case for natural inequality and accepts it, even though he is of the lower caste. Dworkin remarks, "An inegalitarian political system does not become just because everyone wrongly believes it to be." However, he provides no justification for the use of the adverb "wrongly" in regard to Amartya's belief.
26. A suspicion shared by Patrick Riley, *Will and Political Legitimacy* (Cambridge, Mass.: Harvard University Press, 1982), especially pp. 125–62.
27. This would seem inconsistent with Dworkin's remarks regarding the "deep theory" underlying Rawls' theory of justice; *Taking Rights Seriously*, Chapter 6.
28. Dworkin, "Liberalism," pp. 128–36, 141–3, and see the argument above.

3   A Liberal Theory of the Good?

Assuming that the argument of the previous chapter is correct, a puzzle arises. If it is indeed a relatively straightforward path of argument that leads to the conclusion that liberalism is not neutral with regard to the question of the good life, then why do so many liberals remain convinced that it is?[1] Why, when liberals and their critics debate the issue of neutrality, do they so often seem to talk beyond one another? It seems to me that instances of these debates ought to come off better than they do, and in this essay I attempt to describe how they might. Leaving aside the consequences of state action and inaction in relation to the ideal of neutrality, I focus instead upon the two-tiered structure of liberal thinking about the idea of the good and the ideal of neutrality. My claim is that this structure inclines liberals to subtly but powerfully distort the nature of non-liberal ideals through the way in which the notion of "conceptions of the good" is itself conceptualized.

One argument often made in support of liberal political morality is that liberalism, both as a theory and as a practice, is neutral in regard to the question of the good life.[2] In this chapter I shall criticize and reject this argument. Since I maintain that liberalism is not neutral with regard to the good, I suppose that my argument must aim at being put such that a liberal can agree that it has been fairly presented, and yet continue to adhere to liberalism. Now this continued adherence could not, of course, be based upon liberalism's (supposed) neutrality regarding the good. My account must be wide enough to undermine the neutrality thesis without being so wide as to undermine liberalism itself in the process. The decision to proceed in this manner embodies something more than merely strategic considerations, for I remain unsure whether liberalism is the most defensible form of political life. However, the argument presented here suggests that if it is, it is not because it is neutral in regard to the question of the good, and if it is not, it is not simply because it fails in being neutral with regard to the good. In criticizing those liberals who maintain the thesis of neutrality, I mean to imply that liberalism stands in need of a better defense than that which it receives from them.

Let us begin with liberal theory. First, we need to address the objection that liberal theory is not monolithic. One could argue that while deontological, or rights-based, versions of liberalism attempt to maintain the neutrality thesis by arguing that the right is prior to the good, teleological versions of liberalism, that is, utilitarianism, openly proclaim a conception of the good in defining the right as that which maximizes the good. Perhaps then, we should simply look in front of us, that is, at utilitarianism, to find a liberal theory of the good.

Now, in a sense this is true; utilitarianism does contain a theory of the good, and it is, for all intents and purposes, *the* liberal theory of the good. I maintain, however, that this theory is also characteristic of deontological versions of liberalism, be they contractarian or libertarian. In maintaining this, I mean to question the unfortunate tendency prevalent in Anglo-American political theory, which is to suppose that rights-based and utilitarian theories of justice are the fundamental alternatives open to reasonable consideration as viable accounts of justice. Other accounts of justice, which are said to differ fundamentally from both deontological and teleological versions of liberalism in that they posit and advocate the pursuit of some substantive conception of the good, are lumped together under the heading, "perfectionism." It is worth noting here that "perfectionism" is a concept used by "non-perfectionists" (that is, liberals) to describe non-liberal theories of justice; it is doubtful that those categorized as "perfectionists" would be comfortable with the characterization (not to say evaluation) that accompanies this apparently innocent labelling. Aristotle and Nietzsche, two "perfectionists" mentioned by Rawls, would surely be surprised to find themselves in the same bed, and would likely wonder whether they had not ended up there simply because they were not liberals.[3]

The utilitarian theory of the good is not a perfectionist one, or at least is not in the prevailing contemporary form of utilitarianism, which I shall call, following Dworkin, "preference" utilitarianism. Preference utilitarianism has come to replace what Dworkin labels "psychological"[4] utilitarianism, of which Bentham may be taken as the prime exemplar. Psychological utilitarianism aimed at maximizing satisfactions which were conceptualized as (at least in principle) empirically verifiable, quantifiable and capable of comparative measurement; in short, amenable to representation within a felicific calculus. This version of utilitarianism foundered on the shoals of the impossibility of interpersonal comparisons of utilities. Preference utilitarianism is, in its way, more modest; it takes the aim of social policy to be that of maximizing the satisfaction of individual preferences, leaving aside the attempt to quantify levels of individual satisfaction in terms of happiness or pleasure. The good which preference utilitarianism, or hereafter simply utilitarianism, sets out to maximize in some sense (whether it be total or average or some variant thereof) is the satisfaction of individual preferences. "Preferences," on this theory, is a concept capable of universal content; all desires, ends, interests or goals which an individual may have can be consumed under the formal category of "preferences." So, according to utilitarianism, can all conceptions of the good which an individual may have. So the utilitarian theory of the good is of a special kind; it is not a substantive, or perfectionist, conception of the good, in that it does not refer to some conception of human excellence which all individuals are morally obligated to pursue or enhance. Nor need it refer to the satisfaction of existent desire. Rather, individuals are to define for themselves what is good, and no such conception of the good is intrinsically privileged over any other; from the point of view of the state, a preference for the life devoted to pushpin is to be treated as equal to the preference for a life devoted to poetry. Now this sounds a great deal like a doctrine of neutrality regarding the good, and indeed it is. What, then, do deontological liberals have against utilitarianism? Partly, and superficially, the complaint is that the status of individual rights is insecure within utilitarianism, in that the maximization of preference satisfaction might conflict with claims of individual liberty. This, of course, begs the question at hand, since the priority of liberty is what utilitarianism denies. The more fundamental complaint is that utilitarianism does not take seriously the separateness of persons, that it treats preferences rather than the persons having preferences as of decisive moral importance. Utilitarianism is said not to take seriously the dignity and autonomy attendant to moral personality, to be unable to account fully for the fact that the satisfaction of preferences has value only insofar as these are realized in the course of self-directed human activity. On a utilitarian theory of justice, it does not matter, except indirectly and contingently, how the sum of satisfactions is distributed among individuals.[5]

Now our question is how deontological versions of liberalism differ from utilitarianism in regard to the question of the good. In one sense, they clearly differ. Deontological liberalism limits the pursuit of the good, understood as the collective satisfaction of preferences, by prior principles of right, which are understood to yield basic individual rights or liberties which constrain the maximization of the satisfaction of preferences. Rights are trumps (Dworkin) or boundaries (Nozick) setting strict limits to what the state can legitimately do with regard to individuals. However, in regard to the question of the good understood as the question of what constitutes the good life for individuals, these versions of liberalism are similar, in maintaining that the state must be neutral in regard to this question. No conception of the good life held by an individual is politically privileged; all are to be treated equally. The two versions differ in regard to what it means to treat individuals equally, but cohere in treating the question of the good life as a matter of free individual choice. The only legitimate limit upon an individual's liberty to define and pursue his or her conception of the good is that he or she allow others the same liberty. The state is to provide a neutral framework for these pursuits by enforcing those measures necessary to their being carried out peacefully and orderly. There are, of course, differences between liberals as to what properly constitutes "enforcement" here, ranging from defenses of the minimal state preventing force and fraud and securing contracts to defenses of the welfare state providing the material means necessary to the successful practical pursuit of individual ends. All agree, however, that the state is not to enforce or pursue any substantive conception of what constitutes the good life; individuals must be free to do this themselves.

Yet if this is so, how can we speak of a liberal conception of the good? Apparently, liberalism prevents no one from pursuing his or her conception of the good; it simply prevents anyone from imposing his or her conception of the good upon anyone else, or from harming anyone else in the process of pursuing his or her conception of the good. Liberalism seems to be uniquely privileged in relation to other political theories, which, insofar as they do presume some substantive conception of the good as an ideal to be pursued, not only threaten the freedom of individuals as a matter of practice, but also take on the theoretical burden of somehow justifying and explaining just why what is therein conceptualized as the good life is in fact that. The appeal of liberalism thus has both a practical and theoretical aspect. Practically, liberalism asks us to ask ourselves if we really want our lives structured by an elite; would it not be better to be masters of our own destinies? Theoretically, liberalism beckons us to hold on to our powers of critical reason, and avoid the temptation of succumbing to the doctrines of absolutism and their expositors who claim privileged insight into the meaning of the good. Where, after all, is the proof?

Now the first thing which ought to make us, and I mean liberals, too, skeptical about this characterization of the state of affairs in political theory is that it comes close to maintaining that liberalism is the only reasonable political morality there is. It is not seen as one among many political doctrines potentially open to reasonable assent, but as a uniquely privileged one which makes no controversial or substantive assumptions about the good life (admittedly a highly controversial question) where other political theories do. If this were true, it might well be unreasonable not to be a liberal. Liberals ought to reflect upon whether anyone devoted to the exercise of critical reason, as they understand themselves to be, would want to commit themselves to such a position. Can we really be so sure that all those Thomists, Marxists, Straussians and neo-variants thereof are just misguided (at best; subversive at worst)? In any case, the characterization is not accurate. The liberal theory of the good may be defensible, but it does need defending, because prima facie it is no more plausible than any other.

How then does the liberal fail to be neutral regarding the question of the good? In a very special way – for although liberalism is neutral with regard to *conceptions* of the good, it has a very distinct *conceptualization* of what it means to have a conception of the good. At the second-order level of individual conceptions of the good, we may say that liberalism advocates and embodies the principle of neutrality. But there is nothing neutral about the first-order conceptualization of conceptions of the good which obtains in liberal theory. Liberalism, if it does not have a theory of the good, certainly has a meta-theory of the good.

On liberal theory, you can, at the second-order level, define for yourself and pursue any conception of the good which does not violate the liberty of others to do so as well. However, there are at least three things which are non-neutral about this conceptualization of conceptions of the good. They are (a) the way it conceptualizes the relation between a "conception of the good" and those who possess or bear it, (b) the way it conceptualizes the meaning of "a conception of the good," and (c) the way it does linguistic, and hence theoretical, violence to alternative, non-liberal conceptualizations of "conceptions of the good" when they are translated into the language of liberal meta-theory.

Within liberal meta-theory, it is individuals who have, or possess, or bear conceptions of the good. These are conceptions of what ends they desire to pursue in the course of their lives. Now these ends can be shared with other individuals, but only in a particular sense. They can be shared *contingently* and *aggregatively* but not *essentially* and *collectively*. Let us explain these distinctions.

On the liberal meta-theory of the good, each individual is responsible for defining his or her conception of the good. Now it may happen that the ends of life defining my good turn out to be the same as those defining yours. We may then be said to share a conception of the good. This sharing is, however, contingent upon our having chosen, as separate selves, ends which happen to cohere. Moreover, it may be that I define my ends with reference to yours, that is, that I understand my good to consist in the furtherance of those ends which you define as your good. This point is important; liberal meta-theory requires that individuals define for themselves their own good, their own ends. However, your conception of the good need not be selfish, or self-interested in the narrow sense of egoistically desiring to maximize the successful pursuit of *your* desires or preferences at the expense of others'. Your conception of the good, your ends, may amount to attempting to maximize the successful pursuit of my ends. Liberal meta-theory, then, need not necessarily lead to egoism in the narrow sense.

You can, then, on liberal meta-theory, be a liberal altruist, desiring that my, or others', substantive ends be successfully pursued. However, what you cannot do is cease to have a conception of the good which is understood as being *primarily* possessed and defined by you as an individual, as a separate self. If you desire above all else to see me achieve the successful pursuit of my ends, then that is what *you* have chosen to define as your good. The point is that this is your conception of the good, and only yours. It is not mine, and it is not ours, except in the special sense outlined above. We share certain ends because you as an individual happen to have contingently chosen to define your good with reference to my conception of the good. On liberal meta-theory, we cannot essentially share a conception of the good.[6]

What does this mean, exactly? It means that you and I cannot speak, or understand ourselves, in the following way: we cannot say that we as separate selves have no conception of the good because we cannot understand ourselves (our selves) except insofar as we are allowed to define and speak of them with reference to the conception of the good we (claim) to share. If we speak this way, we are claiming to share a conception of the good essentially, and not just contingently. We are saying that in the absence of the substantive relation between us (which we take to define our good), we are not selves, and cannot coherently understand ourselves as such. We are saying that we cannot, as separate selves, say what our good is, because we have no sense of self in the absence of the good we share, that good being the intrinsic value of the relation between us. Liberal meta-theory prevents us from speaking this way because it requires that individuals be the primary bearers of conceptions of the good, whatever their substance may be. We are violating this requirement by reversing the order of ontological priority, claiming as we do that essentially shared conceptions of the good yield and define selves, and that in their absence there can be no separate selves to serve as the bearers of conceptions of the good.

Liberal meta-theory does not, however, simply silence those who wish to speak the language of essentially shared conceptions of the good. If this were the case, the non-neutrality of liberal meta-theory would be far easier to pinpoint and describe than it is. Liberalism continues to allow us to speak, but asks that we *translate* our self-understanding, which, as I have outlined it, violates the grammatical rules of liberal meta-theory, into the language of that meta-theory.

Now there is no question that this can be done. All non-liberal meta-theories of the good can be translated into the language of liberal meta-theory so as to conform to the rules of expression therein. The question is whether such transformations can be carried out without violence being done to the languages thereby assimilated. If this could be done, then the claim of neutrality upon the part of liberalism would be buttressed. But it seems to me that it clearly cannot be done.

Consider our previous example. You and I wish to maintain that we share a conception of the good essentially, that is, in a way which is essential and prior to our understanding of ourselves as selves. Liberal meta-theory is perfectly willing to accommodate the conception of the good we act upon; neutrality requires it (so far as it does not harm others, which we assume here it does not). All that is demanded of us is that we alter our self-understanding so that we conceptualize ourselves as partners who, as individuals, have chosen (freely, let us say) each of us to pursue a conception of the good which involves some degree, perhaps a very large one, of consideration, perhaps even sympathy and benevolence, for the aims and ends of the other. We can even go so far as to understand ourselves as liberal altruists toward each other, in that I define my good to consist of you achieving your ends, and you define yours reciprocally. What, aside from the curious prospect that as altruists on this model we may wind up frustrating ourselves in attempting to maximize the successful pursuit of each other's ends, is so bad about this? What has been lost in the translation?

From the point of view of liberal meta-theory, nothing. We are simply being asked to understand ourselves, each of us, as free and equal moral beings, each with conceptions of the good we wish to pursue. But from our point of view, we have lost something more, for our claim is quite simply that we cannot understand ourselves, we cannot make sense of ourselves as selves, in this way. From our point of view, *we cannot express who we are* in the language of liberal meta-theory. To put the point another way: liberal meta-theory sees *two* selves and *therefore* sees necessarily *two* conceptions of the good (even if they are identical in substance, they still constitute two conceptions of the good); we see *two* selves *because* there is *one* conception of the good essentially shared by the two selves who understand themselves in terms of this shared relation.

Let us consider the case of Ralph. Ralph says that his conceptualization of conceptions of the good, his meta-theory of the good, differs fundamentally from the liberal one. Ralph maintains, let us say, that his conception of the good is the collective pursuit of those virtues understood as excellences within the Athenian polis. The liberal says this is fine; Ralph may pursue those virtues, whatever they are, and in company with others who choose to do so, just so long as he leaves other individuals free to pursue their ends. But Ralph objects; he claims that what is noteworthy about these virtues is not merely their substance, but the meta-theory of the good they presuppose. He claims that these virtues cannot be pursued within the neutral framework of the liberal state, and he therefore claims that the framework is not in fact neutral. They can be pursued, the good as he understands it can be pursued, only insofar as this pursuit is collectively undertaken upon the basis of essentially shared ends which are understood by the participants to be definitive of themselves as selves. Ralph claims that it is a necessary condition of his pursuing virtue that everyone else pursue a conception of the good which serves to identify these virtues as such.

The liberal objects; Ralph, it is said, simply wants to impose his conception of the good upon everyone else. If Ralph has a preference for a certain set of virtues, he is free to pursue them as best he can; but Ralph is supposing himself superior to others in wanting to impose these virtues, his conception of the good, on everyone else. But Ralph will object that this is not what he is saying, or at least trying to say. Ralph claims that it is not a conception of *his* good, of his preferences, which he is trying to express, but rather a meta-theory of the good, one which holds that the good for *any* individual cannot properly be understood as the personally possessed set of ends he or she desires to pursue, but must instead be understood as a set of essentially shared collective ends. Ralph claims that he cannot pursue the good *as he understands it* within a liberal framework because his conceptualization of conceptions of the good denies the very thing which liberalism presupposes: that conceptions of the good are born primarily by separate selves.

Ralph will be at pains to try to get the liberal to see the following crucial point; that he is not, in advocating such a meta-theory of the good, pressing his personal interests, his individual ends as a separate self. He is pressing not a conception of the good, but a conceptualization of conceptions of the good, which, he submits, is not applicable simply to him but to everyone. Ralph is arguing not for the satisfaction of his ends, but for a meta-theory of the good. Yet it is just this distinction which is denied him from within the language of the liberal meta-theory of the good, for therein no such distinction can be made. The liberal will be prone to translate Ralph's first-order, meta-theory of the good into an expression of a second-order conception of the good and situate it within the universe of individually defined and possessed ends. Again, there is no question that this can be done; but what happens is that an alternative meta-theory of the good is not allowed to express itself as such. Now, we may judge this a good thing, or we may not; but judgment is required here, because the translation of Ralph's meta-theory of the good into the liberal language of neutrality is not itself neutral. It is, if anything, neutralizing.

It may be objected here that "essentially shared conceptions of the good" which define selves need not necessarily be good in an evaluative sense.[7] I, let us say, may not be able to understand myself except in terms of the essentially shared relation of love which characterizes my marriage; but you, and perhaps even I at some future point in time, may not be able to understand yourself (myself) and express who you are (I am) except in terms of an essentially shared relation of hatred with your (my) spouse. The relation may turn out to be an essentially shared evil rather than an essentially shared good. However, it is questionable whether the liberal can marshall the linguistic resources necessary to consistently level this complaint. He rules out essentially shared conceptions of the good not because they are good or evil, but because they are essentially shared. I have thus far followed liberalism in defining "the good" formally, without content, as that which is preferred. I have simply claimed that to understand "the good" even in this formal sense as individually defined and possessed by separate selves is to rule out a conceptualization of the good as essentially shared and definitive of selves.

But this in itself is a bit curious. It is bound to strike common sense as odd that the liberal conceptualization of the good makes no distinction between good and bad conceptions of the good. The good which I define and pursue as a separate self may encompass any and all ends; except those the pursuit of which entails overriding the liberty of others. This refusal to discriminate amongst ends in terms of their substantive meaning is, of course, necessary if there is to be neutrality at the second-order level of individually possessed and defined conceptions of the good. But the non-liberal will complain that this is to assimilate the language of good to the language of preferences. "Good," within liberal meta-theory, is severed from its relations with the family of concepts within which it is embedded in ordinary discourse, such as the antonyms "evil" and "bad," and the synonyms "proper" and "righteous." And it is no accident that the terms synonymous with "good" in ordinary language are normatively positive, the terms antonymous normatively negative. These conceptual relations reflect and constitutively express our practices of normative assessment and judgment, wherein the concept of "good" finds its home in practical life. "Preferences," on the other hand is, as one should expect given its role in liberal meta-theory, a concept without any straightforward attachment to these normative practices. We may hold that it is a good thing, prima facie, that preferences be satisfied rather than frustrated, but "preferences" has no relation with synonyms or antonyms which are clearly normative. Indeed, it is not clear that "preferences" has any antonyms at all. While it is not manifestly absurd to say that "John's ends are bad," or that "John's ends are evil," it would seem absurd to say that "John has no preferences," and it is nearly impossible to cite a word which is the antonym of "preferences" and which has a normatively negative meaning such that one could replace "bad" and "evil" in the locutions above with it. The only thing I can come up with is something like "John has anti-preferences," but I don't know what this could mean.

I do not wish to argue here that these considerations somehow demonstrate the absurdity of liberal theory. The point is that when the concept of "good" is translated into the language of liberal meta-theory so that "conceptions of the good" become equivalent to *preferring* some ends and desiring to see them achieved, a dimension of the meaning of this concept as it occurs in practical language is purged. The dimension is that of the normative assessment and judgment of ends qua ends. In the language of liberal meta-theory, no one can have a conception of the bad; they can have only a conception of the good. Other individuals may be of the *opinion* that one's conception of the good is normatively good or bad, but this is simply an expression of their preferences regarding the preferences of others, and is not to receive public expression through the state practically, or through the terms of liberal meta-theory.

Now this purging may, all things considered, turn out to be a good thing. But that is just the point. It is a purging, or, if you wish, a translation which is less than neutral (or pure) in that it changes the meaning of the concepts involved, and this translating activity stands in need of explicit defense. To put the point another way: the translation of the good as normative concept into the good as neutral concept equivalent to "preferences" is not itself neutral, but rather normative in that the meaning of the concept is changed thereby.

This problem of translation can be seen as well with regard to other conceptualizations of concepts which non-liberals fail to share with liberals. Consider, for example, the apparently innocent conceptualization of "teleological" theories of justice as those which define the right as that which maximizes the good. But then accounts which differ fundamentally in terms of their conceptualizations of "the good" are rendered similarly to one another for purposes of analysis. Once "teleology" is translated into a neutral, formal term, it is detached from the other linguistic and theoretical contexts from within which it takes on particular meanings. In being formalized, the concept is *not*, however, left without a context; it is rather placed in a particular context, that of the formal grammar of liberal meta-theory. So, for example, Aristotle comes to be understood as advocating the maximization of a substantive conception of the good which he happened to hold and desired to pursue; Aristotle, like everyone else, had some preferences. Yet it is highly questionable whether Aristotle's understanding of the good can be so conceptualized without losing its essential character. The good, as I understand Aristotle to have understood it, must be seen within the context of a teleological conception of nature, goodness being the imminent unfolding of the purposes therein, virtue being the active recognition and affirmation of these through the recognition of oneself as a participant part of that nature. This caricature may do less than justice to Aristotle, and even insofar as it is accurate there is much within that is contentious; yet it would seem to me that to translate this meta-theory of the good into the language of personally defined and possessed ends is to eviscerate it. Aristotle becomes a teleologist without what he would understand to be a teleology; a utilitarian who happens to have advocated the maximization of a substantive conception of the second-order good, in contrast to those utilitarians who advocate the maximization of preference satisfaction generally. Compared to them, Aristotle cannot help but appear as narrow-minded, as one whose preference is simply to see others prefer his preferences.

Let me now try to sum up the point I have been trying, in various ways, to express. Liberalism understands itself to be a political theory which permits no substantive conception of what constitutes the good life for individuals to take public, political priority over any other; it is hence neutral with regard to the question of the good. I have argued that this liberal theory of neutrality regarding the good presupposes a meta-theory of the good which is not neutral. That meta-theory holds that conceptions of the good are properly understood as the individually defined and possessed ends which separate selves pursue. Whether they are shared and pursued collectively, or dissimilar and pursued antagonistically, is a contingent question of fact depending upon what substantive ends happen to have been chosen. This meta-theory is non-neutral because it necessarily rules out any alternative meta-theory which denies that a "conception of the good" can be properly understood as the ends which separate selves define and pursue. One such alternative is that I ascribed to Ralph, who maintains that "conceptions of the good" are properly understood as essentially, and not just contingently, shared relations which are primarily definitive of, and not primarily defined by, individual selves. Ralph does not say conceptions of the good are chosen; he says they are recognized.

The reason this point is so easy to miss, and by implication the reason debates between liberals and their critics in regard to neutrality often go awry, is that it is so easy, not to say tempting, to translate alternative first-order meta-theories of the good into the language of liberal meta-theory as second-order conceptions of the good, and transform them thereby into what they are not – the substantive ends thought worthy of pursuit by a particular individual.

Now it is possible for translations to be carried out in the other direction, as, say, when it is claimed that the liberal meta-theory of the good is in fact a rationalization of an impoverished form of life, say that of consumerist capitalism. Nothing I have said thus far provides grounds for this, or any other, normatively negative assessment of the liberal meta-theory of the good. Of course, nothing said thus far necessarily lends support to liberal meta-theory either.

The choice, if choice is the proper word here, between alternative meta-theories of the good is in (at least) one key respect different from the individual choice of the conception of the good within liberal meta-theory. The choice of a conception of the good, of personal ends, within the language of liberal meta-theory leaves every other individual at liberty to do the same. It is understood as a private choice, one without public, political consequence for the choices of others. But the decision to speak the language of that meta-theory is not without public consequence; for if the good is a matter for private individual choice, then it is not a matter for public political determination. There is no neutral ground here, no "meta-meta-"theory to which further appeal in the name of neutrality can be made. If we are to speak of the good, then we have to speak; only the skeptic has the false luxury of remaining silent. Alternative meta-theories provide different languages for speaking of the good; but to speak any one of them is not to speak the others, and this is as true of the language of liberal meta-theory as it is of any other. The politics of neutrality is conducted within a language which is, like its competitors, non-neutral; those who do not speak it as a matter of course in liberal societies are provided, sometimes against their wishes, with a translator. In the last analysis, that translator is the state. I want now to conclude by raising the issue of how a liberal might abandon the thesis of neutrality and yet remain a liberal by defending the language of liberal meta-theory. This is, I believe, what Hobbes does in *Leviathan*. Hobbes has as good a claim as anyone to be the father of the liberal meta-theory of the good. In Chapter 15, he writes:

> For Moral Philosophy is nothing else but the Science of what is *Good*, and *Evill*, in the conversation, and Society of mankind. *Good*, and *Evill* are names that signifie our Appetites, and Aversions; which in different tempers, customes, and doctrines of men, are different: And divers men, differ not onely in their judgment, on the senses of what is pleasant, and unpleasant to the tast, smell, hearing, touch, and sight; but also of what is conformable, or disagreeable to Reason, in the actions of common life. Nay, the same man, in divers times, differs from himselfe; and one time praiseth, that is, calleth Good, what another time he dispraiseth, and calleth Evill: From whence arise Disputes, Controversies, and at last War. And therefore so long as man is in the condition of mere Nature, (which is a condition of War,) as private Appetite is the measure of Good, and Evill: and consequently all men agree on this, that Peace is Good, and therefore also the way, or means of Peace....[8]

Good and Evil, then, are names used by individuals to describe their appetites and aversions, or, if we strip away the psychology here, their preferences.

Now although Hobbes says, in this passage, that "consequently all men agree on this, that Peace is good," and that therefore they accept his moral philosophy as true and speak its language owing to this happy contingent sharing of at least one big end, he knows perfectly well that this is not so, that there is nothing this obviously neutral about the neutral language of the good he proposes to have everyone speak. That is why Leviathan requires a sword. And Hobbes also knows that, in spite of his efforts toward rationally explaining to everyone why it is in their interest to speak this language, not everyone will. That is why the sword is a sharp one – the force of words being too weak not only to hold men to the performance of their covenants, but too weak to force men to make them in the first place. The coercion endemic to political practice based upon the liberal meta-theory of the good is open and explicit in Hobbes, not obscured within the language of neutrality. So, for example, Hobbes does not translate Aristotle into the language of liberal meta-theory and allow him to speak as a "perfectionist;" he declares him an enemy of the state and banishes him. In the same Chapter 15 where he says that "consequently all men agree on this, that Peace is Good," he spends most of his time trying to rationally persuade those who manifestly do not agree with this (the fool, the rebel and the saint)[9] of the folly of their ways.

Those arguments are unconvincing, or at least will convince only those who are not fools, rebels and saints to begin with. But Hobbes is aware of this. The real argument against fools, rebels and saints, or against anyone who resists the language of liberal meta-theory, is the *Leviathan* considered as a rhetorical whole, which I understand to be the attempt to jolt resisters into a transformation of their self-understanding through the vicarious experience of their own death, an experience with which Hobbes attempts to provide them. However powerful that attempt, the vicarious experience of death is not the real thing. So the ultimate argument against fools, saints and their fellow travellers is no argument at all – it is the sword. Those who fail to heed the lessons of *Leviathan*, and refuse either to speak the language of liberal meta-theory or avail themselves of a translator, will learn the lessons the hard way – from Leviathan, who imposes silence.

Hobbes' case in support of the language of liberal meta-theory, whatever one's judgment may be, has its merits. It *is* an argument, in that it is conscious of the need to defend the language of the good it propounds. It is conscious that the language is a particular one. And it makes no bones about the coercion necessary to endure that the language be rendered practically effective in the "Conversation and Society of Mankind." It is, to my mind, one of the most powerful arguments in defense of liberalism yet expounded; the Bill 101 of the liberal way of life, designed to ensure its survival.

Liberals need not agree with that judgment; but if not, they ought to offer an argument in its stead, one which purports to explain why it is not only good to speak the liberal language of the good, but to require others to do so as well. At the least, they ought not suppose that the language of neutrality regarding the good is itself neutral – and that not simply because they are thereby less than neutral toward their critics, but because they do less than justice to the liberalism they would defend.

NOTES

1. One liberal who does not endorse neutrality is William Galston, "Defending Liberalism," *American Political Science Review*, vol. 76 (1982), pp. 621–9.
2. See, for example, Ronald Dworkin, "Liberalism," in S. Hampshire, ed., *Public and Private Morality* (Cambridge: Cambridge University Press, 1978), pp. 113–42.
3. On perfectionism, see John Rawls, *A Theory of Justice* (Cambridge, Mass.: Harvard University Press 1971), pp. 325–32.
4. Ronald Dworkin, *Taking Rights Seriously* (Cambridge, Mass.: Harvard University Press 1977), pp. 231–9.
5. These criticisms are developed at length in Rawls, *A Theory of Justice* and Robert Nozick, *Anarchy, State and Utopia* (New York: Basic Books, 1974).
6. A variation on the idea of shared relations and its significance within the liberal-communitarian debate is presented in Patrick Neal and David Paris, "Liberalism and the Communitarian Critique: A Guide for the Perplexed," *Canadian Journal of Political Science*, vol. 23, no. 3 (September, 1990), pp. 419–39.
7. See, in this regard, D.J.C. Carmichael, *Agent-Individualism: A Critique of the Logic of Liberal Political Understanding* (Ph.D. Dissertation, University of Toronto, 1978).
8. Thomas Hobbes, *Leviathan*, C.B. Macpherson, ed. (Harmondsworth: Penguin Books, 1968), Pt. I, ch. 15, p. 216.
9. Hobbes speaks explicitly of the Foole in Chapter 14. "Rebel" and "Saint," however, are my terms; were Hobbes to give a personified label to his arguments, he would surely choose different terms, that is, what I have labelled the argument of the saint, he would label the ravings of a (dangerous) fanatic.

Part II

Rawls and
Political Liberalism

4   In the Shadow of the General Will: Rawls, Kant and Rousseau on the Problem of Political Right

This is the first of three chapters focusing upon the thinking of John Rawls, the leading contemporary liberal political thinker. The relationship between Kant and Rawls is apparently an obvious one; Rawls himself acknowledges the Kantian foundations of his approach to questions of justice and political right, and identifies the precise points at which his theory departs from that of Kant. This chapter attempts to show that when one examines those points of departure carefully, they turn out to point not merely away from Kant, but directly and inexorably toward the account of political right given by Rousseau in The Social Contract. *The essay argues that it is impossible to fully understand Rawls' theoretical project until one sees the (unstable) position it occupies between the Kantian and Rousseauean accounts of political right. Moreover, it argues that the theoretical project undertaken by Rawls, that of revising the Kantian conception of autonomy in an attempt to show how it could be coherently "expressed" politically, was actually undertaken and "completed" by Rousseau – though with ironic, and unsettling results.*

I

How are we to understand the theoretical project undertaken by John Rawls over the past two decades?[1] Some will wonder at the utility of raising such a question; the world wants for many things, but surely not another attempt to take the measure of justice as fairness. Yet it seems to me that for all that has been said about Rawls, the project he continues to pursue has not been adequately understood for what it is. The voice missing from the conversation Rawls has initiated is that of Rousseau, and my claim herein is that our critical vision with regard to justice as fairness must of necessity remain clouded until we bring clearly before the mind's eye the image that casts a long shadow over it: the general will.

My concern here is with what Rawls calls the Kantian interpretation of justice as fairness, and I take "justice as fairness" to refer neither to the substance of Rawls' two principles of justice nor to their application to existing institutions. Instead, I focus, as Rawls has done in his post-*A Theory of Justice* writings, upon the "general concept of justice" from which these more specific aspects of his work are derived. "Justice as fairness," then, I take to refer to the idea that principles of justice morally binding upon citizens are those that would be unanimously agreed to from a point of view that represents and gives expression to their capacities as free and equal moral persons. It is perhaps worth noting here that this idea, and Rawls' project generally, presuppose an ideal conception of the person as their starting point, that is, the conception of persons as free and equal moral persons capable of expressing their capacities as autonomous beings. Rawls readily acknowledges this point,[2] and I take no issue here with this presupposition. My aim is not to criticize the Kantian foundation of Rawls' project from a point without; I accept that foundation, and attempt to work from within his project as a means of bringing to light its distinctive character. The criticisms I shall later raise in regard to justice as fairness I understand to be immanent criticisms made from within the framework of argument set by the Kantian foundation of Rawls' project. I would hope they might also be constructive to the degree they succeed in being immanent.

In elaborating the distinctive features of the Kantian interpretation of justice as fairness, Rawls highlights not only the Kantian features of his project but also the features that depart from Kant's views. He acknowledges that "Justice as fairness is not, plainly, Kant's view strictly speaking; it departs from his text at many points."[3] Now some have wondered whether his deviations from Kant are not more significant than Rawls appears to believe, and hence wonder whether justice as fairness can be properly said to be a "truly" Kantian account of justice. I am not terribly concerned with this issue, for I do not wish to give a "truly" Kantian critique of Rawls' appropriation of Kant. Indeed, I approve the general direction of the departures from Kant that Rawls makes. However, I do believe it highly significant for understanding Rawls' project that he concentrates his discussions on the similarities and differences between *his* view of justice as fairness and Kant's specific views. I shall argue that Rawls' departures point not only *away* from Kant, but necessarily *toward* the account of right given by Rousseau in *The Social Contract*. My claim is, minimally, that it is impossible to fully understand Rawls' project, within its own terms, until one sees how it is situated not merely in relation to Kant, but how it is situated *between* Kant and Rousseau. Finally, I want to suggest that the project undertaken by Rawls is actually carried through to its completion in *The Social Contract*.

I shall attempt to establish these claims in the following manner. In Section II, I explicate the Kantian interpretation of justice as fairness, and highlight the points at which Rawls departs from Kant. In Section III, I sketch the account of right given by Rousseau in *The Social Contract*, and highlight the similarities between this account and justice as fairness, especially those that contrast with Kant's views. In Section IV, I explain how Rawls, Kant, and Rousseau present three alternative solutions to the same problem, and in Section V, I argue that the project pursued by Rawls, that of revising the Kantian conception of autonomy to show how it could be politically expressed and realized, was actually undertaken and "completed" by Rousseau, though with ironic results.

II

The first full discussion of the Kantian interpretation of justice as fairness occurs in Section 40 of *A Theory of Justice*. Rawls notes that "this interpretation is based upon Kant's notion of autonomy."[4] Autonomy is obedience to a law one gives to oneself. The original position, Rawls says, is a procedural interpretation of Kant's conception of autonomy,[5] and the original position is said to make good a central defect of Kant's ethics. That defect concerns the concept of *expression*. Citing Sidgwick's charge that the Kantian conception of autonomy results in the (unfortunate) conclusion that the lives led by both the saint and the scoundrel may be said to be autonomous insofar as each may be understood as the free choice of a noumenal self, Rawls writes:

> Sidgwick's objection is decisive, I think, as long as one assumes, as Kant's exposition seems to allow, both that the noumenal self can choose any consistent set of principles, and that acting from such principles, whatever they are, is sufficient to express one's choice as that of a free and equal rational being.... The missing part of the argument concerns the concept of expression. Kant did not show that acting from the moral law expresses our nature in identifiable ways that acting from contrary principles does not. This defect is made good, I believe, by the conception of the original position. The essential point is that we need an argument showing which principles, if any, must be applicable in practice. A definite answer to this question is required to meet Sidgwick's objection.[6]

Now "Sidgwick's objection" is simply a version of the familiar charge that Kant's ethics are formal and give rise to no substantive duties, or conversely, give license to any and all substantive duties as a consequence of their formality. The Kantian interpretation of justice as fairness, and the concept of the original position that is at the heart of it, are nothing less than an attempt by Rawls to put meat on the bones of Kant's ethical concepts.

The principles of justice substantially determined through the original position do not give rise to merely hypothetical imperatives; rather,

> ...these principles are indeed those defining the moral law, or more exactly, the principles of justice for institutions and individuals. The description of the original position interprets the point of view noumenal selves, of what it means to be a free and equal rational being. Our nature as such beings is displayed when we act from the principles we would choose when this nature is reflected in the conditions determining the choice. Thus men exhibit their freedom, their independence from the contingencies of nature and society, by acting in ways they would acknowledge in the original position.[7]

So the original position may also be said to give *expression* to the Kantian concept of autonomy in that it allows for the substantive determination of that moral law that autonomous beings must *both* give to themselves and obey if they are to practically express their capacities as autonomous beings. Rawls understands the original position to be nothing less than "a procedural interpretation of Kant's conception of autonomy and the categorical imperative."[8] This is the first departure Rawls makes from Kant's specific views, and it is indeed a major one. (I shall hereafter refer to it as Departure 1.) For Kant, the concept of autonomy is an idea of reason, a concept we, as theoretical observers of human action, must attribute to ourselves if we are to make sense of our ordinary moral consciousness, wherein we experience conflicts between the demands of duty and those of interest. Kant does not say we have a duty to be autonomous; he teaches that we must understand ourselves as at least potentially autonomous beings if we are to make coherent sense of our engagement in moral practices. The point is epistemological, not political. Rawls, on the other hand, is proposing a procedure we can use to actually express and realize our capacities as autonomous beings. Such expression requires both a substantive or determinate set of particular principles defining justice (there must be some meat on the bones of Kant's formal concepts) and the delineation of a procedure designed to yield such principles (a means of putting the meat on the bones).

This is not, however, Rawls' only significant departure from the letter of Kant's ethics. At the conclusion of Section 40, he mentions two other ways in which he has departed from Kant. The second of these (Departure 3) has drawn the most attention from Rawls' commentators, but I believe the first (Departure 2) is ultimately the more significant one for understanding Rawls' project.

The second departure (Departure 3) mentioned by Rawls at the end of Section 40 is his assumption that agents to the original position proceed with the knowledge that they are subject to the "circumstances of justice," that is, to conditions of moderate scarcity and competing claims to these moderately scarce resources.[9] Commentators have wondered whether Departure 3 does not violate the spirit and not just the letter of Kant's views. Michael Sandel, for example, questions whether one can legitimately replace Kantian metaphysics with Hume's doctrine of the circumstances of justice and still claim a Kantian heritage. "Deontology with a Humean face," he argues, is something of an oxymoron.[10] Other critics wonder whether Rawls has not revealed his (liberal) ideological biases by assuming the condition of moderate scarcity.[11] I believe reasonable Rawlsian responses can be given to these questions; here, I propose that we assume for the sake of argument that this can be done, and that we focus our attention instead upon the much less discussed Departure 2.

Rawls notes that "the person's choice as a noumenal self I have assumed to be a collective one. The force of the self's being equal is that the principles chosen must be acceptable to the other selves.... This means that as noumenal selves, everyone is to consent to these principles."[12] Then, almost as an aside, Rawls goes on to say of this collective choice that it "in no way overrides a person's interests as the collective nature of the choice may seem to imply. But I leave this aside for the present."[13]

In acting so as to obey principles of right substantively determined through participation in the original position, we express our autonomy, our capacity to obey that which we give to ourselves. The statement that this collective choice "...in no way overrides a person's interests..." is not puzzling if we bear in mind the distinction between our (highest order) interest in expressing our autonomy and our (lower order) interests as phenomenal beings. Autonomy is realized not through satisfaction of desire, but when desire itself is ordered according to self-willed principle. Collective choice of principles of right through the original position, then, far from overriding a person's interests, is actually the means by which a person's highest-order interest is expressed and realized. Utilitarians, or generally anyone who treats "interests" as all of one order, will likely take Rawls' aside with as much chagrin as they take the more famous (and more provocative) aside which it so closely resembles. A Rawlsian gloss on that aside would run as follows: he who refuses to obey principles of right resulting from the original position will be rightfully constrained to do so by the whole social body; which means he will be forced to be autonomous.

The importance of Departure 2 is that we see that not only is Rawls using the original position to give a procedural rendering of the Kantian conception of autonomy, but that he is also doing this at the level of politics, not at the level of private life. Hence the original position is actually a response to *two* perceived defects in Kant's views. The first, leading to Departure 1, is the formality of the ethical concepts themselves; the second leading to Departure 2, is the fact that within Kant's system these concepts are understood to apply to individual actors apart from their political relations with one another. Politics, for Kant, is a realm of instrumentality, a practice that, if it serves the ends of morality, does so in spite of itself, as a consequence of that "hidden plan of nature" that experience fortuitously suggests to him.[14] Rawls, however, is rendering Kantian ethical conceptions into distinctly political terms; he departs from Kant not only in providing a procedural means for autonomy to be *expressed*, but also in providing a means for it to be expressed *politically*. He is attempting not merely to provide a means for allowing the formal concepts of Kant's ethics to be substantively determined, but also to make these concepts directly relevant to the practice of politics. The collective nature of the choice of substantive principles of justice indicates the political nature of the choice. The original position is, above all, a political institution; to obey the principles determined therein is to express ourselves as autonomous citizens.

Lest there be any doubt about the political nature of this departure from Kant, I quote at length from one of Rawls' more recent descriptions of it:

> Another observation is that although I regard justice as fairness as a Kantian view, it differs from Kant's doctrine in important respects. Here I note that justice as fairness assigns a certain primacy to the social; that is, the first subject of justice is the basic structure of society; and *citizens must arrive at a public understanding on a conception of justice for this subject first*. This understanding is interpreted via the unanimous agreement of the parties in the original position. By contrast, Kant's account of the Categorical Imperative applies to the personal maxims of sincere and conscientious individuals in everyday life.... Thus Kant proceeds from the particular, even personal case of everyday life; he assumed that this process carried out correctly would eventually yield a coherent and sufficiently complete system of principles, including principles of social justice. *Justice as fairness moves in quite the reverse fashion: its construction starts from a unanimous collective agreement regulating the basic structure of society within which all personal and associational decisions are to be made in conformity with this prior undertaking.*[15]

The primary expression of autonomy, then, is taken by Rawls to occur at the level of politics rather than private life. The original position regulates the "basic structure" of society, and individual projects are subject to the constraints engendered by the collectively binding principles determined therein. Now the (or at least one) rationale behind Departure 2 is this: it allows

Rawls to meet a criticism often leveled against contractarian accounts of justice, that which complains that such accounts ignore the degree to which individually defined preferences and ends are shaped by the social system within which individuals live. Justice as fairness meets this objection through the requirement that principles of justice regulate the basic structure of society. Rawls acknowledges that, "it has always been recognized that the social system shapes the desires and aspirations of its members; it determines in large part the kind of persons they want to be as well as the kind of persons they are."[16] Yet contractarian accounts of justice have often ignored, or at least failed to fully appreciate the significance of, these mundane facts. In "The Basic Structure as Subject," Rawls criticizes the contractarian theories of Hobbes and Locke (and by implication, Nozick) on just these grounds. "From a Kantian viewpoint," he writes, "Locke's doctrine improperly subjects the social relationships of moral persons to historical and social contingencies that are external to, and eventually undermine, their freedom and equality."[17] Justice as fairness takes neither the existent preferences of individuals nor even their naturally given attributes and talents as morally relevant "givens." Since the formation of substantive preferences as well as the differential values and meanings of individual talents are the consequence of social forms of life, the principles must regulate the basic structure of social forms of life.

The problem we encounter here is this: if indeed the aims and preferences of existent individuals are at least partly the products of the particular form of social life in which they live, how are these individuals to detach themselves from that form of life in order to assess and evaluate it? Rawls' proposal is that they reason about the basic structure of the form of life that is constitutive of their identity from the point of view of the original position, which is the point of view of free and equal autonomous beings. This does not, of course, ontologically detach them from the society in question, for that is, *ex hypothesi*, impossible. It does, however, provide one plausible means of modeling a procedure whereby socially constituted individuals might consciously reflect upon and assess the qualities of the society with which they are constitutively bound. I shall have more to say about the coherence of this idea later; for the moment, I want only to point out that Rawls' formulation of the idea proceeds from recognition, not ignorance, of a point often mistakenly raised against him, that is, that insofar as he is a contractarian he too commits the "original sin" of such theories, that of imagining that individual identity precedes and generates social relations and structure. Not least among the distinctive features of justice as fairness is that it is a version of contractarian theory which affirms that which much contractarian theory denies (the social constitution of individual identity) without abandoning contractarian ideas altogether.

Rawls' forerunner in this regard is Rousseau, and the importance of Departure 2, for our purpose of understanding Rawls' project, lies not so much in how it departs from Kant's contractarianism, but in how it approaches that of Rousseau. *The Social Contract*, I shall argue, may be read, if we may speak anachronistically, as an attempt to do exactly what Rawls sets out to do in Departure 2: provide an account of how the Kantian conception of autonomy can be given expression at the collective level of politics. Of course, Rousseau's account is in important ways very different from that given by Rawls, and I shall try to show presently that these differences may be understood to rest upon differing conceptions of what it could mean to "express autonomy" or, what is the same thing, what it could mean to determine and obey the general will. For the moment, however, I want to describe the striking similarity between their respective accounts of political right, with an eye toward explaining how it is that justice as fairness finds its theoretical resting place *between* Kant and Rousseau.

III

In *The Social Contract*, Rousseau identifies three forms of freedom: natural, civil and moral. Beings in the state of nature are naturally free; through the social contract, natural freedom is exchanged for civil and moral freedom. However, this is only part, and not the most important part, of Rousseau's teaching in regard to the three forms of freedom. In fact, the *exchange* of natural for civil and moral freedom corresponds to and indicates a *transformation* of those beings to whom the forms of freedom are attributed; this is the transformation of "a stupid and ignorant animal into an intelligent being and a man."[18] We cannot fully understand Rousseau's account of right if we think of the shift from state of nature to political society as merely a change in the environment of stable beings or an exchange of one form of freedom for others. Rather, in changing their environment, they change themselves, their very nature. Beings in the state of nature, let us call them "natural beings," possess natural freedom, that is "an unlimited right to anything which tempts him and which he is able to attain."[19] Natural freedom is hence equivalent to natural power; Rousseau's account here is equivalent to that of Hobbes. This natural freedom is lost with the shift to political society. What is gained is, first, civil freedom, that is "property in all that he possesses."[20] Property as right exists only within political society; within the state of nature, "property" is merely "possession, which is nothing but the result of force or the right of the first occupant."[21] The exchange of natural for civil liberty is not, however, the essence of the change from the state of nature to political society. What is also gained thereby is "moral freedom, which alone renders man truly master of himself; for the impulse of mere appetite is slavery, and obedience to a law one prescribes to one's self is freedom."[22]

It is the constitution of moral freedom, or what we have been calling autonomy, that signifies the full extent of the transformation in man that is wrought by the institution of political society. The transformation of natural beings into moral persons is described by Rousseau as follows:

> This passage from the state of nature to the civil state produces in man a very remarkable change, by substituting in his conduct justice for instinct, and by giving his actions the morality that they previously lacked. It is only when the voice of duty succeeds physical impulse, and law succeeds appetite, that man, who till then had regarded only himself, sees that he is obliged to act on other principles, and to consult his reason before listening to his inclinations.[23]

One might then say that the social contract adds a noumenal dimension to human existence that was, by nature, purely phenomenal. Moral consciousness does not exist in the state of nature. Thus it is that human animals can become moral persons only through their social relations. They become beings capable of ordering their activity and relations according to standards of right, where previously they had been slaves of appetite and desire. Moral freedom, then, is constituted by social man developing the capacity of consulting "his reason before listening to his inclinations."[24]

There is nothing surprising about finding that the dualism between natural will and moral reason in Rousseau's thought bears a similarity to the dualism between interest and reason in Kant, who, after all, gratefully acknowledged an intellectual debt to Rousseau. A conventional understanding of their relationship is expressed by Hans Reiss, who writes, "Kant differed from Rousseau in his interpretation of nature and the general will. Above all, whereas Rousseau is frequently ambiguous, he (Kant) is clear."[25] Stephen Korner, in a similar vein, remarks that Rousseau's doctrine of the general will suffers in comparison with Kant because it is obscured "...often by a too narrow concern with purely political issues of philosophy."[26] I shall presently argue that it is just this concern with politics that marks the strength, not the weakness, of Rousseau's account relative to that of Kant. It is worth pointing out, however, that Rawls too sees Kant as superior to Rousseau in this respect. He states that "among other things, Kant is giving a deeper reading to Rousseau's remark 'to be governed by appetite alone is slavery, while obedience to a law one prescribes to oneself is freedom'."[27] As we have seen, Rawls understands justice as fairness to be an attempt to go Kant one better in this respect by developing a procedural interpretation of the Kantian conception of autonomy so that it might be expressed in practical political terms. However, Korner's critical remark concerning the overly political character of Rousseau's treatment of the notions of autonomy and the general will alerts us to the point that I wish to stress – that Rousseau may well have already done what Rawls sets out to do.

The conceptual distinction at the individual level between natural freedom and moral freedom is expressed at the collective level through the opposition between the general will and the "will of all." The "general will" is not the amalgamation of individual interests; it is, rather, the standard of political right. The amalgamation of individual interests by means of a process of mutual competition and conciliation yields the will of all. The general will, to the contrary, signifies the result of deliberation aimed at answering the question, "What is it right for us as a community to do?" Our image of Rousseau as the champion of participatory legislation is apt to mislead us here unless we are careful to qualify it.[28]

The procedure of participatory legislation may take either of two radically different forms, depending upon three interrelated factors: (1) the nature of the question raised and addressed by those participating, (2) the end or purpose of the legislation, and (3) the motivations of the agents involved therein. In each case, the conceptual oppositions at the individual and collective levels previously referred to are reflected in dichotomous dimensions of these aspects of the procedure linking the two. Hence, the procedure leading from the particular wills of individuals to the will of all is characterized by (1) individuals raising and addressing themselves to the question of how a collective policy will advance or hinder their particular interest, (2) political action undertaken toward the end of advancing one's particular interests upon (3) the motivation of satisfying these interests to the greatest possible degree. Conversely, the procedure linking the moral will of the individual with the general will is characterized by (1) individuals raising and addressing themselves to the question of what collective policy is morally right, (2) political action in the form of deliberation aimed at determining a specific and substantive answer to this question upon (3) the motivation of determining such an answer so that each might then also obey it as a means of *expressing* one's moral freedom, that is, the capacity to obey law one has given to oneself. In regard to the procedure whereby the general will is determined substantively in a particular case, one's particular interests are simply irrelevant to the issue at hand. The Rousseauean citizen participating in the determination of the general will is not, by definition, pursuing his particular interest. To do so is to participate in another procedure entirely, that of arriving at the will of all. Let me note here that we are speaking entirely at the level of *the conceptual structure* of Rousseau's account in *The Social Contract*. The practical possibility of such arrangements is not our concern at this point. Instead, I wish to emphasize the structural similarities between this account and that of Rawls, before proceeding to such practical questions.

Recall that Rawls' departures from Kant aim at both (1) giving an account of how autonomy can or could be expressed and (2) giving such an account at the level of collective, public life. These aims require that one define or construct a procedure such that one might express one's autonomy through participation within. Such a procedure serves a threefold purpose. It is the means by which one (1) *gives oneself* (one is a legislator) (2) *a law* (the content must be substantively determined so as to be known) (3) *one is to obey* (obedience to self-prescribed legislation is an essential component of autonomy or moral freedom; to fail to obey such law is to fail to be free, for duty and freedom are not antithetical but mutually presupposing).

Rousseau too can be understood as attempting to define a procedure such that what he calls moral freedom (or what Rawls calls autonomy) can be expressed at the level of collective, public life. Citizens engaged in common deliberation aimed at determining the general will in substantive terms under specific circumstances are thereby expressing their capacities as morally free beings. Insofar as they both define and obey the law determined, they realize the highest of human capacities – those defining morally free citizens.

IV

Having identified the bare structural similarity between the theories of Rawls and Rousseau, we turn now to the substantive differences between them. Here it will prove useful to reintroduce the figure of Kant. To this point, we have taken at face value Rawls' departures from Kant, and also the criticism implied within them. For in proposing that the Kantian conception of autonomy stands in need of revision so as to render it capable of expression at the level of public life, Rawls is supposing that Kant himself failed to do this. Yet this is not really to put the matter accurately. While it is true that Kant provides no account of a procedure for the expression of autonomy that would satisfy Rawls' criteria of what is required in this regard, it is not the case that Kant provides no such account whatsoever. He does provide an answer to the question that motivates Rawls' theorizing, that which asks, "what are the political consequences of the view that persons are free and equal moral beings whose autonomous capacities are expressed through obedience to self-prescribed law?" That answer is plainly insufficient to Rawls' political sensibilities, but it is an answer nonetheless. Indeed, once we look at the divergent answers given to this same question by Kant on the one hand and Rousseau on the other, we can see how Rawls' answer to that question rests precariously and uneasily between the two.

Kant's answer to this question may be seen in the following passage from his essay, "On the Common Saying, 'This May be True in Theory, But It Does Not Apply In Practice,':"

> This, then is an *original contract* by means of which a civil and thus completely lawful constitution and commonwealth can alone be established. But we need by no means assume that this contract (*contractus originarius* or *pactum sociale*), based on a coalition of the wills of all private individuals in a nation to form a common, public will for the purposes of rightful legislation, actually exists as a *fact* for it cannot possibly be so. Such an assumption would mean that we would first have to prove from history that some nation, whose rights and obligations have been passed down to us, did in fact perform such an act, and handed down some authentic record or legal instrument, orally or in writing, before we could regard ourselves as bound by a pre-existing civil constitution. It is in fact merely an *idea* of reason, which nonetheless has undoubted practical reality; for it can oblige every legislator to frame his laws in such a way that they could have been produced by the united will of a whole nation, and to regard each subject, in so far as he can claim citizenship, as if he had consented with the general will. This is the test of the rightfulness of every public law. For if the law is such that a whole people could not *possibly* agree to it (for example, if it stated that a certain class of *subjects* must be privileged as a hereditary *ruling class*), it is unjust; but if it is at least *possible* that a people could agree to it, it is our duty to consider the law as just, even if the people is at present in such a position or attitude of mind that it would probably refuse its consent if it were consulted. But this restriction obviously applies only to the judgement of the legislator, not to that of the subject.[29]

Here one sees Kant's articulation of a "test" by means of which one may, in principle, determine whether or not some particular institutional arrangement may be said to satisfy the requirements of political right. If a community of citizens could have agreed to it, then it can be said to be a rightful law. It is made abundantly clear here that consent is to be understood in a hypothetical, not an empirical, sense. The hypothesis supposed is that of rationality; whether a body of citizens in actuality do or do not consent to some institutional arrangement is, strictly speaking, irrelevant to the question of whether that arrangement is right. What matters is whether or not they could (hypothetically) consent to it insofar as they were to rationally evaluate it. The "general will" referred to here is a rational, not necessarily an empirical, will, and is general to the extent that citizens generally are represented as (hypothetically) rational.

The test of whether some institutional arrangement is an expression of the general will is, from the point of view of twentieth-century representative politics, not a terribly stringent one. All that is necessary for some institutional arrangement to satisfy the requirement of right and hence give rise to a categorical duty of obedience upon the part of subjects is that the arrangement meet the hypothetical test specified. There is no requirement that citizens actually participate in the process resulting in the substantive proposal, only the requirement that the proposal *could* have been agreed to *had* the citizens been consulted and *were* they fully rational. Moreover, for Kant, "citizen" and "subject" are not, as they are for Rousseau, dual attributes of the status of citizenship, but rather comprise different elements of the community itself. Only adult male property owners are eligible for citizenship and legislation.[30]

The hypothetical aspects of Kant's test are not, however, those that move Rawls to develop an alternative. Rather, the fact is that even as a hypothetical test, Kant's proposal is so weak that one could, as Rawls does, take it to amount to no test at all. For example, Kant makes the test apply "only to the judgement of the legislator, not to that of the subject."[31] Moreover, Kant makes no sustained attempt to elaborate the procedural requirements entailed by the test, beyond stating the requirement that "if it is at least possible that a people could agree to it, it is our duty to consider the law as just."[32] Rather than devoting systematic attention to a more detailed elaboration of this formulation, that is, rather than taking up Rawls' concern with "expression," Kant simply mentions two institutional arrangements that, he asserts, violate the test, and leaves it at that.[33] Finally, Kant makes it clear that institutional arrangements failing the test give rise to no right upon the part of citizens to disobey, another point that reflects what I have called the "weak" character of the test. Considering the case of a law that declares permanently valid an ecclesiastical constitution, Kant argues that this would fail the test of political right, and remarks, "Thus a law of this kind cannot be regarded as the actual will of the monarch, to which counter-representations may accordingly be made."[34] Yet he follows this by saying, "In all cases, however, where the supreme legislator did nevertheless adopt such measures, it would be permissible to pass general and public judgements upon them, but never to offer any verbal or active resistance."[35] I shall not take up the perplexing question of how it could be that one could pass "general and public judgements" upon unjust laws without having thereby offered at least verbal resistance to them. The main points I hope to have established here are that (1) Kant does provide an account of a test for determining whether institutional arrangements satisfy the requirements of political right and (2) that this test is both hypothetical and weak in the senses specified.

By way of comparison, we may say that Rawls' test is a more stringent one than Kant's, while keeping in mind that it is at the same time hypothetical. It is more stringent in the following ways. First, Rawls' articulation of the original position is an attempt to specify a procedural test for determining the rightness of institutional arrangements in such a way that citizens can be said to have expressed their autonomy insofar as they participate within it. Second, the account of the original position and the constraints upon deliberation therein (constraints that are liberating in being the necessary or enabling conditions of expressing our capacities as autonomous beings) are worked out to a far more extensive degree than is the case with Kant. Third, admission to the original position is not restricted to (male, property owning) legislators and denied to subjects,but rather open to citizens who, by determining the law they are to obey, express their autonomous citizenship as self-legislating subjects. In sum, whereas Kant gives us at best a minimal account of what it could mean to express autonomy at the political level, Rawls delivers on his promise to take up the problem of expression and provide what we can call a full or at least a fuller account of this problem.

Still, Rawls' account remains hypothetical. Autonomous citizenship means obedience to a law we *could have* given to ourselves from the point of view of the original position. Institutional arrangements respecting the capacities of autonomous citizens need not necessarily be the actual result of activity undertaken by autonomous citizens, or to put it another way, expressing our autonomy means *thinking* about our institutions in a certain way. While Kant is different from Rawls in requiring only a part of the political community to submit legislation to a test of right, both conceive the test at the level of hypothetical reflection. In this, they differ from Rousseau. Like Rawls and unlike Kant, Rousseau does not separate the political community into legislators and subjects; but unlike both Rawls and Kant, Rousseau conceives the procedural test determining the rightfulness of institutional arrangements as one that must actually be institutionalized at the level of practical politics.

Rousseau argues that sovereignty, the right of legislation aimed at determining the general will, cannot be represented. Institutional arrangements respecting the moral freedom of autonomous citizens must actually be the product of citizens expressing in political activity their capacities as autonomous beings. Like Rawls, Rousseau may be said to give an account of what it means to *express* autonomy politically. But whereas for Rawls this turns out to mean "express your autonomy by obeying those laws and institutional arrangements you could have, or would have, given to yourself while reasoning from the point of view of the original position," for Rousseau it means "express your autonomy by obeying those laws and institutional arrangements you actually have given to yourselves through your participation in the procedure aimed at determining the general will." The original position is a hypothetical political institution that makes possible vicarious political participation; Rousseau takes the idea of autonomy literally, and argues that political right requires actual participation in the making of that which we are to obey.

Granting this, it may nevertheless seem that Rousseau's account of what it could mean to have autonomy expressed politically has little to recommend it relative to the account given by Rawls, for Rousseau's argument runs headlong into an apparently intractable paradox. If institutional arrangements satisfying the requirements of political right must actually be the product of the political activity of autonomous citizens, then we must presuppose the existence of such citizens, that is, a political community composed of citizens who leave aside their particular interests and devote themselves to the task of determining the general will so that they might obey it and express thereby their autonomy. We have to thus presuppose autonomy as a realized human capacity, not as an ideal, not an "idea of reason." Such citizens are rare indeed, and Rousseau doubts whether we might be speaking here of gods, not men. Be that as it may, it is nevertheless clear that such citizens, if they were to exist, could only be expected to be found where institutional arrangements themselves nurtured and developed their capacities as autonomous beings. Autonomous citizens, then, presuppose rightly ordered institutional arrangements, but rightly ordered institutions presuppose autonomous citizens capable of constructing them, and we are left in a conundrum. As Rousseau puts it, "it would be necessary that the effect should become the cause; that the social spirit, which should be the work of the institution, should preside over the institution itself, and that men should be, prior to the laws, what they ought to become by means of them."[36] One is not surprised at the element of exasperation in Rousseau's remarking that, "it would require gods to give laws to men."[37]

V

Might we not conclude, then, that Rawls gives us a more viable account of the requirements of political right than does Rousseau? If pushing the idea of "expressing autonomy" from Rawls' hypothetical-proceduralist rendering to Rousseau's literal and practical rendering results in what we might label "the Rousseauean dilemma," aren't we better off with Rawls? One wants to say "yes," on the grounds that Rawls takes the idea of citizens being their own masters as far as one can go without pushing it to an extreme that results in political impracticability and theoretical confusion. Rousseau's account culminates in a view we might term "the political self in permanent revolution."[38] If (1) the self is at least partly constituted through the institutions of which it is part, then (2) to protect its autonomy it demands that these institutions be its own creation. This means the self must constitute itself through the medium of these self-created institutions. But this simply asks too much. The self is (necessarily) already constituted through the medium of institutions that it did not create. The self has existence, has an identity, only in relation to these. Yet they are not its autonomous creation, and indeed cannot be, *in a literal sense*. This would require that the self create itself, but it is already "created." "The self in permanent revolution" is simply no self at all, it has no identity. Autonomy interpreted this way literally breaks down into solipsism, for the self that would create itself is a literal impossibility.

Rawls seems altogether more sober and practical here. Aware that we cannot be fully autonomous in Rousseau's literal sense, he nevertheless appears to provide us with a means of trying to get at Rousseau's problem without lapsing into theoretical incoherence. That is, granted that the "basic structure" of society intimately and constitutively affects who we are, we need not, as it were, acquiesce in our identities (à la Kant) or suppose we must somehow create ourselves anew (à la Rousseau). Rejecting Kant in the name of expressing autonomy, Rawls may also be said to reject Rousseau in the name of recognizing the limits that constrain our ability to express autonomy. Occupying a happy middle ground, Rawls' delineation of a hypothetical thought procedure for determining a hypothetical general will governing the basic structure of society seems to be at once the most we can practically expect of a political theory that takes autonomy seriously and yet avoids the twin "extremes" of Kant's conservative acquiescence to the status quo and Rousseau's revolutionary condemnation of it.

It seems to me, however, that this appearance is ultimately illusory, for the theoretical space between Kant and Rousseau that Rawls would occupy is groundless. To put it another way, I want to suggest that once one departs from Kant in the manner chosen by Rawls, one cannot legitimately stop short of Rousseau, and hence I would argue that "justice as fairness" is what we might term an unstable theoretical formulation, oscillating between the Kantian and Rousseauean poles that serve to define and situate it.

The source of this unstable oscillation is the concept of autonomy itself, or more precisely, the Rawlsian concern over providing an adequate means of "expressing autonomy." For once Kant is amended so as to satisfy this concern, it is hard to see how one can consistently stop short of Rousseau's conclusions, that serve not so much to show how autonomy can be expressed at the collective, political level, as they serve to show that such expression is impossible.

Consider again the essence of Rawls' Kantian interpretation of justice as fairness. Faced with the fact that who we are is constitutively bound up with the institutions and relations composing the basic structure of our society, and aware that this structure is not our creation but the product of history and circumstance, we suddenly find it difficult to see wherein our autonomy exists. We begin to feel that our identities, our very selves, are not "our own," but are also the product of history and circumstance. Far from being the autonomous creators of ourselves through our institutions and relations, we begin to feel that our institutions and relations have created us, and in the name of autonomy we now undergo the ironic experience of experiencing that which is constitutive of our identity as alien, as the chief threat to our identity rather than the ground of it. In a previous age, such an experience would be described as an essentially sinful one, a manifestation of mankind's all-too-human tendency toward pride, the essence of which is to desire to be one's own creator, that is, equivalent to God.

This, however, is a different age. In response to this experience, let us call it the problem of autonomy, Kant and Rousseau work out alternative theoretical formulations. Kant appeals to a possible meaning in history itself that might serve to reconcile man's phenomenal existence with his autonomous essence, an approach taken up and fully articulated by Hegel. Therein, the autonomy of the individual is "rescued" insofar as he comes to the realization that he is a constitutive part of the gradual expression of the whole just as the whole is that which is constitutive of his particular identity. Or in other words, autonomy is "rescued" when it is transcended, when one no longer (falsely) experiences the constitutive ground of one's being and identity as alien, but simply as what it is.

History as meaningful purpose, however, is an idea that appeals to neither Rawls nor Rousseau. In *The Social Contract*, Rousseau in effect argues that the expression of autonomy would require nothing less than that citizens actually give themselves the "basic structure" of society that would constitute their identity. "The self in permanent revolution" is conceptually equivalent to the permanently revolutionary society, which is no society at all. Rousseau does not solve the problem of "expressing autonomy;" he follows the logic of what this would mean to the point that he forces us to see that the "problem" cannot be solved.

Now what of Rawls' response? We are said to express our autonomy through participation in the original position, by *thinking* about the basic structure of our society under the restraints ("veil of ignorance," for example) outlined by Rawls. Institutions and practices that *could have* been agreed to therein are just and can be said to respect our capacities as autonomous beings. But if our concern is one of *expressing* our autonomy, at the *practical* level, it is hard to see why or how this theoretical formulation can satisfy it. Rawls provides a more *elaborate* rendering of the concept of expression than does Kant, but it remains nevertheless a *hypothetical* rendering, regardless of the degree of elaboration. Were elaboration alone the reason underlying Rawls' departures from Kant, justice as fairness might be said to succeed. As we saw, however, this is not the case. Rawls' efforts at elaboration are aimed not merely at "completing" Kant, but at moving beyond him in the direction of giving an account of what it could mean to express autonomy at the practical, political level. That "moving beyond" points in the direction of Rousseau, and calls into question the hypothetical character of Rawls' elaboration.

What reason do we have to accept Rawls' hypothetical thought procedure providing vicarious political participation over Rousseau's demand for an actual, practical procedure requiring literal political participation, given that our concern is one of having human beings express their capacity to autonomously give to themselves the law they would obey? The answer cannot be that Rousseau's formulation is impractical, for while it indeed is impractical, this fact may simply force us to reconsider whether the very idea of "expressing autonomy" is a coherent one. This is why I maintained that it is illusory to see "justice as fairness" as occupying a *happy* middle position between Kant and Rousseau. Once Rawls departs from Kant, there is no reason to stop short of Rousseau. But to follow Rousseau is to call into question the viability of basing a political theory upon the principle of expressing autonomy. This is the sense in which I began by suggesting that Rousseau's account of expressing autonomy through the general will casts a shadow over Rawls' Kantian interpretation of justice as fairness. Justice as fairness, understood as a theory of political right based upon the central value of autonomy, can indeed be placed between the theories of right articulated by Kant and Rousseau, but it is not a particularly happy resting place. Once we place it there, we see more clearly both its essential nature and the deep questions that confront it. Chief among these is that which Rousseau forces upon us – is the ideal of the autonomous person nothing more than a false God?

NOTES

1. The works upon which I draw in this discussion include *A Theory of Justice* and Rawls' main articles through 1984 elaborating the theory worked out there. John Rawls, *A Theory of Justice* (Cambridge, Mass.: Harvard University Press, 1971); "Reply to Alexander and Musgrave," *Quarterly Journal of Economics*, vol. 88, no. 4 (1974), pp. 633–56; "The Basic Structure as Subject," in *Values and Morals*, ed. A.I. Goldman and J. Kim (Dordrecht, Holland: D. Reidel Publishing Company, 1978), pp. 47–71; "A Well-Ordered Society," in *Philosophy, Politics and Society, Fifth Series*, ed. P. Laslett and J. Fishkin (Oxford: Basil Blackwell, 1979), pp. 6–20; "Kantian Constructivism in Moral Theory; The Dewey Lectures, 1980," *Journal of Philosophy*, vol. 77, no. 9 (1980), pp. 515–71.
2. Rawls, "Kantian Constructivism in Moral Theory," pp. 516–17, and also p. 534 where the role of a "conception of the person" is distinguished from that of a "theory of human nature."
3. *Ibid.*, p. 517.
4. Rawls, *A Theory of Justice*, p. 251.
5. *Ibid.*, p. 256.
6. *Ibid.*, p. 255.
7. *Ibid.*, pp. 255–6.
8. *Ibid.*, p. 256.
9. *Ibid.*, p. 257.
10. Michael Sandel, *Liberalism and the Limits of Justice* (Cambridge: Cambridge University Press, 1982), p. 14.
11. In "Kantian Constructivism in Moral Theory," Rawls allows that "moderate scarcity may possibly be overcome or largely mitigated..." (p. 539), but argues that the circumstances of justice would still obtain due to "deep and pervasive differences of religious, philosophical, and ethical doctrine." Justice as fairness, he grants, does presuppose the existence of such "non-materially based" differences, but it is hard to see how this could be said to be an ideologically biased presupposition.
12. Rawls, *A Theory of Justice*, p. 257.
13. *Ibid.*
14. See Immanuel Kant, "Idea for a Universal History with a Cosmopolitan Purpose," in *Kant's Political Writings*, ed. Hans Reiss (Cambridge: Cambridge University Press, 1970), pp. 41–53.
15. John Rawls, "Kantian Constructivism in Moral Theory," pp. 552–3; emphasis added.
16. John Rawls, "A Well-Ordered Society," p. 9.
17. John Rawls, "The Basic Structure as Subject," p. 68; see also "A Well-Ordered Society," pp. 9–10.
18. Jean-Jacques Rousseau, *The Social Contract*, ed. Charles Sherover (New York: Meridian Books, 1974), bk. 1, ch. 8, p. 31.
19. *Ibid.*
20. *Ibid.*, p. 33.
21. *Ibid.*
22. *Ibid.*
23. *Ibid.* p. 31.

24. *Ibid.*
25. Hans Reiss, "Introduction," *Kant's Political Writings*, p. 11.
26. Stephen Korner, *Kant* (New Haven, CT: Yale University Press, 1982), p. 150.
27. Rawls, *A Theory of Justice*, p. 264.
28. See, for example, Carole Pateman, *Participation and Democratic Theory* (Cambridge: Cambridge University Press, 1970), pp. 22–45.
29. Immanuel Kant, "On the Common Saying, 'This May be True in Theory, But It Does Not Apply in Practice,'" Reiss, *Kant's Political Writings*, p. 79.
30. *Ibid.*
31. *Ibid.*, pp. 79–80.
32. *Ibid.* p. 79.
33. These are "...that a certain class of subjects must be privileged as a hereditary ruling class..." and (2) a law "...which declares permanently valid an ecclesiastical constitution" (*ibid.*, p. 85).
34. *Ibid.*
35. *Ibid.*
36. Rousseau, *Social Contract*, bk. 2, ch. 7, p. 69.
37. *Ibid.*, p. 63.
38. An excellent discussion is Bernard Yack, *The Longing for Total Revolution* (Princeton, N.J.: Princeton University Press, 1986).

5 Justice as Fairness: Political or Metaphysical?

In the two decades after the publication of A Theory of Justice, *Rawls reframed certain aspects of his understanding of the nature of that theory, and also devoted greater attention to the question of the role of political philosophy itself in a democratic society. He now argued that his theory of justice could best be understood as a view that was "political, not metaphysical," and that once this difference was understood, many criticisms of the theory would be shown to be misguided. In this chapter I argue that Rawls' theory is not "political" in the senses he claims it to be, and indeed that it cannot be. Rawls' idea of a "political" conception of justice which is neatly situated between and above the twin pitfalls of "metaphysical" and "modus vivendi" conceptions of justice is in some ways similar to the idea of neutrality about the good. Each notion functions to create the sense that liberalism stands as an ordering principle detached from and superior to the conflicting moral ideas at the heart of alternative political moralities. The temptation to think this way about the views they affirm is one that I counsel liberals to resist. That counsel, of course, is unsolicited.*

I

It is not uncommon to hear John Rawls' post-*A Theory of Justice* writings referred to with sentiments of regret, even disappointment. As has often been remarked, *A Theory of Justice* had an impact upon the Anglo-Saxon intellectual world far beyond that achieved by most academic books. One (certainly not the only) reason for this was a widespread perception that Rawls was therein attempting a project of heroic proportion and classical scope: articulating a comprehensive and universal theory of justice founded on first principles. It is impossible to understand the praise bestowed upon Rawls by friend and foe alike for "reviving" the practice of normative political theory without taking into account this perception. Of course, such praise was usually the prelude to a not so faint damnation, as critic after critic pointed to the gaps, holes and presuppositions in the (apparently not so) architectonic structure of Rawls' theory, which I shall follow him in referring to as "justice as fairness" (JAF). And there is more than a little irony in the fact that some who devoted their criticism to demonstrating the failure of JAF to satisfy the (perceived) aim of universality now bemoan the (perceived) fact that Rawls

71

has retreated from the heroic ambitions of *A Theory of Justice* and settled for "merely" systematizing and giving expression to the dominant opinions of modern liberal democracy. One can't help but wonder whether Rawls would have achieved the fame which is now his had he originally spoken as modestly as he now does regarding the ambitions of his theory.[1]

Making use of the conceptual poles within which he situates JAF in his most recent works, I aim here to take issue with both the contemporary views of Rawls and of those (perhaps including himself) who once perceived his work along the "heroic" lines just mentioned; in short, JAF, I shall argue, while not metaphysical, is not political either. If not metaphysical in its original incarnation in *A Theory of Justice*, neither has JAF become "merely" political in its latest. It was and remains, I shall suggest, a theoretical formulation which has continuously rested uneasily between these poles, due primarily to its inability to fully reflect upon and successfully incorporate into itself the problem constituted by this polar dichotomy. The doctrine of JAF is, I submit, an attempt to articulate a conception of justice which would overcome and transcend alternative articulations which either (a) in seeking universality rest on "metaphysical" propositions which do not admit, *ex hypothesi*, of simple verification or universal public agreement, or (b), in avoiding (a) reduce to relative and non-universal propositions which either (b-1) fail to achieve a critical standpoint with regard to existing opinions, norms and institutional practices, or (b-2) turn out to implicitly presuppose the sorts of propositions under (a) that one set out to avoid. The problem with JAF then is *not* that it amounts to an articulation of type (a) *or* (b), but that it lies uneasily between (a) and (b), unable to move beyond a position of oscillating between the two. To call that a "problem" is not, of course, to define a solution, but an attempt to specify the essential nature of JAF as a theory by defining the deeper structure or context within which it moves. This chapter propounds no solution, for the simple reason that I know of none to propound. It does, however, attempt to reflect on the question of what might and might not constitute such a solution by means of buttressing in detail and elaborating the interpretation of JAF just sketched.

Before setting upon that task, three preliminary considerations are in order. First, the decision to speak of JAF rather than of "Rawls' theory" is a necessity generated by Rawls himself. For while he is the author of the works considered here, he has from the start followed the practice of distinguishing various possible interpretations of JAF, often on particular points elaborating one without necessarily criticizing or denying possible others. In light of this, it is difficult at points to clearly distinguish Rawls the proponent of JAF from Rawls the interpreter of JAF. I have chosen, for purposes of discussion, to separate the doctrine of JAF from its author.

Second, by the "doctrine of JAF", I do *not* mean to refer to the substance of Rawls' two principles of justice nor to the application of those principles to existing institutions. Rather, I focus, as Rawls has done in his post-*A Theory of Justice* writings, upon the "general concept of justice" from which these more specific aspects of his works are derived. JAF, then, I take to refer to the idea that principles of justice morally binding upon citizens are those to which they would unanimously agree from a point of view which represented and gave expression to their capacities as free and equal moral persons. Third, my aim herein is not to criticize, in the sense of rejecting, Rawls' idea of justice as fairness. It is rather to bring to light problems and questions which seem to me to remain unresolved in his most recent elaboration of that idea. For whatever it is worth, I am in many ways sympathetic to Rawls' basic views regarding justice; the analysis undertaken here is thus at least intended to be an expression of immanent and constructive criticism.

II

In his most recently published articles, Rawls offers an account of "how I now understand the conception of justice that I have called justice as fairness."[2] This understanding is designated as "political." There are three key senses in which JAF is said to constitute a political account of justice. (1) It is interpreted in such a way that it is made independent, as far as possible, of any "controversial philosophical and religious doctrines" or "claims to universal truth, or claims about the essential nature and identity of persons."[3] It is then independent of any particular conception of the good, or as Rawls puts it, any "comprehensive moral ideal." (2) As a consequence, a political account of justice is said to be subject to different standards of "justification" than other accounts. A metaphysical account of justice would be one which defined justice in terms either of the conception of the good or the metaphysical theory of the self it held to be ultimately true. Justification of such an account would be an "epistemological or metaphysical problem," for it would ultimately turn on the question of whether the moral ideal from which it was derived was indeed the true rational good for human beings or whether the metaphysical theory of the self was indeed true. On the other hand, Rawls says that for a political conception of justice, justification is "a practical social task."[4] That "task" is specified as follows:

> Thus the aim of justice as fairness as a political conception is practical, and not metaphysical or epistemological. That is, it presents itself not as a conception of justice that is true, but one that can serve as a basis for

informed and willing political agreement between citizens viewed as free and equal persons.... To secure this agreement we try, so far as we can, to avoid disputed philosophical, as well as disputed moral and religious questions.[5]

(3) The third sense in which JAF is defined as political is that it is self-consciously rooted in a particular historical context, and is understood to arise as a response to a practical problem existing within that context. In the case of JAF, the context is "modern constitutional democracy," and the problem is that "...as a practical political matter no general moral conception can provide a publicly recognized basis for a conception of justice in a modern democratic state."[6] JAF is not a "general moral conception," but a conception of justice designed to secure fair terms of agreement regulating the basic structure of a democratic society consisting of adherents to alternative general moral conceptions, or conceptions of the good.

Now in order to evaluate Rawls' claim that JAF is political and not metaphysical, we need a clear grasp of what distinguishes these two categories of conceptions of justice. Yet a perplexing feature of Rawls' account is that while he devotes much attention to explaining the sense in which JAF is a political conception of justice, he devotes relatively little to explicitly elaborating the distinction between political and metaphysical conceptions generally.

In a moment, I shall attempt to construct that distinction, reasoning from the three senses of "political" outlined above. Before elaborating the substantive differences between political and metaphysical conceptions of justice, however, we need to take note of two formal aspects of that distinction. First, it is unclear from Rawls' account whether these categories are taken to be exhaustive of possible conceptions of justice or not. Rawls says nothing explicitly about this, and I shall proceed on the assumption that they are exhaustive categories, on the further assumption that did he understand there to be some third (or fourth, or so on) category, he would have discussed them. Second, and more importantly, we note that as *categories* of conceptions of justice, one would suppose that there would, or could, be a number of conceptions within each category. This mundane consideration turns out to be quite important in terms of assessing JAF, which is after all *a* political conception of justice on Rawls' understanding, and presumably not the only one. One level of assessment of JAF would involve an evaluation of it relative to alternative political conceptions in terms of how well each satisfied the aims of such conceptions. Rawls does not undertake such a task, and what is at issue here is more than simply a matter of unfinished business. As we shall see, Rawls defines the general category of political conceptions of justice in such a way that JAF comes to be treated as a uniquely privileged political conception of justice, for crucial attributes of JAF, a particular conception of justice, are (unwittingly, I think) read into the criteria defining the more general category in an ad hoc manner. This makes it difficult to evaluate JAF at the level just specified, for it is given an inherent advantage over its competitors as a political account of justice.[7]

Let us first turn to the problem of distinguishing political from metaphysical conceptions of justice. Taking the three aspects in which Rawls speaks of JAF as a political conception of justice, we can set out to derive the distinguishing features of a metaphysical conception.

Let us label these three aspects of political conceptions as (1) independence of controversial philosophical claims, or *non-controversial foundations*, (2) justification in practical terms, or *practical justification*, and (3) *historical rootedness*. If we define metaphysical conceptions by contrast, we arrive at the conclusions shown in Table 5.1.

Table 5.1: Conceptions of Justice

Distinguishing Criteria	CONCEPTIONS OF JUSTICE	
	Metaphysical	Political
Philosophical Dependence	Dependent claims to truth of controversial philosophical claims; hence *philosophically controversial*	Independent of such claims; hence *philosophically uncontroversial*
Standards of Justification	Epistemological or metaphysical; justified by reference to *truth* of basic premises or axioms	*Practical*; justified in terms of securing fair agreement among free and equal persons
Scope of Application	*Universal*; applicable to all historical societies, not relative to one	*Historically limited*: arises from a particular historical situation, applicable only to it

It is important that we understand Rawls' use of the concept of "metaphysical" in the works under consideration here, and not confuse it with meanings that terms takes on in different contexts. Rawls uses the term in a straightforward, though perhaps unconventional, way. It refers most generally to controversial philosophical claims purporting to be true. We are liable to be misled if we confuse this meaning with the idea of metaphysics as, say, that "branch of philosophy that systematically investigates the nature of first principles and problems of ultimate reality...including the study of being (ontology) and, often, the study of the structure of the universe (cosmology)."[8] For while "metaphysics" thus understood certainly comprises controversial philosophical claims, Rawls is using it in a wider and looser sense to refer to any doctrine entailing controversial philosophical claims, not simply ontological or cosmological ones. The significant point is that doctrines expressing moral ideals or conceptions of the good can fall within this category. JAF is said not to rest upon any such doctrine, and hence assessment of it is said not to be a matter of determining the truth value of its basic premises or axioms, its "first principles."

Now given the distinctions outlined in Table 5.1, there are two levels of assessment in which we might engage. One would proceed from asking – How successful is JAF as a political conception of justice? The litmus test would ultimately be practical; would a society in which citizens approached and settled questions of justice along the lines outlined by JAF be a peaceful and harmonious one, relative to possible alternatives? The second level would involve raising a logically prior question; rather than taking the category of "political" accounts of justice as the given starting point for analysis, we would assess the rationale for adopting that starting point in the first place. In short, it would proceed from asking – What are the reasons for preferring political accounts of justice to metaphysical ones, and are they sound ones?

Taking up this latter question, we can identify two sorts of considerations which might lead one to undertake to replace metaphysical accounts of justice with a political one. The common root of such an enterprise is the fact of long-standing intractable disagreement between alternative metaphysical accounts of justice and the comprehensive moral systems of which they are part. Following Rawls, let us speak of this condition as "the fact of pluralism."[9] But responses to this fact can be described as either "theoretical" or "practical" depending upon the sources to which this intractability is attributed. The "theoretical" response would be that metaphysical accounts of justice (and the comprehensive moral systems of which they are part) cannot meaningfully be said to be true or false, and hence should be abandoned. This response would take the form of philosophical skepticism. The "practical" response would abandon metaphysical accounts without denying that such an account might ultimately and actually be true. Such a response would hold that whatever the correct answer to metaphysical questions relating to justice might be, the fact remains that for all practical purposes one should treat metaphysical accounts *as if* they are intractable, for the fact of pluralism shows that people do disagree about them and there is no practically known method, short of the autocratic use of state power, of publicly adjudicating these disputes; hence the need for a political account of justice.

A great deal hinges upon which of these considerations motivates the preference for a political account of justice over a metaphysical one. One proceeding from the "theoretical" consideration would in effect be a metaphysical argument against the viability of metaphysics, insofar as its skepticism regarding truth failed to extend to itself. One proceeding from the practical consideration would be a less skeptical, more overtly political, argument, "bracketing out" the metaphysical questions in the name of the need for agreement. It would seem, however, that this "bracketing out" would presuppose the value of agreement itself (or the value of freedom underlying it), and must at least rate it as of higher value than truth. Once this evaluation is called into question, the "practical" respondent would be pushed back to the sort of metaphysical issue he or she sought to avoid, for if agreement is of greater value than truth, it is by no means self-evidently so.

It is clear that Rawls rests his case for a political understanding of JAF upon the "practical" considerations. He is careful to make it clear that he wishes to leave metaphysical level questions open; as he modestly puts it, "...Justice as fairness deliberately stays on the surface, philosophically speaking."[10] This "staying on the surface" is what Rawls calls "the method of avoidance," wherein "we try, so far as we can, neither to assert nor to deny any religious, philosophical or moral views, or their associated philosophical accounts of truth and the status of values."[11] He stresses the point that JAF as he now conceives it is *not* premised upon philosophical skepticism, including skepticism about what is truly good for human beings. It is meant to allow the possibility of an objectively true metaphysics, without affirming or denying any particular account. Aware that the "method of avoidance" might be understood as resting upon philosophical skepticism, he argues, to the contrary, that "...it would be fatal to the point of a political conception to see it as skeptical about, or indifferent to, truth, much less as in conflict with it."[12] It is the overriding value of, and need for, agreement that serves to justify this conscious superficiality. To go beneath the surface would be to begin inquiring into the truth value of the doctrine at hand, and this would threaten the possibilities of agreement, not to say consensus. Rawls writes:

> Thus, the aim of justice as fairness as a political conception is practical, and not metaphysical or epistemological. That is, it presents itself not as a conception of justice that is true, but one that can serve as the basis of informed and willing political agreement between citizens viewed as free and equal persons. This agreement when securely founded in public political and social attitudes sustains the good of all persons and associations within a just democratic regime. *To secure this agreement we try, so far as we can, to avoid disputed philosophical, as well as disputed moral and*

*religious, questions. We do this not because these questions are unimportant
or regarded with indifference, but because we think them too important
and recognize that there is no way to resolve them politically. The only
alternative to a principle of toleration is the autocratic use of state power.*
Thus, justice as fairness deliberately stays on the surface, philosophically
speaking. Given the profound differences in belief and conceptions of the
good at least since the Reformation, we must recognize that, just as on
questions of moral and religious doctrine, public agreement on the basic
questions of philosophy cannot be obtained without the state's infringement
of basic liberties. Philosophy as the search for truth about an independent
metaphysical and moral order cannot, I believe, provide a workable and
shared basis for a political conception of justice in a democratic society.

We try, then, to leave aside philosophical controversies whenever
possible, and look for ways to avoid philosophy's longstanding problems.[13]

Now it is doubtless true that public agreement upon disputed moral issues
is the last thing to be expected in contemporary liberal-democratic societies.
Any critic of Rawls, indeed any observer of such societies, would surely agree
with that. What is open to question is not this sociological fact of pluralism,
but rather the precise philosophical significance which Rawls attributes to
it, and correspondingly, the philosophical weight and argumentative burden
it carries in his account of justice.

The fact of pluralism alone cannot justify adherence to a political conception
of justice rather than to a metaphysical one. While it is true that in
contemporary liberal-democratic societies no conception of metaphysical
justice would be universally agreed to by "citizens viewed as free and equal
persons," a resulting preference for political accounts presupposes the value
of viewing one another in this way, that is, in respecting each citizen's right
(as a free and equal moral person) to, as it were, veto any metaphysical
conception which would be incompatible with his or her own conception.
My point here is not to quarrel with that "basic value", but simply to point
out that it *is* just that. When Rawls remarks that "the only alternative to a
principle of toleration is the autocratic use of state power," this point is
obscured. State enforcement of a comprehensive moral ideal is "autocratic"
insofar as we accept the primary value of equal individual liberty at issue
here. The point is that the mere fact of pluralism is not sufficient to ground
the acceptance of that value. Hence the preference for avoiding controversial
philosophical issues commits one to affirming a position on a controversial
philosophical issue, in this case an affirmation by Rawls of the priority of
the value of liberty. However much the "method of avoidance" may allow
us to avoid affirming or denying particular moral judgments, what is

unavoidable is the affirmation of the value which would justify the choice to employ it in the first place.

It is this necessity which generates what I see as the as yet unresolved problem of oscillation in Rawls' account. To argue for the affirmation of the value of the individual's liberty to define and pursue his or her own conception of the good is to risk moving to a "metaphysical" level position; yet to avoid that risk in the name of avoiding controversy is to leave the method of avoidance without justification itself. To be sure, Rawls has a good deal more to say than we have thus far considered, and we need now to take up his arguments in greater detail. In doing so, I shall attempt to show that even as Rawls deepens his account of JAF as a political conception of justice in ways designed to resolve the "problem of oscillation," that problem reappears at another level.

III

"Justice as fairness deliberately stays on the surface, philosophically speaking."[14] This notion bears thinking through. A deliberate superficiality is something more than a naive one; it presupposes a ground or rationale which would serve to explain it, and we are thus led to seek the nature of the deliberation behind it. At first glance, we might suppose that the threat of civil conflict, along with the corresponding desirability of civil peace, are the operative values here. On this reading, a political conception of justice would constitute an antidote to the dangers of civil strife constituted by the spectre of a politics of competition amongst comprehensive moral doctrines. For ease of reference, let us refer to such a reading as the "Hobbesian version" of a political account of justice.

Initially, it appears that Rawls is moving in the direction of interpreting JAF in such a manner, given the emphasis placed upon avoiding controversy over substantive moral disagreement. This seems even more evident when he goes on to explain the sense in which he understands JAF to constitute a liberal account of justice. For while Rawls explicitly characterizes JAF as a liberal account of political justice, he is careful to distinguish it from the "liberalisms of Kant and J.S. Mill," which are said to stem from the "comprehensive moral ideals" of autonomy and individuality respectively. Just because of this commitment to comprehensive moral ideals, these "liberalisms" are said to be "unsuited for a political conception of justice," for each thus understood is said to express "...but another sectarian doctrine."[15] JAF, to the contrary, is committed to no such comprehensive moral ideal; rather, it "...seeks to identify the kernel of an overlapping consensus"[16] *amongst* comprehensive moral ideals.[17] It would appear, then, that a further (fourth) key sense in which JAF is to be interpreted as "political" is that of eschewing substantive moral commitment altogether, aiming instead at specifying the procedures which make possible a prudentially based peace treaty amongst adherents of alternative moral views.

However, this appearance is mistaken. Immediately upon distinguishing the political interpretation of JAF from any conception of justice founded upon a comprehensive moral ideal, Rawls turns to distinguish it on the other hand from a "merely prudential" account of justice, and it is therefore worth looking carefully at Rawls' statements in this regard. He argues that while JAF is "political" in the sense that it presupposes no commitment to any comprehensive moral ideal, it is *not* to be interpreted as "political" in the sense that it is an a-moral conception of procedural justice. He remarks that while the idea of an overlapping consensus amongst comprehensive moral ideals "...may seem essentially Hobbesian,"[18] it is not to be understood in this way. So, while it may appear that "...the public acceptance of justice as fairness is no more than prudential; that is, a *modus vivendi* which allows the groups in the overlapping consensus to pursue their own good subject to certain constraints which each thinks to be to its fair advantage given existing circumstances,"[19] Rawls argues that this is mistaken and that in fact JAF "...*is* a moral conception."[20] Now in purely formal terms, it is easy enough to identify the boundaries of the idea of a "political" conception of justice Rawls is pursuing here; "political" is not defined in opposition to "moral," but at the same time it is to be understood as something other than a conception of justice founded upon a comprehensive moral ideal. In "The Idea of an Overlapping Consensus," Rawls describes this balancing aim of JAF as follows: "...this view steers a course between the Hobbesian strand in liberalism – liberalism as a *modus vivendi* secured by a convergence of self- and group-interests as coordinated and balanced by well-designed constitutional arrangements – and a liberalism founded on a comprehensive moral doctrine such as that of Kant and Mill."[21]

But while it is clear that this is what Rawls *wants* of a "political" conception of justice, it remains unclear how one could achieve this desideratum of a moral conception of justice which presupposes no controversial philosophical arguments establishing its particular moral character. As a means of trying to explain how this achievement is possible, Rawls gives two arguments designed to show that the political interpretation of JAF does not make of it a merely prudential, or Hobbesian, account.

First, Rawls reminds us that JAF *is* a moral conception; "....it has conceptions of person and society, and concepts of right and fairness, as well as principles of justice with their complement of the virtues through which those principles are embodied in human character and regulate social and political life."[22]

Second, Rawls claims that,

...in such a consensus each of the comprehensive philosophical, religious, and moral doctrines accepts justice as fairness in its own way; that is, each comprehensive doctrine, from within its own point of view, is led to accept the public reasons of justice specified by justice as fairness. We might say that they recognize its concepts, principles and virtues as theorems, as it were, at which their several views coincide. But this does not make these points of coincidence any less moral or reduce them to mere means. For, in general, these concepts, principles and virtues are accepted by each as belonging to a more comprehensive philosophical, religious, or moral doctrine.[23]

We will take up the latter argument later in this chapter. In regard to the former, it seems to me that the precisely *moral* character of the overlapping consensus aimed at by JAF remains obscure, and that Rawls' remarks here constitute more a (re)statement of what a political conception must amount to than an explanation of how such an account can be given. The polar oppositions which Rawls seeks to avoid are clear enough; JAF must not be premised upon a *comprehensive* moral ideal of individual character, for it would then fail to qualify as a non-controversial conception of a procedure capable of adjudicating conflict amongst moral ideals. Rawls' insistence that it not on the other hand be conceptualized as a modus vivendi proceeding from prudent self-interest is more difficult to understand. Given the stress he lays upon the practical functions of JAF as a political, rather than a metaphysical, account of justice, one wonders why, exactly, he is so uneasy with the Hobbesian rendering of the idea of overlapping consensus. What could account for the insistence upon Rawls' part that JAF not be so understood?

One supposes that the insistence proceeds from an underlying Kantian notion of the separation between morality and prudence, and the resulting fear that a Hobbesian reading of the "political" character of JAF would fail to provide a sufficiently *moral* account of the citizen's obligation to accept and obey the institutional practices which would result from the original position. On a Hobbesian reading, the account of obligation would take on a decidedly prudential and utilitarian flavor; adherents of opposing conceptions of the good would accept the terms of the cease-fire yielded by JAF insofar as they reckoned that, outright victory being unobtainable, it would be preferable to peacefully coexist with their opponents rather than engage in a (presently?) futile effort to remove or "convert" them. Within the terms of Rawls' project, then, one can identify a first rationale for resisting the "Hobbesian interpretation" of JAF. Were Rawls' argument understood along these lines, it could not plausibly be said to fulfill the avowed Rawlsian aim of providing "...an alternative to the dominant utilitarianism of our tradition of political thought."[24] Instead, it would have become a prudential version of it.

Yet this rejection of the "Hobbesian interpretation" calls into question the "political" character of JAF, even as it saves it from being rendered as a prudential doctrine. If we reject the Hobbesian reading, it would seem that we are forced into the position of supposing some kind of "metaphysical level" foundation for JAF sufficient to give an account and defense of the moral value of tolerance itself. Now, liberalism has offered such accounts, notably in the theories of Kant and J.S. Mill.[25] Yet the very feature which would make them attractive in this respect is that which leads Rawls to place them in the category of "comprehensive moral ideals" expressing "sectarian doctrines." How can one have it both ways?

Now Rawls does anticipate this problem, and provide a response to it. But I think it can again be shown that the response, rather than resolving the dilemma, simply gives expression to it at another, deeper, level of analysis. To see this, we need first to look at Rawls' conception of moral personality, for it is through the explication of this idea that Rawls provides a response to the manifestation of the problem of oscillation just sketched.

JAF, understood as a model procedure capable of accommodating an overlapping consensus amongst alternative conceptions of the good, is premised upon a particular conception of the person. Most notably, participants in the original position are defined as "free and equal persons." Rawls explains each attribute as follows:

> The basic intuitive idea is that in virtue of what we may call their moral powers, and the powers of reason, thought, and judgement connected with these powers, we say that persons are free. And in virtue of having these powers to the requisite degree to be fully cooperating members of a society, we say that persons are equal.[26]

He continues by elaborating this conception of the person: "Since persons can be full participants in a fair system of cooperation, we ascribe to them the two moral powers connected with the elements in the idea of social cooperation noted above: namely, a capacity for a sense of justice and a capacity for a conception of the good."[27] As well as being premised upon this conception of the person, the procedure advanced by JAF is designed not to yield a basis for social cooperation simply, but for *fair* social cooperation.[28] The original position is the element of JAF wherein these ideas receive their procedural expression.

> ... The fair terms of social cooperation are conceived as agreed to by those engaged in it, that is, by free and equal persons as citizens who are born into the society in which they lead their lives. But their agreement, like any other valid agreement, must be entered into under appropriate conditions. In particular, these conditions must situate free and equal persons fairly and must not allow some persons greater bargaining advantages than others. Further, threats of force and coercion, deception and fraud, and so on, must be excluded.[29]

Hence we arrive at what Rawls calls the "fundamental question of political justice: namely, what is the most appropriate conception of justice for specifying the terms of (fair) social cooperation between citizens regarded as free and equal persons, and as normal and fully cooperating members of society over a complete life."[30] Now in light of the above, we see that JAF does qualify as a moral theory of justice, at least in the descriptive sense that it rather obviously comprises moral premises: the conception of persons as free and equal, and the further requirement that terms of social cooperation must satisfy a condition of fairness, which they will do just insofar as they result from a procedure which respects and embodies this conception of the person. It would seem however, that this would undermine the claim that JAF qualifies as a political account of justice, given the apparently Kantian basis of this conception of moral personality which is admitted to be its very heart. In the earlier Dewey Lectures, Rawls seemed to accept as much. As William Galston aptly summarizes the argument therein, "...the Dewey lectures can be seen as resolving the tension, which runs through *A Theory of Justice*, between the Kantian and the rational-prudential account of human agency, by offering a thoroughgoing reconstruction of justice as fairness along frankly Kantian lines."[31]

In his recent work, however, Rawls distances himself from such a reading of JAF. To be sure, from a purely descriptive point of view the quasi-Kantian notion of moral personality remains at the heart of JAF. To argue for it *in these terms*, however, by appealing to the "Kantian interpretation," would make JAF a "sectarian doctrine," and undermine any interpretation of it as a political account of justice capable of accommodating the range of sectarian doctrines which receive expression in modern democratic culture. Aware of this tension, Rawls offers no direct philosophical argument in support of this conception of moral personality; instead, he argues that "...the conception of persons as having the two moral powers, and therefore as free and equal, is also a *basic intuitive idea assumed to be implicit in the public culture of a democratic society.*[32]

With this move, Rawls avoids the charge that JAF is a metaphysical account of justice. The justification for the "moral" elements of JAF is now articulated in the form of an *empirical* proposition about the self-understanding of persons in democratic societies. JAF is thus said to derive its conception of the person not from any Kantian or quasi-Kantian philosophical foundation, but rather from the (alleged) fact that this conception of the person is accepted as more or less a given in the "public culture of a democratic society." But if we allow that this interpretation succeeds in detaching JAF from any controversial metaphysical foundation, it does not follow that the new, "empirical," foundation is any less controversial.

To begin, one might question the validity of the empirical proposition itself. Is it true that, whatever the ultimate metaphysical merits of the Rawlsian conception of moral personality, this conception is the (at least implicit) self-understanding of contemporary liberal citizens? Granting that it is the predominant one, Rawls himself recognizes that it is something less than universal.[33] This recognition can be glimpsed by looking at Rawls' explanation of those conceptions of the good which are *impermissible* within the terms of JAF. He openly acknowledges that in JAF, "...the concept of justice is independent from and prior to the concept of goodness in the sense that its principles limit the conceptions of the good which are permissible."[34] Echoing the rejection of perfectionist doctrines which extends back to the incarnation of JAF in *A Theory of Justice*, Rawls excludes from consideration those conceptions which "...hold that there is but one conception of the good which is to be recognized by all persons, so far as they are fully rational."[35] This turns out to be, to say the least, a rather expansive category, and Rawls himself describes it as including the "dominant tradition since classical times."[36] He explicitly mentions Plato, Aristotle, and the "Christian tradition as represented by Augustine and Aquinas," as theorists or theories falling under it. Liberalism, on the other hand, of which JAF is an example, is said to be,

> ...a political doctrine (which) holds that the question the dominant tradition has tried to answer has no practical answer; that is, it has no answer suitable for a political conception of justice in a democratic society. In such a society, a teleological political conception is out of the question: public agreement on the requisite conception of the good cannot be obtained.[37]

By my lights, this seems a remarkable argument. But in the present context, I leave aside the question of whether Rawls has done justice to the "dominant tradition" by so characterizing it as what amounts to narrow-mindedness. Instead, I note only that the argument circumscribes sharply the range of conceptions of the good which might find their place within the "overlapping consensus" provided by JAF. That consensus, we now see, will comprise only those doctrines which can accept the Rawlsian conception of moral personality. Those doctrines which do not accept or embody that conception of moral personality are, as Rawls bluntly puts it, "out of the question." Hence we see that it is, strictly speaking, false to say that JAF serves to fairly adjudicate amongst competing conceptions of the good simply. By Rawls own account, JAF serves to adjudicate amongst those conceptions of the good which, whatever their other differences, share an underlying consensual acceptance of the Rawlsian idea of moral personality. Any other doctrines are ruled out prima facie.

Adherents of those doctrines who also happen to be citizens of liberal societies will surely wish to point out to Rawls that, however predominant his conception of moral personality is in such societies, it is something less than universal. Were Rawls more willing to embrace the Hobbesian interpretation of JAF, he would have a ready reply to any complaints that such adherents might voice, roughly along the lines of "grin and bear it." In the absence of that, it is hard to see what sort of moral, as opposed to prudential, reply could be given, especially when we recall that Rawls' project here prevents him from asserting and arguing the philosophical inadequacy of any such doctrine; that would be to pursue a strategy of "metaphysical", not political, argument. One could, of course, claim that no such doctrines are actually held by citizens of contemporary liberal societies; but the manifest absurdity of that proposition would be evident to no one more than a professor of political theory whose book elicited public howls of complaint from just such fellow citizens.[38] Barring an ad hoc refusal to address the issue at all, another alternative would be to pursue the strategy Rawls (unwittingly?) slips into when he remarks at one point that the basic ideas of JAF "...are likely to be affirmed by each of the opposing comprehensive moral doctrines *influential* in a reasonably just democratic society."[39] But here again, Hobbesian prudentialism would seem to have reared its ugly head; adherents of "non-influential" comprehensive moral doctrines will surely wish an account of the *moral* basis for imposing the legal order sanctioned by JAF upon them simply because they lack the *power* to make their views influential.

In "The Idea of an Overlapping Consensus," Rawls revises this strategy by speaking of the bounds of the consensus as excluding *unreasonable* moral views rather than *non-influential* ones. He writes:

Certain truths, it may be said, concern things so important that differences about them have to be fought out, even should this mean civil war. To this we say, first that questions are not removed from the political agenda, so to speak, solely because they are a source of conflict. Rather, we appeal to a political conception of justice to distinguish between those questions that can be reasonably removed from the political agenda and those that cannot, all the while aiming for an overlapping consensus. Some questions still on the agenda will be controversial, at least to some degree; this is normal with political issues.[40]

Now if our primary worry was that an overlapping consensus provided by a political conception of justice would be "too tight" in the sense that it dissolved too many, or all, sources of political disagreement, this would, perhaps, satisfy us. But if our worry is the prior one of understanding (so as to be able to assess) the justification for requiring adherents of moral conceptions which do not fit within the overlapping consensus provided by JAF to nevertheless obey the legal order consistent with that consensus, this doesn't help. It merely labels such conceptions as unreasonable, without explaining why we should accept the appropriateness of the label. That such conceptions are *illiberal* is, of course, clear beyond a doubt; but that is surely no argument against their reasonableness. Were I an adherent of one of these illiberal conceptions living under the (state-enforced!) legal order consistent with JAF, I would suspect that although the language of Rawls' account has shifted here from non-influential to non-reasonable, the operative idea has remained the same; that is, there aren't enough of us illiberal sectarians with enough *power* to prevent the more powerful liberals from erecting a legal order reflecting *their* values and requiring us to live by it as well.

A further strategy of response by Rawls to adherents of moral ideals falling outside the overlapping consensus is contained in the second of his explanations as to why the political interpretation of JAF is not merely a Hobbesian modus vivendi. To recall, Rawls argues that

...in such a consensus each of the comprehensive philosophical, religious, and moral doctrines accepts justice as fairness in its own way; that is, each comprehensive doctrine, from within its own point of view, is led to accept the public reasons of justice specified by justice as fairness. We might say that they recognize its concepts, principles and virtues as theorems, as it were, at which their several views coincide. But this does not make these points of coincidence any less moral or reduce them to mere means. For, in general, these concepts, principles and virtues are accepted by each as belonging to a more comprehensive philosophical, religious, or moral doctrine.[41]

This idea, first articulated in "Justice as Fairness: Political not Metaphysical," is elaborated in "The Idea of an Overlapping Consensus." After briefly explicating that elaboration, I want to examine and assess it at two levels: (1) as a response to the charge that a political conception of justice is merely prudential and (2) as an explanation of the moral grounds for enforcing a liberal legal order upon adherents of illiberal moral ideals. As we shall see, the two levels are closely linked.

A key element of the idea is that a political conception of justice is limited in scope to the political framework of the *state*; it allows for, and is indeed built upon, the recognition and acceptance of a diversity of comprehensive moral ideals and conceptions of the good operative within *society*. Following Rawls, let us define community as "...an association or society whose unity rests on a comprehensive conception of the good."[42] It follows that while JAF as a political conception of justice rules out the possibility of the state as a community in this sense, it does allow for communities to exist at the level of society, as Rawls says "...in the various associations which carry on their life within the framework of the basic structure and second in those associations that extend across the boundaries of nation-states, such as churches and scientific societies."[43] JAF as a political conception of justice is said to make no judgment regarding the truth of any of "the comprehensive conceptions of the meaning, value and purpose of human life, or conceptions of the good," operatively shared in any of these private communities.[44] "They are all equally permissible, *provided they respect the limits imposed by the principles of political justice.*"[45]

Would, then, an overlapping consensus amongst such communities to accept JAF as regulating the basic structure of political society be a moral and not merely prudential agreement? The answer to this question is indeterminable in the abstract. Rawls' claim, recall, is that "...in such a consensus each of the comprehensive philosophical, religious, and moral doctrines accepts justice as fairness in its own way...they recognize its concepts, principles and virtues as theorems, as it were, at which their several views coincide."[46] This would be accurate in regard to those doctrines, or communities built upon shared adherence to such doctrines, which contain somewhere within themselves a commitment to the value of individual liberty *as that value is understood in JAF*. Doctrines or communities without such a commitment, though, would by definition be unable to be a part of such a consensus, at least on moral grounds. Presumably, they would either be simply excluded from it, or would accept it (and be accepted within it) upon prudential grounds only. So the degree to which the overlapping consensus of JAF would be moral rather than prudential would depend upon the particular society in question, and upon the substantive nature of the "private" communities within it.

The "model case" of an overlapping consensus Rawls utilizes for illustrative purposes is not likely to answer our questions in this respect. He describes it thus:

> It contains three views: one view affirms the political conception because its religious doctrine and account of faith lead to a principle of toleration and underwrite the values of a constitutional regime; the second view affirms the political conception on the basis of a comprehensive liberal moral doctrine such as those of Kant and Mill; while the third supports the political conception not as founded on any wider doctrine but rather as in itself sufficient to express political values that, under the reasonably favorable conditions that make a more or less just constitutional democracy possible, normally outweigh whatever other values may oppose them.[47]

The disappointing feature of this example stems from the fact that all three exemplars of comprehensive views are "easy cases" for JAF. One is not surprised, after all, to find that those who find the political conception acceptable in itself as a moral view (the third case) are able to affirm it morally! And there is no difficulty in accepting that the other two exemplars can morally affirm JAF, as each contains within itself a deep commitment to the value of equal individual liberty. One wishes that the religious group imagined by Rawls (the first case) would have been drawn more from the model of Amish or Mennonites or Jehovah's Witnesses than from, as appears to have been the case, Unitarians.

I conclude that as a reply to the suspicion that the overlapping consensus of JAF is merely prudential rather than moral, Rawls' idea of alternative doctrines affirming JAF each in its own way is, if not unsuccessful, at least ambiguous and incomplete.

How shall we assess it as an explanation of the moral grounds for enforcing the law upon adherents of illiberal conceptions of the good? I think the answer must be the same. Such citizens (and their doctrines) either are or are not to be treated as part of the overlapping consensus. If not, then a *moral* justification for requiring them to obey the legal order of a liberal state must ultimately rest upon the adequacy of the philosophical defense which can be given in support of liberalism (and hence against their illiberalism). But to engage such a task would be to abandon a political conception of justice for a metaphysical one. On the other hand, if we treat them as part of the overlapping consensus, it can be so only on prudential, not moral, grounds. The first strategy would allow Rawls to maintain the thesis of the moral character of the overlapping consensus provided by JAF, at the cost of sacrificing a degree of inclusiveness, as well as the cost of entailing controversial moral judgments, or "metaphysical level" arguments. But if to avoid these costs we take the latter strategy, we undermine the thesis of the moral character of JAF, and its overlapping consensus becomes prudential instead.

At one point in "The Idea of an Overlapping Consensus" Rawls appears to consciously endorse this latter, prudential, interpretation with regard to "illiberal" groups. He writes:

> Nevertheless, in affirming a political conception of justice we may eventually have to assert at least certain aspects of our own comprehensive (by no means necessarily fully comprehensive) religious or philosophical doctrine. This happens whenever someone insists, for example, that certain questions are so fundamental that to ensure their being rightly settled justifies civil strife. The religious salvation of those holding a particular religion, or indeed the salvation of a whole people, may be said to depend on it. At this point we may have no alternative but to deny this, and to assert the kind of thing we had hoped to avoid. But the aspects of our view that we assert should not go beyond what is necessary for the political aim of consensus.[48]

This would seem to let the (Hobbesian) cat out of the bag. If this is taken as Rawls' considered position on the question, then the moral interpretation of JAF would have been unequivocally abandoned, for no attempt is made to justify the exercise of power envisioned in this example, as "we" liberals "deny" the views of those outside our consensus and "assert" our own over them. It is true that in discussing this case, Rawls reminds "us" to assert as little as possible. It is noteworthy, however, that this constraint is advocated not out of concern with the question of the moral status of those outside the consensus, but out of concern to maintain the consensus among those already within. But that *they* share a set of moral beliefs is not in question; what is left unanswered is the question of what would morally justify their imposition of these beliefs upon those who do not share them. In the absence of an attempt to answer that question, it is difficult to see how the overlapping consensus of JAF can be called a moral, rather than prudential, one. In short, the problem of oscillation characterizes Rawls' account here again.

IV

Suppose, for the sake of argument, we ignore the problem of the unsettled moral status of those whose moral commitments leave them outside the consensus offered by JAF. It seems to me there is yet a further and deeper, and final, sense in which JAF oscillates between its metaphysical and political interpretive poles. I want now to try and show this.

Supposing all citizens of a contemporary liberal society do accept the Rawlsian idea of moral personality, and thence and therefore accept JAF as a procedural framework designed to yield principles governing the basic structure of their society, the moral character of the overlapping consensus remains an obscure notion. By making JAF a metaphysically innocent construction, Rawls leaves us to wonder why we should accord moral significance to the *beliefs* about moral personality held by citizens in a democratic culture. It is not enough to say that this is simply in keeping with the political character of JAF. That *might* be enough, if Rawls were to pursue the Hobbesian line of interpretation.

As we have seen, however, Rawls does not wish to render JAF in this manner. And there is more than squeamishness at work here. A genuinely Hobbesian, or prudential, reading of JAF would ultimately eviscerate it, for JAF, through the veil of ignorance, *requires* that parties to the original position be situated with equal amounts of power to determine the final outcome. On a Hobbesian reading, however, parties would have reason to accept this *morally-based* constraint of equal power only insofar as it actually obtained in social reality, a rather doubtful state of affairs to say the least. That is, on the Hobbesian reading, parties to the original position would have no reason not to drive a hard bargain on the terms of social cooperation insofar as they had the power to do so. This is simply to say that they would refuse to have the veil of ignorance placed over them. (Relatively weaker parties would, of course, happily accept the veil of ignorance.) We see, then, a further rationale behind Rawls' insistence that JAF not be conceived as a political doctrine of justice along Hobbesian lines. To do so would be to remove a central component of the theory, the requirement that no party to the original position have a bargaining advantage over any other. But that is just to say that a central moral premise of JAF is the value of equal individual liberty.

However, we are then left to wonder again what argument Rawls could give to *support* this aspect of the theory, remembering that any argument appealing to "metaphysical" grounds is ruled out. Presumably, the argument would be that doing so is a means of working out a procedure whereby competing comprehensive moral ideals (or their adherents) can establish *fair* terms of social cooperation. But this argument, depending upon how it is understood, establishes either too much or too little. Too much, if "fair" is read as equivalent to "terms acceptable to free and equal moral persons deliberating under the conditions of equal power established by the veil of ignorance." This argument is either circular, in that fairness is thus defined in terms presupposing JAF, or dependent for its plausibility upon one of the more controversial arguments advanced by Rawls, that which maintains that inequalities of social power are morally arbitrary and unrelated to personal desert.[49] On the other hand, the argument establishes too little if, leaving aside the question of how to interpret "fairness", the claim is the minimal one that JAF is a means of establishing terms of social cooperation simply in a morally pluralistic society. Granted that it is *a* means of doing so, it does not follow that it is the only means. A theory specifying a procedure which allowed social inequalities of power to be replicated within (say, an original position without the veil of ignorance) could surely result in an agreement establishing terms of social cooperation.[50]

Now to be sure, such an agreement would legitimate social inequalities which are unacceptable to Rawls, but it could achieve the minimal desideratum of peace in a morally pluralistic society. What argument could Rawls then give for excluding any such procedure in favor of that specified by JAF? It would have to be one which purported to show that such a procedure would fail to yield genuinely *fair* terms of social cooperation insofar as it allowed morally arbitrary factors to be reflected in the choice situation. But here we would be back to the circular argument which established too much. How could one break the circularity? One could, as Rawls seemed to do in the Dewey Lectures, appeal to a Kantian foundation as a ground for his *particular interpretation* of "fairness" as requiring a veil of ignorance in the original position. I think there is much to be said for this strategy, but it would again make JAF a metaphysical, not a political, account of justice. But if one tries to break the circularity by moving in a political direction, one again runs into the problem that JAF is not the only procedure capable of generating terms of social cooperation, and that there is no purely political rationale for preferring the procedure specified by JAF to any other that could do the job. Rawls closes "Justice as Fairness: Political not Metaphysical," with the following remark: "...in a society marked by deep divisions between opposing and incommensurable conceptions of the good, justice as fairness enables us at least to conceive how social unity can be both possible and stable."[51] But the problem is that it is not the only procedural model of social cooperation enabling us to conceive these things. In the absence of an argument which appeals back to (admittedly) controversial "metaphysical" grounds for its moral commitments, we have no reason to prefer JAF to any other such procedural model.

At this point, Rawls could argue that while alternative procedural models can account for the *possibility* of terms of social cooperation, JAF is uniquely suited to account for *stable* terms of social cooperation. Rawls does make such an argument for JAF on grounds of stability in "The Idea of an

Overlapping Consensus," suggesting that because adherents of alternative moral ideals which do fit within the overlapping consensus generated by JAF will have affirmed it for moral reasons, it is likely to be more stable than a consensus resting merely upon a balance of power. Referring to the "model consensus" described previously, he writes:

> ...those who affirm the various views supporting the political conception will not withdraw their support of it should the relative strength of their view in society increase and eventually become dominant. So long as the three views are affirmed and not revised, the political conception will still be supported regardless of shifts in the distribution of political power.[52]

This argument seems highly doubtful in supposing, in effect, that power will not corrupt. Rawls begs the question in tautologically saying that "so long as the three views are affirmed and not revised, the political conception will still be supported regardless of shifts in the distribution of political power." Surely the question is whether one of those "views," or groups, might not begin to "revise" its sense of moral obligation once it no longer found itself in the position of not having the power to advantage itself by doing so. One need not think mankind a race of devils to fear that it might, and to fear that Rawls is overly optimistic here in supposing that a dominant "majority faction" will not dominate. And as the allusion to Madison suggests, the expression of that fear is certainly within the liberal tradition. Indeed, if we accept Rawls' supposition about human behavior here, we are led to wonder why he includes the veil of ignorance, which ensures equality of power, as a component of JAF. To be sure, there are those genuinely virtuous liberal characters, who, as it were, don't need to have the veil of ignorance placed upon them to ensure that they treat others as equal unto themselves; whether there are enough of them to lend credence to Rawls' argument quoted above is another question. We can recall that Hobbes too recognized that there were those who would keep their word regardless of the advantages to be gained from breaking it; but he also remarked that this "...is a generosity too rarely found to be presumed on, especially in the pursuers of Wealth, Command, or sensuall Pleasure; which are the greatest part of mankind. The passion to be reckoned upon is fear...."[53] Without claiming that a balance of roughly equal power is an absolutely necessary condition for underwriting the stability of an egalitarian liberal regime, it seems at the very least fair to say that Rawls' supposition above that it is not is open to serious doubt, even (or especially?) from within the framework of liberal thought. The attempt to ground JAF through an appeal to stability is thus open to the same doubt.

V

I have tried to show throughout this chapter that JAF may be said to oscillate between its metaphysical and political interpretations. Interpreting it along political lines, Rawls must be careful to keep it from being rendered too politically, lest it become Hobbesian. Yet the remedy for the spectre of Hobbesianism is a dose of Kantianism, and this serves only to take JAF beneath the surface, philosophically speaking, raising the spectre of controversial metaphysical arguments, or of turning JAF into a "sectarian moral ideal."

Is this oscillation a necessary feature of Rawls project? It seems to me that at this point in the development of that project, it is. Failing a return to the explicitly "Kantian interpretation" of JAF, I cannot see how Rawls' present arguments provide a systematic and convincing basis for rendering a political interpretation of JAF which does not collapse into the "Hobbesian interpretation." Yet one can see an alternative path of argumentation which might be pursued in an attempt to work out something like the political interpretation of JAF Rawls is after.

Granting that the Rawlsian idea of moral personality is the predominant (though not universal) self-understanding held by contemporary citizens of liberal-democratic societies, and granting that any practically viable principles of justice will have to accept and proceed from this fact, then what is necessary to the Rawlsian project is the articulation of an argument designed to explain why we should accord moral significance to this empirical state of affairs. Only then would we have an account which "settled" the moral status of those whose moral ideals exclude this conception of moral personality. I have tried to demonstrate in this chapter that Rawls has yet to provide such an account. Thus far, he has shown only that insofar as (most) contemporary citizens do (at least implicitly) understand themselves this way, any principles of social coordination which could govern and order their relations in a manner agreeable with their moral intuitions will have to accept and build upon such intuitions. But one would have reason to accept such principles of coordination as *moral* principles only insofar as those intuitions carried moral force. What is needed, then, is an argument to show why contemporary beliefs about moral personality (and hence justice) are something more than simply beliefs; we need an explanation of their rationality, of their genuinely moral, and not merely empirical, force.

In short, if JAF is to remain a moral theory, as Rawls wishes, the conventional beliefs of contemporary citizens must be shown to be something more than mere conventions; and thus one comes to imagine the possibility of an "Hegelian interpretation" of JAF, an interpretation that would make of it not a doctrine which "steers a course between"[54] Hobbes and Kant, but one that transcends both even as it retains each within itself. JAF needs to be interpreted or rendered in such a way that its aim is not that of *balancing* Kant and Hobbes, but of *synthesizing* them. Hegel may be said to have attempted just such a project.

Hegel, like Rawls, transposes the Kantian idea of the free and equal moral personality from the timeless realm of transcendental reason to the realm of history.[55] But unlike Rawls, Hegel continues on to offer an account of the rationality of history, an account purporting to explain how the empirical reality of the modern constitutional state embodying this conception of moral personality ("subjective freedom") is part of the larger, rational and morally developmental, process of Spirit coming to self-consciousness through the historical action of the human species ("objective freedom"). Hegel, through his philosophy of history, offers us grounds for according rational and moral significance to the subjective beliefs of the modern liberal mind. To be sure, Hegel's philosophy of history is, to say the least, both controversial and demanding of a rather large degree of metaphysical commitment. My point here is not that its truth is somehow evident, for rather obviously it is not. Rather, I am suggesting that in the absence of some sort of philosophy of history along Hegelian lines, there is no obvious *reason* to accord moral significance to the subjective beliefs about moral personality held by contemporary liberal citizens. And without that, Rawls' political interpretation of JAF is left hanging between instrumental Hobbesian prudence and austere Kantian reason. My claim, then, is that Rawls' project of developing an interpretation of JAF which avoids both Hobbesian heteronomy and Kantian autonomy points, strange as it may seem, directly toward Hegel. To put it bluntly, one needs to moralize history if one is going to develop a moral theory of justice out of historical circumstance. Otherwise, the moral character of the political interpretation of JAF is left unexplained and ungrounded.

The irony of this conclusion, if indeed it is a valid one, is evident. Rawls' attempt to ground JAF in an empirical foundation, motivated by the desire to avoid any controversial philosophical commitments, turns out in the end to presuppose a level of philosophical commitment (that is, to a philosophy of history) which, if it is non-controversial today, is so only because it is so widely dismissed as absurd. Reflecting upon that irony perhaps gives one reason to wonder whether the "cunning of reason" is as absurd an idea as contemporary liberal "intuitions" would doubtless perceive it to be.

NOTES

1. The three most important of Rawls' post-*A Theory of Justice* writings, in the sense that they elaborate, extend, and in some ways modify the argument advanced in the book, I take to be "Kantian Constructivism in Moral Theory: The Dewey Lectures 1980," *Journal of Philosophy*, vol. 77, no. 9 (September, 1980), pp. 515–72; "Justice as Fairness: Political not Metaphysical," *Philosophy and Public Affairs*, vol. 14, no. 3 (Summer, 1985), pp. 223–51; and "The Idea of an Overlapping Consensus," *Oxford Journal of Legal Studies*, vol. 7, no. 1 (Spring, 1987), pp. 1–27. This chapter focuses upon the latter two articles; the former is discussed in William Galston, "Moral Personality and Liberal Theory," *Political Theory*, vol. 10, no. 4 (November, 1982), pp. 492–519.
2. Rawls, "Justice as Fairness: Political not Metaphysical," p. 233.
3. *Ibid.*, "The Idea of an Overlapping Consensus," pp. 6–7.
4. Rawls, "Justice as Fairness: Political not Metaphysical," p. 224.
5. *Ibid.*, p. 230; see also "The Idea of an Overlapping Consensus," p. 8.
6. Rawls, "Justice as Fairness: Political not Metaphysical," pp. 224–5.
7. In brief, the problem is this. Rawls speaks of the aim of political conceptions as that of "...specifying the terms of social cooperation between citizens regarded as free and equal persons." ("Justice as Fairness: Political not Metaphysical," p. 234.) Regarding citizens as free and equal persons is the fundamental constitutive component of JAF, presumably only one of many possible political conceptions of justice. But here that component is read into the criteria of political conceptions generally, giving JAF a uniquely privileged status.
8. Entry for "metaphysics," *The American Heritage Dictionary of the English Language* (New York: Houghton Mifflin Company, 1971), p. 825.
9. Rawls, "The Idea of an Overlapping Consensus," p. 1.
10. Rawls, "Justice as Fairness: Political not Metaphysical," p. 230.
11. Rawls, "The Idea of an Overlapping Consensus," p. 13.
12. *Ibid.*, p. 12. As the succeeding analysis will reveal, I am doubtful that Rawls' account of JAF as a political conception of justice satisfies these self-imposed conditions. Granting that it is not skeptical about truth, I am not so sure that it is not indifferent to or in conflict with it. Everything hinges, of course, upon what constitutes "indifference" or "conflict." Insofar as a political conception of justice weighs the value of agreement to be greater than that of truth, it would seem plausible that from the point of view of those who would weigh truth the greater value, a view such as Rawls' could be seen as being indifferent to truth or in conflict with it in the sense that it does not comprehend or accept (what this latter view sees as) the full and proper weight of the value of truth. Hence one would have to decide which of these two views is true itself before one could say that Rawls' view is not indifferent to or in conflict with the value of truth.
13. Rawls, "Justice as Fairness: Political not Metaphysical," p. 230; emphasis added.
14. *Ibid.*
15. *Ibid.*, p. 246.
16. *Ibid.*
17. See also "The Idea of an Overlapping Consensus," pp. 4–5.
18. Rawls, "Justice as Fairness: Political not Metaphysical," p. 279. See also "The Idea of an Overlapping Consensus," pp. 9–12.

19. Rawls, "Justice as Fairness: Political not Metaphysical," p. 279.
20. *Ibid.*, p. 247.
21. Rawls, "The Idea of an Overlapping Consensus," pp. 23–4.
22. Rawls, "Justice as Fairness: Political not Metaphysical," p. 247.
23. *Ibid.*
24. *Ibid.*, p. 226.
25. Locke might also be mentioned, but there is a question as to whether Locke's well-known defense of toleration in *A Letter Concerning Toleration* does not stem from considerations similar to the Hobbesian interpretation sketched above; in this regard, see the interesting argument in Robert Kraynak, "John Locke: From Absolutism to Toleration," *American Political Science Review*, vol. 74, no. 1 (March, 1980) pp. 53–69.
26. Rawls, "Justice as Fairness: Political not Metaphysical," p. 233.
27. *Ibid.*
28. *Ibid.*, pp. 234–5.
29. *Ibid.*, p. 235.
30. *Ibid.*, p. 234; note that the criteria of JAF are here read into the criteria of a political account of justice.
31. William Galston, "Moral Personality and Liberal Theory," *Political Theory*, vol. 10, no. 4 (November, 1982), p. 497.
32. Rawls, "Justice as Fairness: Political not Metaphysical," p. 234; emphasis added.
33. For the purposes of this chapter, I concentrate upon the foundations of this concept of moral personality, not its interpretation. I thus assume (as does Rawls) that when we say citizens think of themselves as "free and equal moral persons," we have a more or less clear idea of what this means, sufficient to enable such citizens to reach agreement on at least constitutional level issues. It is, however, highly doubtful that this assumption is true. Consider, for example, that Nozick too appeals to this concept of moral personality, but works out a very different conception of it, one that grounds a libertarian regime very different than the regime imagined by Rawls. It may well be that even if we ignore the foundational problems treated in this chapter, JAF as a political conception of justice entails a particular conception of the concept of "free and equal persons" which is rejected by many contemporary *liberals*. To the extent that this is so, the overlapping consensus of JAF would be even more circumscribed than I assume it to be for purposes of this chapter. See, in this regard, David Paris, "The Theoretical Mystique: Neutrality, Plurality and the Defense of Liberalism," *American Journal of Political Science*, vol. 31, no. 4 (November, 1987), pp. 909–39.
34. Rawls, "Justice as Fairness: Political not Metaphysical," p. 249.
35. *Ibid.*, p. 248.
36. *Ibid.*
37. *Ibid.*, p. 249.
38. One such example, of many, is Allan Bloom, "Justice: John Rawls vs. The Tradition of Political Philosophy," *American Political Science Review*, vol. 69, no. 2 (1975), pp. 648–62.
39. Rawls, "Justice as Fairness: Political not Metaphysical," p. 247; emphasis added.
40. Rawls, "The Idea of an Overlapping Consensus," p. 13.
41. Rawls, "Justice as Fairness: Political not Metaphysical," p. 247.
42. Rawls, "The Idea of an Overlapping Consensus," p. 10.
43. *Ibid.*, p. 9.

44. *Ibid.*
45. *Ibid.*; emphasis added.
46. Rawls, "Justice as Fairness: Political not Metaphysical," p. 247.
47. Rawls, "The Idea of an Overlapping Consensus," p. 9.
48. *Ibid.*, p. 14.
49. Rawls' argument can be found in *A Theory of Justice*, pp. 65–82; notable criticisms include those of Robert Nozick, *Anarchy, State and Utopia* (New York: Basic Books, 1974), pp. 213–31, and Michael Sandel, *Liberalism and the Limits of Justice* (Cambridge: Cambridge University Press, 1982), pp. 77–103.
50. A view developed most fully in David Gauthier, *Reasons and Morals* (Oxford: Oxford University Press, 1986).
51. Rawls, "Justice as Fairness: Political not Metaphysical," p. 251.
52. Rawls, "The Idea of an Overlapping Consensus," p. 11.
53. Thomas Hobbes, *Leviathan*, C.B. Macpherson, ed. (Harmondsworth: Penguin Books, 1968), Pt. 1, ch. 14, p. 200.
54. Rawls, "The Idea of an Overlapping Consensus," p. 23.
55. The sketch of Hegel's political philosophy given here is admittedly nothing more than that. The sketch is drawn primarily from my understanding, limited as it no doubt is, of *The Philosophy of Right* and the *Phenomenology of Mind*.

6   Does He Mean What He Says?
(Mis)Understanding Rawls' Practical Turn

*This chapter continues the analysis of Rawls' practical turn as expressed in his post-*A Theory of Justice *writings. Here, however, the focus shifts to Rawls' distinctive, and often perplexing, views in regard to the role of political philosophy and the political philosopher within a democratic society.*

John Rawls' writings since 1985 have been marked by an increasing emphasis upon and concern with what he calls the "practical task of political philosophy in a democratic society."[1] Whatever their assessment of the cogency of the arguments advanced by the "later Rawls,"[2], most commentators have understood his practical turn to have resulted in a less ambitious and less provocative political theory than had been advanced in *A Theory of Justice*. I am not concerned, at least directly, with trying to measure the distance between Rawls' earlier and later works. Instead, I want to focus attention directly upon the later works and certain ideas concerning the activity of political philosophy introduced there. More specifically, I want to examine the way those ideas are being interpreted and understood by the larger community of political theorists, for it is my contention that in that process Rawls' ideas are being misunderstood in significant ways.

Given that hardly anyone is happy about the direction Rawls' later work has taken, it may be thought that my contention is part of an effort to defend Rawls' later writings against his discontented critics. That is not necessarily so. There are both puzzles surrounding and problems confronting the ideas that constitute Rawls' practical turn. However, because leading interpreters of Rawls tend to misidentify the nature of that turn, my critical reactions to it differ from theirs.

I shall proceed as follows. In Section I, I explain briefly the elements of Rawls' later thought which comprise the practical turn of his theorizing. I then focus more directly upon Rawls' understanding of the relationship between politics and philosophy, attempt to explicate fairly what he is saying, and then explain why it is that no one believes him when he says it. In Section II, I critically analyze in detail the interpretations of Rawls' later work offered by two of his most adept and respected readers: those of Charles Larmore and Joseph Raz. Having thus explained why Rawls' theory is not especially vulnerable to the criticisms raised by those readers, I turn in Section III to explaining what I take to be the genuine problems confronting Rawls' theorizing. Consideration of these leads us to wonder, ironically enough, whether the "later Rawls" may not be more audacious and ambitious in aim than was the original.

I

The Practical Turn: Conceptual Elements

The distinctive features of Rawls' later work can be explained in terms of three phrases which were absent from *A Theory of Justice* but now figure centrally in his thinking. The theory of justice is to be understood as (1) "political, not metaphysical," as (2) "political, not comprehensive," and (3) as designed to pursue the "practical task of political philosophy in a constitutional democracy."

Political/Metaphysical
JAF is said to be non-metaphysical in three distinct senses. Failure to distinguish these and the contexts in which Rawls uses them can lead to misunderstandings of the logic of his theory. The first refers to the form of the theory and is what we might call a structural sense. Many think of a theory of justice as being necessarily built upon a basis of ideas imported from other, foundational, areas of philosophy. Thus, for example, it is often said that the key to understanding X's political theory is to see how it rests upon a theory of human nature, or a meta-ethical theory, or a theory of epistemology, or theology, or so on. Rawls sometimes uses the term "metaphysical" to refer to the class of these other domains generally. Thus to say JAF is not metaphysical is to say that it neither rests upon nor presupposes any particular thesis from any of these domains.[3] That JAF is, in this structural sense, free-floating rather than anchored will turn out to be an important aspect of its ability to fulfill the practical task Rawls designates for political theory.

A second sense in which JAF is non-metaphysical refers to the domain of relevance the theory claims to occupy. Here, "metaphysical" denotes a theory's claim to universal spatial and temporal relevance, to be applicable for all times and places. JAF is said to be "political" in eschewing such a claim. It claims to apply only to "the basic structure of a modern constitutional democracy."[4] The domain is thus limited both spatially and temporally.

The third sense in which JAF is non-metaphysical is that of eschewing a claim to truth on its own behalf. In these contexts, "metaphysical" is used by Rawls to connote a theory's claim to truth, and JAF is said to be "political" in not claiming such a status for itself. Summarizing, then, to say that JAF is political and not metaphysical means variously that it is (i) free-floating,

(ii) contextually limited in applicability, and (iii) detached from any truth claim on its own behalf.

Political/Comprehensive

Specifying the spatial and temporal dimensions of a theory's applicability results in a definition of the subject population to which the theory is understood to apply. Rawls refers to this as the degree of "generality" of a theory; the greater the range of subjects, the more general the theory.[5] Another way of classifying moral theories is in terms of their *comprehensiveness*. A comprehensive theory is defined by Rawls as one that goes well beyond specifying the terms of *political* interaction amongst *citizens*; instead, it "...includes conceptions of what is of value in human life, ideals of personal virtue and character, and the like, that are to inform much of our non-political conduct (in the limit our life as a whole)."[6] The underlying sense of the distinction here is again a structural one. It is possible to think of a political theory as a component part of a larger entity, of a complete and systematic philosophical conception. Indeed, this is probably the most common way of thinking spatially about political theories. Rawls argues that "there is a tendency for religious and philosophical conceptions to be general and fully comprehensive; indeed, their being so is sometimes regarded as an ideal to be realized."[7] But JAF is not to be understood in this way. It is not derived from or tied to any comprehensive moral conception, but is rather free-standing and formulated to apply to the political realm only. It simply does not speak to issues of non-political value and virtue (or vice); as Rawls puts it, "it consists in a conception of politics, not of the whole of life."[8] Thus to say that JAF is "political" in the sense of being "non-comprehensive" is to say variously two things: (i) that it is, so far as possible, independent of particular comprehensive moral conceptions and (ii) that it addresses only the political sphere of life. These two features are closely tied to the idea that JAF is a free-floating political theory, unanchored in any metaphysical discourse or claim.

Practical Tasks of Political Theory

The understanding of JAF as "political" is motivated by Rawls' attempt to fulfill what he has come to speak of as a very important practical task of political philosophy in a constitutional democracy. This twofold task is to "...provide a shared public basis for the justification of political and social institutions (and to) help insure stability from one generation to the next."[9] This task is conceived as both urgent and difficult due to "the fact of pluralism" and its permanence, that is, to the existence of a diversity of competing comprehensive moral views and values.[10] The task is nevertheless conceived as achievable insofar as there is, beneath this diversity, a deeper (perhaps not fully conscious or explicit) level of consensus upon fundamentals. A political conception of justice will found itself upon these consensually held "fundamental intuitive ideas," and articulate from them a charter of principles of justice which, hopefully, will attract the support of most if not all of the adherents of the various comprehensive moral views obtaining in society. To articulate the terms which successfully elicit such an "overlapping consensus" of support would be to have succeeded at the practical task of political theory. It would be to have provided citizens with a common political language by means of which they might authoritatively assess their institutions and practices. In taking what is common, yet latent and inarticulate, and shaping it into a publicly recognized and practically utilized account of justice, a political conception would have contributed to social unity and stability by reminding us of the tie that binds.

JAF can be understood as a political conception attempting to meet these aims. Upon this understanding, evaluation of JAF is a matter of whether it does meet them or not. Whether JAF is true or correct or right in any other senses is left, purposely and self-consciously, as an unaddressed open question.

The Practical Turn: Questions

With the basic conceptual elements which constitute Rawls' practical turn now before us, we can examine more deeply certain aspects of these ideas which are especially important to a full understanding of his thinking.

Eschewing is not Denying
It is important to note that in eschewing claims to universal relevance and truth, Rawls does not understand JAF to involve the denial of such claims. Rawls does not say that a political theory or a theory of justice cannot apply universally, nor does he say that a political theory or theory of justice cannot be true in a deep and metaphysical sense. He doesn't even say these things about his own theory, JAF. JAF may or may not be universally applicable, and it may or may not be true. Rawls simply does not speak to these issues, and it is a mistake to read him as doing so.[11] When he says he "understands" JAF to be a political theory in the senses specified above, he is making a descriptive statement, not announcing the conclusion of an argument. He is also choosing his words very carefully. The "understanding" of JAF articulated in the later works is not to be taken as exhaustive of the theory itself; it is *an* understanding, which does not preclude other possible ones. On *this* "understanding," that is, the particular one John Rawls has been pursuing

and advancing in these later articles, JAF is being *described* as political and not metaphysical or comprehensive. That is not an argument against or a criticism of metaphysical theories generally, nor is it even, rightly considered as Rawls understands it, an argument against or a criticism of a metaphysical "understanding" of JAF itself. Rawls' present "understanding" of JAF is a function of the practical task of political theory he has chosen to pursue; other choices and other tasks might make another "understanding" a more appropriate one. Clarity regarding this point is complicated even more by the fact that the person advancing a specific (but non-exclusive) understanding of "the theory" happens to be the same person who gave birth to the theory itself. In everyday life, we ordinarily think of an author's statement of intention and meaning as decisive when it comes to matters of interpretive disagreement. If you and I disagree about what Jane meant when she spoke of Tom, we settle the matter by going and asking her what she meant. But John Rawls the interpreter of JAF tends not to appeal to John Rawls the author of JAF for, as it were, inside information regarding intention and meaning. More often, he treats JAF (it is never referred to as "my theory") as if it were, for all intents and purposes, a body of theory composed anonymously. This is not altogether fortuitous on his part; it is a mode of treatment which accords well with the idea that JAF is a theory whose deepest sources are latent in the public culture of which it is part.

The Political and the Non-political
The distinction between JAF as a political theory and other political theories which are part of more general and/or comprehensive moral conceptions supposes a distinction between the political and non-political aspects of life which can be more or less clearly made. While I want to grant that for the purpose of the analysis to be pursued here, it may nevertheless be worth noting that the point is a contentious one, and that reliance upon it does generate a difficulty for Rawls.

The bone of contention is clear and familiar; what is the basis of the (posited) line of demarcation between political and non-political, or more colloquially, between "public" and "private"? Of course, any liberal theory would face the problem of specifying, at least roughly, the boundary constituted by the line of distinction. But the difficulty the distinction creates for Rawls is something beyond this generic problem of specification. The problem is that the contrast between political/non-political spheres of life is necessary to underwrite the contrast between theories of justice which are "only" political and those which are parts of comprehensive moral theories. However, the contours of the political/non-political distinction may themselves be an issue of contention between adherents of different comprehensive moral conceptions. Consider, for example, the institution of the family, and the vigorous and ongoing debate over its relation to the public/private line of demarcation.[12] Our answers to the questions of whether it is political or non-political, and in what exact ways, will not be a matter separate from our thinking about justice.

Recognition of this symbiotic (rather than deductive) relation between the two issues casts the distinction Rawls trades upon in a somewhat less flattering light than that with which he ordinarily bathes it. JAF as a non-comprehensive conception of justice appears to have a great practical advantage over comprehensive competitors. This is its flexibility in being able to attract support from diverse sources. As Rawls frames the discourse, to accept the theory of justice which is a component part of some comprehensive conception X, I have to be willing to affirm more or less the whole of X; consensus at such a deep and thoroughgoing level is not to be expected under the conditions of modern pluralism and free institutions which allow, and indeed nurture, diversity of moral belief and commitment. Short of countenancing the "autocratic use of state power," we ought, Rawls argues, abandon appeals to comprehensive moral conceptions in our quest for principles by which to order our political lives.[13] Political conceptions, such as JAF, hold greater promise of securing consensus, for they do not require agreement all the way down, as it were. Different comprehensive moral views may be able to agree to accept JAF as a political conception of justice, though their particular reasons for doing so may differ. This aspect of flexibility, the capacity to attract what Rawls calls an "overlapping consensus" of support, is, by definition, absent from a comprehensive moral conception. This apparent advantage is rendered questionable, however, when we notice how utterly dependent its force is upon the notion that there is a clear and distinct, *pre-theoretical*, line of demarcation between the political and non-political. If a political conception serves to define, rather than merely to be defined by, the contours that distinguish the political realm, it loses what had appeared to be its structural advantage over comprehensive theories generally. The difficulties this raises for Rawls' theory will be considered in Section III.

Philosophy and Politics
Probably no aspect of Rawls' work has attracted as much hostile reaction as his conception of the practical task of political philosophy. Those of a "metaphysical" bent dislike what they see as the somewhat shallow pragmatism of Rawls' views in this regard, and bemoan the historical and contextual, that is to say non-foundational, approach to justification he appears to have adopted. On the other hand, many of those disposed to support the view that political philosophy ought to be cognizant of and

practically relevant to the actual political problems existent in the world are nevertheless unimpressed with Rawls' practical turn. That seems at first a surprising reaction, but is explained, I think, by the following consideration. Those who want political philosophy to be practical and politically relevant tend to want it to be so in a particular way – as critical of and reformist (at least) with regard to the status quo. My impression is that Rawls' present views are seen, rightly or wrongly, as quite conservative politically. His theory is perceived as being "practical" in the sense of aiming at performing the essentially conservative political function of *legitimizing* the existent institutional structure of liberal society, not as subjecting it to deep critical scrutiny. Hence the coolness of the reception granted him by many who share with him the idea that political philosophy needs be practical.[14]

What, exactly, is Rawls' understanding of the relationship between political philosophy and politics as human endeavors? Near the end of "The Idea of an Overlapping Consensus" he acknowledges that "some may think that to secure stable social unity in a constitutional regime by looking for an overlapping consensus detaches political philosophy from philosophy and makes it into politics."[15] Rawls gives a cryptic response to this charge. He writes:

> Yes and no: the politician, we say, looks to the next election, the statesman to the next generation, and philosophy to the indefinite future.... Thus political philosophy is not mere politics: in addressing the public culture it takes the longest view, looks to society's permanent historical and social conditions, and tries to mediate society's deepest conflicts.[16]

This passage is difficult to interpret at least partly because it frustrates our expectations about what an answer to this question should look like. We expect that Rawls will distinguish political philosophy from politics according to a qualitative difference in terms of the nature of each activity. That, at least, is the familiar form of answers to the query, where the contrast usually boils down to truth (validity, correctness, rightness) versus power (consensus, agreement, stability). Rawls refuses to invoke the distinction in this way. The difference is expressed instead in terms of the scope and extent of the time-frame being worked within. What is thereby assented to is the notion that the politician and the political philosopher are performing essentially the same activity. This is just what many of Rawls' critics had expected, and indeed feared.

Now the notion that the political philosopher is performing the same activity as the politician usually occurs in the context of a discourse designed to debunk (what are seen as) the pretentious claims of some political philosopher who insists upon a qualitative distinction between the two activities. An artful and witty maker of such discourses today is Richard Rorty.[17]

Some have been tempted to interpret Rawls in this way, but it would be incorrect to do so. However pragmatic the task Rawls sets for his theory to pursue, he scrupulously avoids pronouncing judgment on the issue of whether it is the *only* task appropriate to "political philosophy." Thus he is careful to, as they say, "neither confirm nor deny" the rationality and/or possibility of assessing a particular political theory in terms of its truth content. He simply insists that *given the aim he is pursuing*, the issue of truth is irrelevant. That is quite different than proposing (as, say, the debunking pragmatist does) that the issue of truth is irrelevant to political philosophy, because "truth" so understood is non-existent.

The motivation behind his practicing of the "method of avoidance" is simply, and innocently, the desire to get on with the job he has chosen to undertake. Rawls wants (rightly or wrongly, foolishly or wisely) to pursue the attainment of an overlapping consensus in support of a political theory of justice. He does not want, and does not have to, or need to, produce a discourse justifying that choice over some other. His choice does not coerce anyone else's choice, nor does the task he chooses exclude other tasks from being pursued. This (surely perfectly understandable?) desire to get on with (what he thinks, rightly or wrongly) is an important job shows the motivating spirit behind the letter of the account advanced above. Rawls is in effect saying to his more metaphysically and foundationalist inclined readers: "relax – different strokes for different folks."

Yet hardly anyone wants to leave him alone. The reason, I think, has less to do with his arguments than with who he is and who we wish him to be. It would be of no particular concern to anyone if Pat Neal had written three or four articles saying that the theory of justice originally advanced by John Rawls could now usefully be understood as a political doctrine of justice which did not claim to be true but aimed instead at gaining the assent of a contextually defined audience. Since no one has ever been moved to say that Pat Neal had resurrected political philosophy from the throes of death, neither would anyone take the least notice of articles which appeared to suggest that it may as well be slain after all. Rawls, on the other hand, frustrates us because in his later work he refuses to play the part we have scripted for him.

When this happens in everyday life, a common result is that observers interpret the actor's words and deeds in such a way as to make them fit the script nevertheless. This phenomenon can be seen at work here. Some insist that Rawls is yet a covert believer in the old foundationalist faith, while others mistake his agnosticism regarding foundational questions for atheism.

Everyone wants to charitably amend his views so as to make him a little more respectable than they fear his present views threaten to leave him. The examples I want to look at here are those of Charles Larmore and Joseph Raz. Larmore and Raz are important political thinkers in their own right, and each is deeply acquainted with and knowledgeable about Rawls' work and liberalism generally. Yet my claim is that each reads, or misreads, Rawls in such a way as to prevent him from being able to say what it is he means, and that this subtle misreading is a consequence of not quite being able to believe that Rawls actually could mean what he says.

II

Saving Rawls from Himself?

Larmore and Raz are worried by what they see as Rawls' new anti-foundationalism, his refusal to recommend liberalism on grounds of truth. They, on the other hand, are willing to recommend the respective versions of liberalism they articulate in such terms. Here I ignore their theories, and am concerned only with their readings of Rawls. Neither is in any deep sense hostile to Rawls; each wishes to show him the way to repairing the (perceived) failings of his theory, the path to salvation from which he has apparently strayed. In both cases, these charitable intentions nevertheless manifest themselves in imperialistic form, for each, I shall argue, distorts Rawls' theorizing in the process of reading it. Rawls is not anti-foundationalist, but simply a-foundationalist. This distinction, however, is one without a difference to a foundationalist, in the same way that the distinction between atheists and agnostics is unacknowledged in the eyes of a kind of believer whose vocabulary separates only believers from heretics.

I shall consider each of their readings in turn, but let me first state how it is I think they are similar in going wrong in reading Rawls.

One can think of a theory as being "foundational," or "having a foundation," in two senses; I'll label these "structural" and "substantive." A theory is structurally foundational in the sense that its component parts, that is, its ideas, concepts, and so on, can be represented as having a formal shape. A component (x) is "foundational" relative to another (y) if (x) is presented as the source of (y), that is to say one argues for (y) by appealing to (x). That component(s) which is structurally most basic in terms of the form of the theory is its "foundation." This is a reference only to the formal structure of the theory; to say that some idea (x) is foundational in this sense says nothing about whether (x) is true or false, right or wrong, wise or foolish. Since any theory can be represented this way, then all theories can be said to be structurally foundationalist.

A theory is substantially foundationalist insofar as it claims to be, or presents itself as, or asks to be assessed in terms of, its truth content. A (substantively) foundationalist theory would claim that its (structurally) foundational premises are true, or at least are to be evaluated in terms of their truth content. In this sense, theories which presented themselves in terms of, or asked to be assessed in terms of, say, their aesthetic qualities or their rhetorical power would not be foundationalist theories.

Thus all theories can be said to be structurally foundationalist, but not all are substantively foundationalist. Rawls' theory understood as presented in his later writings is substantively non-foundationalist. However, from the fact that his theory is structurally foundationalist, Larmore infers that it is substantively foundationalist, while Raz infers that it ought to be so upon pain of internal contradiction and collapse. I believe both are wrong, and that the error stems from a tendency to conflate the two senses of "foundational." That is what I shall now try to show.

Larmore's Reading

Larmore discusses Rawls in the context of defending "political liberalism," the non-comprehensive political theory he joins Rawls in advancing. While highly sympathetic to much of what Rawls has to say, Larmore "insists" that "...political liberalism is to be understood as a correct moral conception and not just as an object of consensus."[18] The insistence derives from Larmore's concern to disassociate his own version of political liberalism from that of Rawls *if* it is interpretively correct (as I have claimed it is) to take Rawls to be saying that political liberalism is grounded upon an appeal to consensus rather than truth. Larmore notes that "many" have so interpreted Rawls' later writings, reading it as constituting "...a retreat to the weaker, but also inadequate and even false view that his theory is simply one on which people in modern Western societies will agree."[19]

Larmore presents a number of considerations designed to show that this is not the correct interpretation of Rawls, and it is these that are of interest to us. While I believe Larmore is wrong about Rawls, he is nevertheless interestingly wrong, and consideration of the points at which he goes astray will help us see more clearly both the peculiar nature of Rawls' understanding of the ways in which political theory can be practical and the reasons why this understanding is easily misunderstood.

Larmore's first argument makes use of the point that in eschewing claims to truth on behalf of his theory Rawls is not therefore saying his theory is not true. Larmore cites the following passage from Rawls:

> The aim of justice as fairness as a political conception is practical, and not metaphysical or epistemological. That is, it presents itself not as a conception of justice that is true, but one that can serve as a basis of informed and willing political agreement between citizens viewed as free and equal persons.[20]

"It presents itself" is the key phrase; in so presenting itself, it does not thereby preclude the possibility of other presentations. Larmore is thus right in thinking that attention to this point is the corrective to interpretations of Rawls which read him as having denied that his theory (or another) could claim to be, or even be, true. However, the point cuts both ways. While it is true that Rawls does not deny that JAF might be true, it does not follow that Rawls affirms, in even the slightest degree, the truth of JAF. To show that Rawls is *not anti-foundationalist* does not translate into showing that he *is foundationalist*.[21] Larmore does claim truth for the foundations of his own theory of political liberalism, and tries valiantly to interpret Rawls as having done the same. However, this first point does not constitute evidence supporting that interpretation.

Larmore's second, and major, argument turns on his understanding of the basic "norm" in Rawls' theory. Larmore describes his own version of political liberalism as resting upon the twin "basic norms" of "equal respect" and "rational dialogue." These norms are unambiguously presented by Larmore as both structurally and substantively foundational. The question is whether Rawls' version of political liberalism is similar.

Now the most (structurally) "basic norm" in Rawls' theory is the idea that justice is that to which free and equal persons deliberating under fair conditions would assent. Larmore reads this as resembling very closely his own notion of "equal respect," and indeed it does. He remarks that he is "convinced that the norm of equal respect lies at the basis of Rawls' own theory of justice," and indeed it does, *if* one understands that "lies at the basis" to be a descriptive statement about the formal structure of Rawls' theory.[22] Larmore, however, means more than that; he wants to claim that in Rawls' theory this norm is "...assumed to be correct and not merely agreed on."[23] That further claim is incorrect. Rawls clearly and unambiguously in all his later works eschews any claim to have argued that the (structurally) basic norm of free and equal persons is grounded in any metaphysical, epistemo-logical, or (substantively) foundational claim or set of claims. Larmore's reading rests upon a mistaken inference from structural foundationalism to substantive foundationalism.

Larmore is misled, I believe, by a very interesting aspect of Rawls' presentation, namely the *usage* to which Rawls puts his basic norm. Contextually grounded, non-foundational, political theories are conventionally thought of as practically quiescent, at least relative to theories which purport to be grounded in deeper truths, which are conventionally thought of as being more practically critical and reconstructive. Rawls, however, breaks the pattern, for he uses the (contextually grounded) idea of free and equal persons as a critical tool for purposes of practical reconstruction. Thus the "overlapping consensus" of support for JAF/political liberalism is treated by Rawls as something to be achieved by, not assumed in, the design of the theory. The theory is not to be understood as defined by the metaphorical "space" of overlap which exists amongst actually held comprehensive moral theories, an understanding which would make it look deeply quiescent. Instead, Rawls says:

> ...we do not look to the comprehensive doctrines that in fact exist and then draw up a political conception that strikes some kind of balance between them. [Instead, JAF]...elaborates a political conception working from the fundamental intuitive idea of society as a fair system of cooperation.... This leads to the idea of a political conception of justice that presupposes no such particular (comprehensive moral) view, and encourages the hope that this conception can be supported, given good fortune and enough time to win allegiance to itself, by an enduring overlapping consensus.[24]

Rawls is thus using a conventional "fundamental intuitive idea" (or "basic norm" in Larmore's vernacular) in an uncharacteristic way, that is, as a tool of reconstruction. Focusing upon that usage, Larmore infers a (substantive) foundational basis, which would indeed be the characteristic pattern. But that misses the peculiar nature of Rawls' enterprise.

A simple way to see it is by analogy to the enterprise of the psychoanalytic therapist. Rawls allows that citizens may not, at an intuitive, pre-reflective level, believe in or assent to the theory of JAF. Nor is JAF to be tailored so as to meet *these* intuitive, pre-reflective beliefs. Instead, "underneath" the citizens' consciously held views of justice is (so it is hypothesized) a deeper, more or less latent, commitment to and belief in the "fundamental" idea of justice as fair cooperation amongst free and equal persons. That is an empirical claim on the part of Rawls, and its truth is assumed (not claimed) for the purposes of further theorizing. The idea is that citizens' conscious-level ideas about politics and justice (call them "level 2 beliefs") may be, and likely are in many cases, inconsistent with their own deepest fundamental commitments ("level 1 beliefs"). It is that divergence which makes it possible for Rawls to use his theory critically and reconstructively. The theory need not be hostage to the level 2 beliefs and opinions of citizens. The fact that citizens do not immediately, as it were, recognize, say, the difference principle as their own is no strike against the difference principle. The theorist acts as a therapist, showing, or better, reminding, the citizens that upon reflection on their own level 1 beliefs, they can see the need to revise and reconstruct their level 2 beliefs. The overlapping consensus sought by Rawls is understood as one which occurs *as a result of* this reconstructive, therapeutic activity. However, no "extra-consensual" basis is ever claimed by Rawls for the level 1, fundamental intuitive idea (or "basic norm"), of fair cooperation amongst free and equal persons.

We can see how this usage misleads Larmore by attending to the following argument he makes. He correctly points out that breadth of agreement is not the only desideratum sought by Rawls' notion of overlapping consensus. The agreement must also be a "free and willing," one between "citizens viewed as free and equal persons." Larmore argues that the use of such phrases by Rawls "...indicate that something like what I have described as the norm of equal respect serves to define the sort of consensus that, for him, counts as a legitimate basis of political principles. This norm is therefore assumed to be correct and not merely agreed on."[25]

The premise is correct but the conclusion doesn't follow. It's true that the "basic norm" of free and equal persons sets, in Rawls' theory, a theoretical constraint upon acceptable practical agreements; that describes the *function served* by the basic norm. It does not, however, speak to the question of how that (structurally) basic norm is to be justified. Larmore is correct in remarking that Rawls believes consensus to be "constrained" by certain principles. The *foundation* of those principles, however, is understood by Rawls to be conventional; the appeal is to (latent) consensus, not the validity of the principles themselves.

We can see the same (interesting) misreading in Larmore's most emphatic statement in defense of his interpretation of Rawls as a (substantive) foundationalist:

> But he seems clearly not to believe, contrary to some of his recent critics, that the commitments on which his political liberalism rests are simply those which people in modern western societies share as a matter of fact. What he holds is that these commitments would be the object of consensus, to the extent that people view themselves, as they should, as free and equal citizens.[26]

Here again to properly understand Rawls we have to draw the distinction between two levels of commitments. The (level 1) commitments on which his theory *rests* are in fact empirically rooted; the (level 2) commitments constituted by his actual theory of justice are not. They are meant to be coercive and reconstructive, along the lines of "if you would be true to your deepest, though perhaps presently unrecognized, self-understandings, you would (change your mind and) commit yourself to my theory of JAF." When Larmore writes, in the final sentence of the passage above, "...to the extent people view themselves, as they should, as free and equal citizens," he is "correct", but ironically so. When he writes "as they should", he means "as they should if indeed they were to follow the dictates of foundational philosophy and commit themselves to valid and true ideas, which happens in this case to be the idea of free and equal persons seeking terms of fair cooperation." However, the correct meaning of "as they should" here is "as they should if they were to reflect deeply enough to come to realize that in fact they already do, and long have, believed in the idea of fair terms of cooperation amongst free and equal persons. Whether that idea is valid and true in a deeper, substantively foundational, sense is completely beside the point." When Larmore uses the conditional tense to express the idea that "consensus" is not presupposed by Rawls' theory, he is half-way right. Consensus at level 2 is not, and therefore must be actively sought; but the seeking of it at level 2 is premised upon the postulate of consensus at level 1.

In effect, Rawls' views have come to strikingly resemble the methodical commitments expressed (and artfully practiced) by Michael Walzer, notably in *Spheres of Justice*. When Walzer wrote the following passage in 1983, he was widely understood to have been defining the difference between himself and Rawls; I believe the passage read now stands as an excellent capsule description of the enterprise Rawls is presently pursuing:

> My argument is radically particularist. I don't claim to have achieved any great distance from the social world in which I live. One way to begin the philosophical enterprise – perhaps the original way – is to walk out of the cave, leave the city, climb the mountain, fashion for oneself (what can never be fashioned for ordinary men and women) an objective and universal standpoint. Then one describes the terrain of everyday life from far away, so that it loses its particular contours and takes on a general shape. But I mean to stand in the cave, in the city, on the ground. Another way of doing philosophy is to interpret to one's fellow citizens the world of meanings that we share. Justice and equality can conceivably be worked out as philosophical artifacts, but a just or an egalitarian society cannot be. If

such a society isn't already here – hidden, as it were, in our concepts and categories – we will never know it concretely or realize it in fact.[27]

Note that Walzer refuses to deny the possibility or meaningfulness of (substantive) foundational philosophy; he rather lets the issue rest at pointing out that it is not his way of "doing philosophy." In this, too, he resembles Rawls, who is not, after all, Richard Rorty – however much Rorty has come recently to think so![28] Walzer and Rawls agnostically abstain from foundational metaphysics; Rorty plays more (though not always) the pragmatic atheist who would debunk it.

Raz's Reading

Raz, unlike Larmore, accepts that Rawls intends a non-foundationalist reading of JAF. "Epistemic abstinence" is the convenient label he places upon Rawls' decision to "...refrain from claiming that his doctrine of justice is true."[29] Raz is, however, quite critical of Rawls' decision to practice such abstention.

His criticism is of a particular type; I shall label it "dissolving criticism." Dissolving criticism purports to show that the argumentative space which the view being criticized understands itself to occupy is not, in fact, there. When successful, dissolving criticism results in showing that, properly understood, it is impossible (conceptually or practically) to consistently advocate the position being advocated. The view being criticized is thus shown to collapse of its own weight, as it were; the ground beneath it is dissolved.

Raz carries this type of argument out against Rawls in the following way. JAF can be mundanely described as a theory of *justice* simply because it concerns itself with matters ordinarily referred to by theories of justice. In this sense, there are many theories of justice. Which one shall we choose? Rawls proposes that we choose JAF. But why? Presumably, because it is especially well designed to secure the terms of an overlapping consensus and thereby contribute to social stability and unity. But why should *those* be the criteria of choice?

Raz's claim is that in implicitly endorsing those criteria as the ones to be employed in choosing amongst possible theories of justice, Rawls is, for all intents and purposes, invoking a claim of truth, or validity.[30] Epistemic abstinence cannot be practiced here, regardless of one's intentions. Rawls fails to practice epistemic abstinence because it is impossible for anyone to practice it. As Raz says, "there can be no justice without truth."[31]

I believe Raz is mistaken, and that his mistake arises from maintaining that one cannot be a structural foundationalist without also being a substantive foundationalist. I shall defend this by first laying out Raz's central argument against Rawls and critically analyzing it, and then giving three examples of how Raz misreads Rawls under the sway of the confusion of structural with substantive foundationalism.

The Central Argument
Here is the text of Raz's central argument against Rawls, which is intended as an exercise in dissolving criticism:

> My argument is simple. A theory of justice can deserve the name simply because it deals with these matters, that is, matters that a true theory of justice deals with. In this sense there are many theories of justice, and they are all acceptable to the same degree as theories of justice. *To recommend one as a theory of justice for our societies is to recommend it as a just theory of justice, that is, as a true, or reasonable, or valid theory of justice.* If it is argued that what makes it *the* theory of justice for us is that it is built on an overlapping consensus and therefore secures stability and unity, then consensus-based stability and unity are the values that a theory of justice, for our society, is assumed to depend on. Their achievement – that is, the fact that endorsing the theory leads to their achievement – *makes the theory true, sound, valid, and so forth.* This is at least what such a theory is committed to.[32]

Raz's claim is *not* that Rawls' advocacy of epistemic abstinence is "not morally justified," but rather that it is "incoherent, for in claiming that this is the theory of justice for us for such-and-such reasons, one is claiming that those reasons show (or make) this the true theory of justice (if truth applies to theories of justice)."[33] Let's examine these claims carefully.

Raz, describing Rawls' views, says "...then consensus-based stability and unity are the values that a theory of justice, for our society, is assumed to depend on." That's literally correct, though one needs to keep in mind two things: (1) Rawls makes this assumption openly and self-consciously, not implicitly or unwittingly, and (2) the "dependence" to which Raz refers is structural, that is, these values can be described as the structurally foundational bases of Rawls' views. Raz, however, reads the passage as implicitly invoking a much stronger (substantive foundationalist) claim, as is evidenced by his next sentence: "...their achievement...makes the theory true, sound, valid, and so forth." But that is unfair to Rawls. Rawls can say: "No, it makes them *consistent* with the values we are *assuming* as our desiderata. I leave open the question of whether those values are properly, in a metaphysical sense, correctly seen as (substantively) foundational. I simply posit their importance in a pluralistic society, and hypothesize that as a matter of empirical fact they are widely assumed to be of great importance. From there we start. Now it may be that there are better places from which to start, that is, better ways to conduct the enterprise of political philosophy. Certainly I have openly recognized that there are *other* ways besides the one I am now pursuing, and as to the question of the best or proper way, I say simply that I am not now interested in addressing that question. It is interpretively wrong to think that because I have chosen one path rather than another I must have thereby necessarily committed myself to the view that the path chosen is the proper or correct one. I cheerfully grant the possibility that my path may be, as a matter of truth, the wrong one."

Raz's error, it seems to me, is to insist that because of the *structural necessity* of a metaphysical level of truth claim, all theories of justice must therefore invoke truth claims about the substance they posit to "fill" this level. But that is mistaken. Rawls does indeed "fill" the foundational level of his theory, as structurally he (and anyone else) must. But he fills it in a particular way which should be distinguished from separate ways of "filling" it. He fills it (1) with an openly announced presupposition, which he does not claim is true. That is a different thing from filling it (2) with a content which is claimed to be true. Raz, as a practioner of dissolving criticism, wants to say that all cases of (1) are really cases of (2). But he argues to this by showing the *structural necessity* of "filling" the metaphysical space of a theory. His critical argument would be effective against someone who wanted to draw a distinction between (a) no metaphysical space to be filled and (b) accepting the necessity of metaphysical space, but (a) is wrong, because all theories of justice have, as a matter of course, a structural foundation; I grant that all (apparent) cases of (a) can fairly be (re)described as cases of (b). However, it does not follow that there is no important distinction to be made at the level of different ways of filling (b). (1) and (2) are different ways of filling (b), and significantly so. Raz reads Rawls as lapsing into incoherence in choosing (a) over (b). He's right in saying that attempt generates incoherence, but wrong in reading Rawls as making it. Rawls is not arguing for (a) over (b), but is rather choosing (1) over (2) as a means of filling (b). Moreover, it seems clear that (1) does not reduce to (2). It is perfectly understandable when someone says "X is the premise from which my arguments build and with which my arguments are designed to be consistent. Whether X is true or not is a meaningful question, but I simply leave it aside here. You might say we are proceeding *as if X* were true, but I do not claim it is actually so." This is different from saying "X is the premise of my argument, and I believe (claim, am willing to speak to the issue of) X is true." There are, of course, criticisms that can be made of the choice of the former over the latter, but Raz is mistaken, in my view, in thinking that Rawls' views in these respects are incoherent. Whatever their vices may be, this is not one of them.

Raz himself seems to glimpse this in the critical passage above, when, after writing the sentence which purports to show that Rawls has unwittingly invoked claims of truth, soundness, validity, and so forth, he then draws back and says, "This at least is what such a theory is committed to." Rawls is indeed (structurally) committed to certain claims at the metaphysical level, but he need not be, and indeed is not, (substantively) committed to the claim that these commitments are *true or valid or sound*.

Raz tries to put Rawls (or show that Rawls has unwittingly put himself) on the horns of a dilemma when he remarks that "...in claiming that this is the theory of justice for us for such-and-such reasons, one is claiming that those reasons show (or make) this the true theory of justice (if truth applies to theories of justice)." The final parenthetical comment is designed to set the trap; either Rawls grants Raz's reading, and abandons epistemic abstinence, or he must commit himself to denying that truth applies to theories of justice, thereby committing himself to a deep and debilitating skepticism. But the dichotomy is a false one, because agnostics are not atheists. Rawls does not deny that truth applies to theories of justice; he simply chooses to bracket that question from his theorizing about justice. He does claim that there are reasons which lead to the conclusion that his theory of justice is the theory for us, but he does not claim that the truth of the theory is one of these, nor does he have to do this to avoid the spectre of skepticism. His claim is that his theory is most consistent with the values of stability and consensus as conceived amongst free and equal persons; the claim is in terms of consistency, not truth. Nor does he claim that those values he seeks to build a theory consistent with are true; he simply starts from them. There is of course no reason why Raz or anyone else cannot legitimately complain about this, or propose different ways of starting. But I do not see anything deeply paradoxical or logically incoherent about Rawls' procedure.

Three Particular Examples
Here are three examples of cases where Raz, in my view, misinterprets Rawls' views as a result of imposing upon those views an interpretive framework which distorts because it denies the distinction between structural and substantive foundationalism.

Accepting a False Theory of Justice. To say there is nothing "deeply paradoxical" about Rawls' views is not to say there aren't some apparently paradoxical features of them. Raz presses one of them against Rawls in the following criticism:

He is willing to contemplate the possibility that there are some who know what the (metaphysically) true theory of justice is, and that it is incompatible with his. He is, in effect, arguing that such persons should nevertheless support his theory rather than the incompatible true theory, for his theory is the theory for us.[34]

It is true that Rawls allows this possibility, and that he must in order to avoid a skepticism which would commit itself to denying that truth is applicable to theories of justice. It is also true that the situation has the air of paradox about it; it seems odd to recommend that one affirm a false theory of justice. However, I think that upon reflection much of that appearance can be dissipated, and that Raz is wrong in thinking Rawls to be advocating an incoherent position here, though Rawls does, in my view, have to modify his views slightly in light of this criticism of Raz.

What Rawls needs is a way to sensibly say "we ought to do X even if X is false and Y is true." And he does have it on hand; it involves breaking the connection between grounds of political obligation and truth.[35] Rawls' claim must be that in living politically in accordance with the principles which represent us as free and equal persons, we achieve integrity, a consistency between our deepest self-conceptions and the *view of* justice which follows from them. However, since those self-conceptions are not evaluated metaphysically in terms of truth, then it is possible that the theory of justice built upon them is not itself true; it is only true to those self-conceptions, in the sense of integrity. The claim of political obligation must be rested upon the force of this view of justice being *ours*, rather than it being *true*. Rawls must, I think, grant this.

But does he then have a theory of *justice*? Raz is pressing the view that he does not, and I think Rawls should grant that claim, to an extent. That extent is this: insofar as "theories of justice" is a locution understood to refer to theories which are to be understood and assessed in terms of (substantively) foundational truth, then Rawls does not, on his present understanding of JAF, have a theory of justice so understood. I believe that this is the dominant and common understanding of what it means to have or propose a theory of justice, and since Rawls does not wish to deny (only to avoid) the possibility that theories of justice can be true in this metaphysical sense, I think he is better off granting Raz's claim here. He does do that implicitly at points in his writing (speaking, say, of a theory of justice "for us") but he does not do it consistently or always explicitly. This generates confusion and ambiguity. By the terms of his practical turn, Rawls' "theory of justice" is best described as a view of justice (allegedly) appropriate to we who dwell in the cave of modern liberalism. It is not a "theory of justice" in the sense of being an attempt to give an account of the sun (that might or might not be) "out there."

On the other hand, I see nothing seriously paradoxical about Rawls recommending to us that we live politically as citizens in accordance with theory X even if it is false. It is seriously paradoxical only if one believes that one's political obligations are dependent upon the truth of the principles governing the life of one's political community. I suppose that view is defensible, but surely it is not the case that alternatives to it are obviously misguided. Walzer's view that "philosophical validation and political authorization are two entirely different things" seems to me highly plausible; at the very least, it articulates a coherent understanding of political obligation which detaches it from truth claims. Rawls' recommendation that we affirm, as citizens, the theory of justice that best accords with our deepest self-understandings even though it may be ultimately and metaphysically false seems to me no more paradoxical than the story related in the *Crito*, where no less a philosopher than Socrates found reason to fulfill his political obligations.

The Task of Political Theory.   Because Raz believes Rawls to have gotten himself stuck between the rock of (substantive) foundationalism and the hard place of skepticism, he considers changes to Rawls' theory which would result in removing the (alleged) incoherence created by the commitment to epistemic abstinence. One such amendment would be to suppose that Rawls "starts from the presupposition that our countries are just."[36] This would mean that (substantive) foundationalist readers of Rawls would now have an explanation of why he seems (from their perspective) so cavalier about the issue of truth, though the price paid would be that such a reader would be supposing Rawls to be extraordinarily naive! It is as if the foundationalist cannot believe that Rawls does not share his anxiety about the truth content of a theory's structural foundations. If we suppose that Rawls assumes our liberal society to be just from the beginning, the (substantive) foundationalist is now satisfied, because Rawls turns out to be a (substantive) foundationalist too – though a rather poor one.

Raz is aware that Rawls does not textually commit himself to any such presupposition. He argues that in maintaining the stance of abstinence on this issue, Rawls erroneously renders his theory "essentially complacent. Any moral and political theory must be open to the possibility that the societies to which it applies are fundamentally defective. Radical criticism of common institutions and common beliefs is, at least in principle, part of the function of such theories."[37]

This criticism misses its mark. First, insofar as "essential complacency" means "not evaluating practices in terms of the truth content of principles," Rawls would be the last to deny that his theory on the understanding he is now*giving it is "essentially complacent." But this is a descriptive point without critical weight; *any* non-(substantively) foundationalist theory is, by mere definition, "essentially complacent" by Raz's terms.

Raz tries to give the point critical force in the succeeding passage. But his regal pronouncements stating what "any moral and political theory must be open to," and what "part of the function of such theories" is, presuppose the necessity of substantive foundationalism in political theory. To say that "radical criticism of common institutions and common beliefs" is a necessary function of moral and political theory, which is what Raz is saying here, simply begs the question Rawls has raised. Performing "radical criticism" cannot be the criterion for judging between foundationalism and non-foundationalism because it exists as a theoretical possibility only within the context of foundationalism. It would be akin to judging football superior to baseball on the grounds that only in football can you score a touchdown.

In addition, it is not true to say that Rawls' theory is not open to the possibility that the society to which it applies is fundamentally defective; I think it more accurate to say that it is neither open nor closed to that possibility, but simply unconcerned with that issue. That means that it is unconcerned with something some (foundationalist) political theorists think is a matter of great concern; that is quite a different thing than being unconcerned with something that a political theory has to be concerned with upon pain of not being a political theory.

The problem here is that Raz is trying to show that Rawls cannot coherently do what he is actually doing; but of course he *can* do it. To mount the criticism in terms of internal incoherence, Raz has to appeal to a list of essential properties and functions of "moral and political theories," which Rawls' theory is criticized for lacking. On reflection however, these "essential" properties and functions are essential only if you are already presupposing the necessity of substantive foundationalism. I think Raz would be better advised to argue that Rawls *should* be doing something else. But that is, admittedly, a difficult thing to get Rawls to argue about; he will say, "do it if you like; but I'm doing something else." Irritating perhaps, but sensible, I think. The alternative is to get oneself into the business of explicitly or implicitly trying to legislate the definitional criteria of "political philosophy." Why should we be so worried about *that*?

A Machiavellian Rawls?   Here I consider a second "imaginary amendment" to Rawls' theory speculated about by Raz as another example of how foundationalists find it so hard to believe that Rawls means what he says that they wind up speaking for him in the course of reading him.

Raz quotes Rawls making the point that some might think that the reflective agreement of an overlapping consensus is itself a ground sufficient for holding the theory of justice which elicits that consensus to be true, or probably true. He notes that Rawls says that he will refrain from taking this further step. Raz then asks why someone might, nevertheless, think reflective agreement constituted truth (a question Rawls, of course, does not ask).

After mentioning one possibility which is irrelevant here, Raz says that:

> ...a second reason, which seems closer to the spirit of Rawls' argument, is that achieving reflective agreement secures the social role of justice (helping to secure consensus-based stability and unity), and this shows that the conception of justice agreed on is true.[38]

Since Rawls has made it clear that he has no desire to speak to the issue of truth, I find it difficult to see why this line of (possible) reasoning is said to be "in the spirit of Rawls' argument." A much greater difficulty is to understand what knowledge Raz is relying on (knowledge about Rawls' "true" motivations?) when he continues on to say:

> It seems that Rawls concurs but fears that saying so would interfere with securing an agreed public basis for justification.[39]

I cannot understand from whence comes this "It seems." Why portray Rawls as a man with one set of beliefs he is "afraid" to announce for fear they might undermine the achievement of stability, when he has explicitly told us that stability is the goal he posits and pursues, that is, he explicitly tells us, in effect, that *that*, and not whatever private, comprehensive views he might or might not have, is the basis upon which he speaks? Raz is led to remark that "what Rawls needs is not epistemic abstinence so much as an esoteric doctrine."[40] Even allowing latitude for rhetorical hyperbole, this characterization subtly distorts Rawls' views; an esoteric doctrine is what Rawls *would* need *if* he pursued the theoretical task Raz urges upon him. But of course he is not pursuing that task, and to speak of him as if he covertly were but is unwilling to say so is evidence of the interpretive lengths to which one can be driven when one feels it necessary to save Rawls from himself.

I think Raz simply finds it hard to believe that Rawls, who, after all, is conventionally acknowledged as one of the greatest living political theorists writing in the English language, can really mean what he says in simply abandoning the whole issue of the truth of his theory. But I think Rawls means what he time and again tells us: that he understands himself to be working upon a practical problem of great import, and that this requires a method willing to abandon epistemic claims of truth. My reservations about this project are different than those of Raz. It is to a discussion of these that I now turn.

III

Supposing the interpretation of Rawls defended above is on the mark, what are the problems confronting the theory rightly understood? In this section, I discuss four central ones. The first two raise issues internal to Rawls' theory, and insofar as they are critical are meant to be immanently so. The latter two raise more speculative issues which arise from considering perplexities generated by Rawls' understanding of the social functions of his own theorizing.

Political and Non-political Revisited

In Section I, I said that one problem confronting Rawls is the dependence of the distinction between political and comprehensive theories upon the logically prior distinction between political and non-political spheres of life. Suppose we ignore that difficulty, and accept as given a more or less theoretically solid boundary between the political and other spheres of life. Still, a difficulty arises.

Recall that one thing making JAF, or political liberalism generally, a practically viable theory under conditions of pluralism is that it demands less by way of allegiance of its citizens than does a comprehensive theory. In accepting the terms of JAF, citizens need not "convert" to an alien moral, religious or philosophical view; as public citizens they affirm JAF, while as private persons they remain free to identify themselves variously as they wish, with reference to any moral, religious or philosophical view so long, of course, as practicing that view does not violate the terms of public justice.[41]

In cases of conflict, the values of the political realm take priority over invocations of non-political value; such an ordering of claims is necessary to secure social order and stability.[42] This view sits uneasily, however, with another of Rawls' views, namely that as a matter of fact, it is our private identities, comprised of attachments and commitments to "thick" theories of the good in the form of various comprehensive ideals, which often, perhaps ordinarily and preponderantly, matter the most to us. He remarks at one point that "...political good, no matter how important, can never in general outweigh the transcendent values – certain religious, philosophical and moral values – that may possibly come into conflict with it."[43]

Political liberalism would thus seem inherently fragile. Private identity in terms of transcendental interests constitutes the (potentially) boiling cauldron upon which political liberalism is the lid. In so describing Rawls' views, I intend no criticism of this aspect of them. Attempts to lessen the fragility of political order would entail more coercive, anxious and impatient attitudes toward pluralism, and a greater willingness to employ the power of the state in the service of comprehensive views.

Attention to this tension can, however, shed interesting light upon aspects of Rawls' thinking. For example, one notices in his later work a (quite uncharacteristic) tendency to rhetorically stress the notion that "...the values of the political are very great values indeed and hence not easily overridden."[44] Elsewhere he remarks that "...the virtues of political cooperation that make a constitutional regime possible are, then, *very great* virtues."[45] The rhetorical stress (arguably) betrays an anxiety arising from the underlying tension between private identities and public commitments. Of course, there is a good deal more than the theorist's preaching/pleading which serves to remind the liberal citizen of the importance of his or her public identity and duty; but reference to the mighty arm of Leviathan, which is always there to underwrite such appeals, would be an admission to or recognition of a failure to achieve consensus.

While it would be unfair to say that Rawls denies or suppresses acknowledgement of this tension, I do think it fair to say he downplays its significance. The sources of fragility for a political liberalism may generate anxiety, but there is no manifestation of despair in Rawls' writing. Nor could there be, for that would throw into question (if not paralyze) the entire project Rawls has now defined and pursued, that of making political philosophy practical by showing how it can contribute to social stability and unity. But the seeds of (potential) despair are sewn in the theory nevertheless, and can be glimpsed even if Rawls, understandably, avoids advertising them. The closest he comes to sounding a note of despair is in remarking that "...in affirming a political conception of justice we may eventually have to assert at least certain aspects of our own comprehensive...religious or philosophical doctrine."[46] The potential sting of this realization is removed, however, when Rawls quickly reminds us that when faced with those who would rather fight than tolerate, we need "state" (that is, impose) no more of our comprehensive view "...than we think would advance the quest for consensus." He even reminds the reader parenthetically that the comprehensive view we must regretfully "state" in such cases need "...by no means (be) necessarily fully comprehensive."[47]

The tension between public and private identity can also be seen in Rawls' ambivalence regarding a type of character I'll label the "too thoroughly liberal citizen."[48] This is the person for whom public identity comes to serve as private identity as well. Rather than affirming JAF politically because his own comprehensive view is sufficiently compatible with it, this citizen "...supports the political conception not as founded on any wider doctrine but rather as itself sufficient to express political values that, under the reasonably favorable conditions that make a more or less just constitutional democracy possible, normally outweigh whatever other values may oppose them."[49] This character appears in the texts from time to time when Rawls discusses how an overlapping consensus is possible. His attractiveness, from that perspective, is clear, though simply to state wherein it lies reveals doubt from another perspective: he is so thoroughly assimilated within and allegiant to the regime of political values that he is without the private identity which might serve as a source of political resistance. A loyal subject, though not a very attractive person; he stands as the latest manifestation of the other-directed organization man who has been a source of liberal unease ever since de Tocqueville and Mill revealed him. His appearances in Rawls' texts mark the temptation, the weaker reflex, which accompanies an entirely legitimate concern with authoritative terms of order. That is the impulse to break the tension between freedom and public order by removing the sources of the former. To love liberal order that much is to have unwittingly betrayed liberalism and the pluralism from which it arises.[50] Rawls does not, let me hasten to add, go so far as to do *that*, but he is in a difficult spot because he can't on the other hand affirm directly a plurality of "experiments in living" as a good thing in and of itself. To do so would be to tie liberal *political* values to a more or less Millean comprehensive conception of good living generally, and thus we would have a "sectarian doctrine" rather than an ecumenical "political" form of liberalism. Either position has its difficulties, and I know of no way of producing a superior synthetic account. Rawls' position entails that from the political point of view, the quality of lives being chosen and lived by liberal citizens is irrelevant, except insofar as they can be shown to bear upon the ability of a constitutional regime to reproduce the degree of political virtue necessary to maintain itself.[51] Such a view seems necessary to avoid oppression (or what Rawls refers to as the "autocratic use of state power"), and yet from another perspective it seems decidedly odd; could it possibly be politically irrelevant if a society becomes comprised of, say, cheerful robots?

Political Liberalism and Politicization

Another interesting and perplexing aspect of Rawls' practical theorizing has to do with a similar tension regarding his attitude toward the politicization of citizens and their interests, values and identities. By "politicization" I mean the process whereby a once unrecognized, unstated or perhaps even non-existent matter becomes an occasion of public consciousness, conflict and concern. There are competing senses in which JAF both does and does not seem to be a view which encourages politicization.

JAF would seem to politicize society in the following way. It is a theory of pre-constitutional principles which are understood to constrain public choices made thereafter, and which calls upon, or at least invites, citizens generally to reflect upon and evaluate such principles. The latter aspect of the theory especially is more pronounced in the later works than it was in the book. There, the citizen was offered the representational device of the original position as a means of reflecting upon pre-constitutional, first principles, of justice. But there was no clear or strong sense in which it would have been correct to say that such activity, on the part of *citizens* (and not simply *theorists*) was encouraged or elicited, much less required. The new idea of eliciting an overlapping consensus of support for JAF carries with it a much stronger commitment to citizen involvement in forging the terms of consensus. While it was possible to meaningfully understand the original theory as one of hypothetical consent, and therefore in such a way that actual citizen activity was irrelevant to the theory, this is clearly no longer the case. JAF is now being presented in terms of contextual acceptability, not rationality; on Rawls' own terms, if citizens do not come to recognize and accept it as their own, it is a failure. The theory thus elicits an active discussion over first principles at the civic level. Since political discourse today rarely cuts to the level of questioning constitutional principle, Rawls' theory would seem to both counsel and be an attempt to contribute to the politicization of citizens and the polity generally. If this were the whole of the story, Rawls would appear more a New Left participatory democrat than a theorist of order and stability.

It is not the whole of the story. For even as Rawls' theory imagines citizens consciously reflecting on the choice of first principles, it does not celebrate the activity or revel in the prospect of it. Indeed, the *purpose* of such activity is, somewhat paradoxically, defined in terms of encouraging depoliticization so as to avoid the spectre of conflict endemic to a pluralistic society. The overlapping consensus of support for JAF (or some other political conception) is said by Rawls to constitute a decision to "...meet the *urgent* political requirement...to *fix, once and for all*, the content of basic rights and liberties, and to assign them special priority."[52] This "fixing" is also described as resulting in the "removal" of potentially divisive matters from the "political agenda."[53]

There is, of course, a rationale for this anti-politicization dimension of Rawls' views. It is articulated succinctly in the following passage, where political liberalism is said to:

> take those guarantees off the political agenda and put them beyond the calculus of social interests, thereby establishing clearly and firmly the terms of social cooperation on a footing of mutual respect. To regard that calculus as relevant in these matters leaves the status and content of those rights and liberties still unsettled; it subjects them to the shifting circumstances of time and place, and by greatly raising the stakes of political controversy, dangerously increases the insecurity and hostility of public life. Thus the unwillingness to take these matters off the agenda perpetuates the deep divisions latent in society; it betrays a readiness to revive those antagonisms in the hope of gaining a more favorable position should later circumstances prove propitious. So, by contrast, securing the basic liberties and recognizing their priority achieves the work of reconciliation and seals mutual acceptance on a footing of equality.[54]

I do not deny the force of the considerations Rawls raises here; depoliticization surely is superior to the war of all against all. I suggest, however, that this is not the whole of the relevant story. The passage above reads benignly insofar as we (tacitly or otherwise) assume that the *identity* of political actors and interests is itself a settled matter. To the degree we are sure that "everyone" is included and no one overlooked, we might sensibly proceed in the manner Rawls outlines above. However, what if this assumption is wrong? What if political actors and interests are thought of not as entities pre-existing the process of political activity, but as properties which emerge and constitute themselves within and through that process? If that is so, then our attitude toward the strategy of depoliticization articulated by Rawls is bound to shift. Now we must be concerned with the possibility that we are in effect closing the channels through which "free and equal persons" manifest themselves in ways recognizable by others. From *that* perspective, Rawls' talk of "fixing once and for all," of "sealing," of taking matters "off the agenda," appears anything but benign. It seems instead to be an impulse to stop the game in the middle of the play; an attractive option to the winners, perhaps, but something else again to the losers, not to mention those (who are they?) yet to succeed in establishing themselves even as players.[55]

Does it make sense to think this way? Consider that if, thirty years ago, there had been something resembling a Rawlsian "pre-constitutional convention" in America, the matter of "gay and lesbian rights" would not only not have been discussed, it would not have *existed* as a political matter.

What has happened in thirty years? Here are two ways of answering that question. (1) Political philosophers (at least some of them) now see aspects of political identity and interests that they overlooked thirty years ago. Those earlier "mistakes," or perhaps, more gently, "oversights," have now been "corrected." (2) Lots of gay and lesbian people *made* themselves and their interests *recognizable* (to political philosophers among others) by engaging in various forms of political activity ranging from letters to the editor to fighting in the streets.

One who finds the second answer the more plausible must, I think, rest uneasy with the depoliticizing dimension of Rawls' views. The constitution and recognition of political identities is not a philosophical problem to be solved, but an historical process whose results are unknown and unknowable. From that angle of vision, "fixing essentials once and for all" is the deadliest of political temptations.

Authority and the Voice of the Theorist

The two previous sections raise matters arising from consideration of tensions in the internal logic of Rawls' theory. Now I want to discuss briefly what I think of as "perplexities" surrounding not Rawls' *conception* of the practical task of political philosophy, but his *practicing* of that task.

Consider in this vein the issue of the authority to speak as a presenter of a political conception of justice. In what capacity does Rawls present JAF as a political conception of justice? To whom is it presented? We can try and answer these questions in two different ways: by examining what Rawls' theory would seem to commit him to doing, or by examining what he actually does.

The terms of the theory do not specify an "office" from which proposals for principles of justice could be advanced. This would, at one level, seem to be a matter of logic; insofar as such principles constrain choice at the constitutional (and successive) levels, they serve to define offices and not vice versa. It would be to put the cart before the horse to imagine a political office to serve as the source of principles which themselves govern the order of political offices. From this perspective, we can see that Rawls' theory is faced with a very old problem: how does one account for the authority of the founder, the legitimacy of the founding?

Perhaps the most natural interpretation of Rawls' theory in this context is a much simpler one; it is to think of each and every citizen as having thereby the authority to advance such principles for consideration by his or her fellows, as he or she is moved to do so. No office (beyond membership – but is even that really necessary?) is required to speak, no institutional procedures define the occasion. The action and the event then seem so "ordinary" (no different really than someone exercising a right to free speech by writing a letter to the editor) that it doesn't occur to one to wonder about the authority of the speaker.

However, this benign picture does not cohere very well with Rawls' view that the achievement of an overlapping consensus of support for a political conception of justice is a matter of great urgency and practical importance, vital to the health and continuing stability of a liberal-democratic order. If it is *that* important that such agreement be reached, the benign reading seems decidedly odd; it would be as if in the midst of World War II the President had invited citizens to develop, at their leisure, plans for conducting the European campaign.

The theory is in my view deeply ambiguous about the authority of the speaker and the nature of the audience. On the one hand, Rawls speaks as if consensus on principles of justice is an urgent practical matter. If this is so, then questions about *who* is suited to and responsible for forging such consensus, under what terms and constraints they are to do this, how the process and moment of ratification can be known and designated, what the consequences of failing at or delaying the completion of this task are – in short, political questions about the location of authority and legitimacy – become matters of significant concern. Think, after all, about the consequences for us of this activity as defined by Rawls' theory; we are binding ourselves "once and for all" to commitments which take priority over and constrain all other social choices. Thus understood, this is no mere philosophers' debate from the armchair; it appears much closer to carving tablets of stone.

On the other hand, the sorts of questions I am pursuing here are not the subject of Rawls' attention or reflection in his later works. It is as if they are non-existent. Under the impact of the recognition of that absence, one begins to think differently about his theorizing, more soberly as it seems, along the following lines. "This talk of authority and 'founding' is wildly misplaced; this is not, after all, Cromwell or Robespierre we are discussing here, but a professional man of the academy! He is engaging in technical discussion and argument with his fellow professionals, not founding, or refounding, a regime. Come to your senses!"

Well, yes and no. Given that Rawls is both an extraordinarily adept and honest thinker, and further that he does not seem to think these questions of authority applicable to his theory, one does begin to doubt that they could be. But then attending to what he says about the urgent practical task of political philosophy in our society, I cannot see how they are not so.

The ambiguity resulting from the tension between the "heroic" and "benign" understandings of the role of the theorist in the theory seems to me irresolvable. There is an interpretation which might resolve the tension and synthesize the two views, but it is one I cannot imagine Rawls actually intending. It would be to suppose that the textual elements supporting the "benign" reading are the sheep's clothing within which are cloaked the ambitions of the heroic founder, who cannot present himself as such precisely because he knows there can be no authority for what he is doing (attempting to do) other than the success which will create it retrospectively. As with Rousseau's Legislator, we find here "...simultaneously two things that seem incompatible: an enterprise threatening to surpass human powers, and, to execute it, an authority that is a mere nothing."[56] But can *that* be Rawls?

Urgency and Practical Political Theory

Here is a related issue which arises from thinking about Rawls' theory in light of his activity as a theorist. To put it bluntly: what could possibly make Rawls think that his degree of success in articulating a political conception of justice *matters* that much *politically*? When one thinks about it, does it really seem plausible to suppose that the future stability of a liberal-democratic society is linked to the labors of academic political theorists?

This feature of Rawls' thinking has puzzled others as well. In an illuminating discussion, Kurt Baier argues that a consensus about constitutional principles is sufficient for stable social unity, and that a further consensus on principles of justice may not only be unnecessary but undesirable.[57] Joseph Raz's doubts run deeper. While charitably acknowledging that a Rawlsian consensus on principles of justice may "contribute" to the goals of social unity and stability, he notes that "given the way the world actually works, the modesty of that contribution raises doubts as to whether Rawls has identified the concerns which should dominate political philosophy today."[58] By "the way the world actually works," Raz is referring to the idea that:

> symbolic and affective identification and a partial cognitive overlap may be a very firm foundation for social unity and stability, especially when we remember that individuals find it both prudentially and morally undesirable to undermine the status quo, or even to try to evade its consequences, given the small chance of success. Of course, many factors contribute to the stability of a country's political system: the nature of the culture, the history of past conflicts, the depth of feeling concerning current rivalries, and so on. The point is that they are only partially sensitive to the existence of *anything remotely like* Rawls' overlapping consensus.[59]

Raz's words are sharp, but to the point. Indeed, it seems (to me at least) so obvious that social unity and stability have little if not nothing to do with Rawls' articulation of a political conception of justice that I again begin to wonder whether he must mean something quite different from what he seems to be saying.

The oddity of this state of affairs is again a result of the disjunction between the role of the theorist as specified in Rawls' theory and Rawls' actual practice as a theorist. By the terms of the theory, the theorist is playing a political role of enormous significance in articulating to his or her fellows a (proposed) political conception of justice upon which they might agree and thereby secure the stability of their political order. But this conceptualization of the social role of the theorist is wildly at odds with what Rawls actually does. Rawls' writings are highly complex and abstract texts; that they serve as the subject of other academics' (highly complex and abstract) interpretive disputes leaves one puzzled at the thought of them serving as the centerpiece of actual civic discourse. The prospect of a campaign of sound-bites in support of the "idea of free and equal persons" is somewhat disconcerting. Consider as well the mundane fact that Rawls writes to an audience comprised of readers of *Philosophy and Public Affairs*, the *Oxford Journal of Legal Studies*, and the *New York University Law Review*. All this is puzzlingly incongruous with the role ascribed to the theorist *in* these writings; it is as if the writers of the Federalist Papers had chosen to publish them in a French encyclopedia.

My point is not that Rawls should begin writing for *USA Today* or appearing on the *McLaughlin Report* (though who does not savor the thought of the expression on Novak's face when he hears about the difference principle?). The theoretical practice in which he is currently engaged seems eminently sensible *if* one understands it as a set of arguments designed to both respond to and advance the lines of argument and advocacy currently characterizing professional, academic discourse *about* politics amongst professors of political philosophy. Indeed, in that context, Rawls' later works can be seen as brilliant tactical advances on a dialectical battlefield. That view looks like this. Setting out to defeat utilitarianism, JAF succeeds but spawns unexpectedly an unanticipated counter-attack; communitarianism generally, and more specifically the critique of the (alleged) "abstract individualism" and "deontological self" said to underpin JAF. Rawls' practical turn and "merely political" reinterpretation of JAF brilliantly meet and trump this attack, by distinguishing the thick, private self from the thin, public self, and thereby accommodating the elements of good sense in the communitarian position.

However, if one views Rawls' theorizing not as a kind of specialized, professional discourse about politics, but rather as political discourse itself, which is what it characterizes itself as being, it appears strange. The issues it conceptualizes, the actual audience it addresses, the vernacular in which it presents itself: all seem vastly remote from civic discourse and practice as it is. None of that matters, of course, if one's aim is making arguments which are superior to those made by one's professional peers, "superiority" being judged by that same body of peers. But Rawls denies that this is what he is best understood as doing, and instead invites us to understand his activity as a contribution to the achievement of political unity and stability. I do not think the promise contained in that invitation can be made good.

I suppose Rawls' theory viewed in this respect might appear less odd if we were to assume, underlying it, a view about the social transmission of ideas roughly like the following. Ideas articulated and debated in elite and specialized intellectual circles ultimately make their way into everyday life. Thus the terms upon which ordinary civic discourse and practice are conducted are the results of such specialized discourses, though it may be unlikely that they are consciously recognized and understood as such. Such a view is captured in Keynes' quip regarding "madmen in authority, who hear voices in the air (and) are distilling their frenzy from some academic scribbler of a few years back."

Rawls does not, so far as I can see, appeal, even obliquely, to such a view in his writings. There are reasons both internal and external to his theory which make it highly doubtful that he would look favorably upon appeal to such a model. Internally, such a view would rest uneasily with his explicit commitment to the "condition of publicity" as it applies to JAF. This is the condition that not only does each citizen know the principles of justice which are to be followed, "everyone accepts and knows that the others accept the same principles of justice" as well.[60] Aside from being crucial to the ability of a conception of justice to generate its own support, this condition rules out any esoteric means of securing political compliance.[61] From an external point of view, reliance upon this view of the social transmission of ideas would imply a need for a substantial degree of consensus amongst political philosophers so that a more or less clear set of ideas could be "transmitted down," or "allowed to trickle down," from the specialized to the ordinary levels of discourse. But this is, upon reflection, both unlikely and undesirable. It is unlikely insofar as argument, disagreement, and difference is the life-force upon which political philosophy as a practice is dependent. Without a plurality of different ideas, political philosophy would not exist. Therefore insofar as consensus is practically possible, it seems to me highly undesirable; it would be a cure worse than the disease.

Conclusion

I can imagine someone saying that with friends like me, Rawls doesn't need enemies. If my reading is correct, then it follows that Larmore is wrong in thinking that Rawls is a (substantive) foundationalist, and Raz is wrong in thinking that he needs to become one lest he leave his theory internally inconsistent. On my reading, Rawls' theory is internally coherent and (substantively) non-foundationalist. However, there are two further consequences of my reading which put Rawls in a less flattering light. First, while it is allowed that Rawls' *theory* is internally consistent, his *theorizing*, in design and execution, is seen to be oddly and strangely incongruent with the provisions of that theory. Second, my reading portrays Rawls as projecting great expectations upon and implicitly attributing heroic dimensions to the practical role of the political philosopher, whose work is made to seem vital to the stability and health of the polity. These expectations seem to me enormously over-exaggerated. If that is right, then my reading entails the unflattering view that Rawls has fallen into a kind of megalomania with regard to the powers of theory. The "practical turn", which most commentators have taken to be a retreat from the ambition embodied originally in *A Theory of Justice*, appears instead as the mark of an even bolder enterprise than the original; an attempt not merely to theorize about justice, but to realize it. Rawls is thus made to appear as more or less akin to the literary critic who, no longer seeing himself as derivatively responding to the primary activity of the writer, has fallen into thinking of literature as the secondary occasion whose function is to make possible the primary activity of criticism. As far as I can see, the stability and health of polities is dependent upon the will, wisdom and prudence of political actors, both leaders and followers. Political philosophers have little to do with it.

I am left uncomfortable with these conclusions my reading of Rawls yields, though they seem to me the inevitable consequence of attending carefully to what he says. Still, I know the feeling embodied in Larmore's and Raz's commentaries; it *is* hard to believe he means it.

NOTES

1. John Rawls, "Justice as Fairness: Political not Metaphysical," *Philosophy and Public Affairs*, vol. 14, no. 3 (Summer, 1985), p. 226. Other works by Rawls drawn upon in this chapter are, John Rawls, "The Idea of an Overlapping Consensus," *Oxford Journal of Legal Studies*, vol. 7, no. 1, pp. 1–25; "The Priority

of Right and Ideas of the Good," *Philosophy and Public Affairs*, vol. 17, no. 4 (Fall, 1988), pp. 251–77; "The Domain of the Political and Overlapping Consensus," *New York University Law Review*, vol. 64, no. 2 (May, 1989), pp. 233–55. Also, John Rawls, *A Theory of Justice* (Cambridge, Mass.: Harvard University Press, 1971).

2. From here on, unless otherwise specified, when I speak of "Rawls" I mean to refer to the author of the articles listed in the previous note. It is cumbersome to have to continually speak of the "original" and "later" Rawls.

3. Rawls, "Justice as Fairness: Political not Metaphysical," p. 231; "The Priority of Right and Ideas of the Good," p. 252.

4. Rawls, "Justice as Fairness: Political, not Metaphysical," p. 224.

5. Rawls, "The Priority of Right and Ideas of the Good," pp. 252–3.

6. *Ibid.*, p. 252.

7. *Ibid.*, pp. 252–3.

8. *Ibid.*, p. 253.

9. Rawls, "The Idea of an Overlapping Consensus," p. 1; see also "Justice as Fairness: Political not Metaphysical," p. 229.

10. Rawls, "The Idea of an Overlapping Consensus," p. 22.

11. See especially his remarks in "Justice as Fairness: Political not Metaphysical," p. 225.

12. In relation to Rawls' work, see especially Susan Okin, *Justice, Gender and the Family* (New York: Basic Books, 1989), especially pp. 89–109; and the insightful commentary on Okin by Will Kymlicka, "Rethinking the Family," *Philosophy and Public Affairs*, vol. 20, no. 1 (Winter, 1991), pp. 77–97.

13. Rawls, "Justice as Fairness: Political not Metaphysical," p. 230.

14. Even Thomas Pogge, a very sympathetic (and enlightening) reader of Rawls, expresses a touch of exasperation regarding Rawls emphasizing "...the importance of his work for enhancing the legitimacy of our social institutions," in *Realizing Rawls* (Ithaca, N.Y.: Cornell University Press, 1989), p. 212.

15. Rawls, "The Idea of an Overlapping Consensus," p. 24.

16. *Ibid.*

17. See, for example, Richard Rorty, "Feminism and Pragmatism," *The Tanner Lectures on Human Values, vol. 13*, ed. Grethe B. Peterson (Salt Lake City: University of Utah Press, 1992), pp. 1–36.

18. Charles Larmore, "Political Liberalism," *Political Theory*, vol. 18, no. 3 (August, 1990), p. 354.

19. *Ibid.*

20. Rawls, "Justice as Fairness: Political not Metaphysical," p. 230.

21. "Foundationalist" here means substantive, not formal, foundationalism.

22. Larmore, "Political Liberalism," p. 354.

23. *Ibid.*

24. Rawls, "The Priority of Right and Ideas of the Good," pp. 275–6.

25. Larmore, "Political Liberalism," p. 356.

26. *Ibid.*

27. Michael Walzer, *Spheres of Justice* (New York: Basic Books, 1983), p. xiv.

28. See especially Richard Rorty, "The Contingency of a Liberal Community," in *Contingency, Irony and Solidarity* (Cambridge: Cambridge University Press, 1989), pp. 44–72, and "The Priority of Democracy to Philosophy," in *Philosophical Papers vol. 2* (Cambridge: Cambridge University Press, 1991),

pp. 279–302; therein (p. 284) Rawls is said to be "thoroughly historicist and anti-universalist;" Rorty is describing himself, not Rawls, here.
29. Joseph Raz, "Facing Diversity: The Case of Epistemic Abstinence," *Philosophy and Public Affairs*, vol. 19, no. 1 (Winter, 1990), p. 9.
30. *Ibid.*, p. 14.
31. *Ibid.*, p. 15.
32. *Ibid.*
33. *Ibid.*
34. *Ibid.*
35. An elegant and persuasive attempt to do this is Michael Walzer, "Philosophy and Democracy," *Political Theory*, vol. 9, no. 1 (August, 1981), pp. 379–97.
36. Raz, "Facing Diversity: The Case of Epistemic Abstinence," p. 19.
37. *Ibid.*
38. *Ibid.*, p. 21.
39. *Ibid.*
40. *Ibid.*, p. 22.
41. Rawls, "The Domain of the Political and Overlapping Consensus," p. 249.
42. *Ibid.*, p. 243.
43. Rawls, "The Priority of Right and Ideas of the Good," p. 275.
44. Rawls, "The Domain of the Political and the Idea of Overlapping Consensus," p. 244.
45. Rawls, "The Idea of an Overlapping Consensus," p. 17 (emphasis in the original).
46. *Ibid.*, p. 14.
47. *Ibid.*
48. My ideas here and in the following section owe a great deal to Bonnie Honig, *Political Theory and the Displacement of Politics* (Ithaca, N.Y.: Cornell University Press, 1993), ch. 5.
49. Rawls, "The Idea of an Overlapping Consensus," p. 9; see also "Justice as Fairness: Political not Metaphysical," pp. 247–50.
50. A theme essayed with much insight in Richard Flathman, *Willful Liberalism: Voluntarism and Individuality in Political Theory and Practice* (Ithaca, N.Y.: Cornell University Press, 1992), especially pp. 166–224.
51. Rawls, "Justice as Fairness: Political not Metaphysical," pp. 271–2.
52. Rawls, "The Idea of an Overlapping Consensus," p. 19.
53. *Ibid.*, pp. 13, 19–20.
54. *Ibid.*, pp. 19–20.
55. See the excellent discussion in Ron Replogle, *Recovering the Social Contract* (Totowa, N.J.: Rowman and Littlefield, 1989), pp. 230–7.
56. Jean-Jacques Rousseau, *The Social Contract*, Book I, Chapter 7.
57. Kurt Baier, "Justice and the Aims of Political Philosophy," *Ethics*, vol. 99, no. 4 (July, 1989), pp. 771–90.
58. Raz, "Facing Diversity: The Case of Epistemic Abstinence," p. 31.
59. *Ibid.*
60. Rawls, *A Theory of Justice*, p. 454.
61. *Ibid.*, n.1.

Part III

Alternative Liberalisms

7   Perfectionism With a Liberal Face? Nervous Liberals and Raz's Political Theory

The views of Rawls and the defenders of the idea of neutrality about the good constitute the mainstream of contemporary American liberal thought. But this procedural-deontological voice is not the only voice in the liberal chorus, even if it is the leading one. This chapter critically analyzes what I take to be an important expression of the minority voice of perfectionist liberalism, the political theory advanced by Joseph Raz in The Morality of Freedom *and other works. In my view, while perfectionist liberalism is correct to abandon the notions of neutrality and deontology as the essence of the liberal project, it nevertheless fails to express the spirit of that project in its most compelling form. This chapter seeks to explain and support these judgments, and along the way to bring to light the sources of appeal of a more modest, pragmatic expression of the liberal spirit which might stand as an alternative to both neutralist and perfectionist expressions.*

I

Introduction

Use of the concept "perfectionism" for the purpose of describing a certain view about the appropriate purposes and actions of the political state began with Rawls' *A Theory of Justice*. Rawls not only coined the term (for use in this particular context, at least), but also elaborated an account of the relationship between liberal and perfectionist political moralities. The relationship was conceived as antagonistic and mutually exclusive; a commitment to publicly authoritative perfectionist principles was deemed incompatible with a commitment to liberal principles of political right. Rawlsian liberalism, in endorsing the priority of the right over the good, relegated perfectionist ideals to the realm of the non-public choice of individual ends, or "life-plans."[1]

For two decades, commentators of various stripes challenged, in different ways, what they saw as the mistaken devaluation of the idea of the good in Rawls' theory and liberalism generally. For the most part, these writers presented themselves as critics of liberalism, thus apparently testifying to the soundness of the view that liberals and perfectionists were horses of a different color. A clear and characteristic expression may be seen in Will Kymlicka's definition of perfectionist theories as ones that "...claim that certain ways of life constitute human 'perfection' (or 'excellence'), and that such ways of life should be promoted, while less worthy ways of life should be penalized. This is unlike liberal or libertarian theories, which do not try to encourage any particular way of life, but rather leave individuals free to use their resources in whatever ways they themselves find most valuable."[2]

There have, however, been challenges to this conventional view, constituted by attempts to articulate a political morality showing liberal and perfectionist principles to be compatible with one another. The most widely discussed and praised attempt to develop a perfectionist liberalism has been that of Joseph Raz, the subject of critical attention herein.

Liberals are sometimes caricatured as nervous and vacillating types, "unable to take their own side in an argument," as it is said. Raz's perfectionist liberalism reflects a very different sort of character; one confident in the rationality of his principles, unafraid of squarely endorsing state action in support of them, willing to walk tall, without guilt about the big stick he carries or the reasonability of swinging it (where warranted only, of course). Such a liberalism would have abandoned the implicit desire, overtly manifested in the discourse of neutrality, to be all things to all people, and would instead dare to speak in its own name.

Understood either as rhetorical performance or as a set of cogent arguments, Raz's liberalism is a powerful and attractive discourse. No liberal worth his or her salt could fail to be tempted by it. Whether, having followed him to the edge of perfectionist waters, one ought to go ahead and drink is another question. I lean toward abstinence, finding through the journey down to the water renewed appreciation for an old-fashioned, nervous and self-doubting, liberalism. My message to fellow travellers is that being tarred as relativists, feathered as irrationalists, and generally condemned for lacking a backbone may simply be the price to be paid for being liberal.

In Section II, I discuss those elements of Raz's political theory which are most likely to make conventional liberals nervous. In III, I discuss those elements of the theory which constitute in effect Raz's effort to take some of the apparently illiberal sting out of the message conveyed through the elements discussed in II.[3] In IV, I discuss Raz's explicit arguments against anti-perfectionist forms of liberal theory. These arguments continue, in a different way, the task pursued by Raz's arguments considered in III; they constitute an effort at relieving the anxiety generated by the perfectionist elements of the theory treated in II. In Section V, I advance a number of reasons explaining why I think liberals ought to decline Raz's invitation to relax and accept perfectionist liberalism. A sentiment underlying this judgment is that the current rush to perfectionism amongst liberal thinkers, at least in the United States, may have less to do with pure and disinterested advances in philosophic reasoning than with the fallout from increasingly moralistic, intransigent and sometimes hysterical strands in American political culture. There has never been, nor in the foreseeable future will there be, a shortage of conservatives willing to exclaim that the barbarians are at (or inside) the gates; liberals might therefore usefully leave that task to them who have traditionally performed it so well, abandon their flirtation with perfectionism, and return to their own traditional, if increasingly neglected, task; that of defending liberty, especially at the margins of what is socially and morally "respectable," "acceptable," and, above all else, "reasonable."

II

Making Liberals Nervous

There are three elements of Raz's political theory likely to strike one as departures from liberalism as ordinarily understood. These are (a) the relation between autonomy and the good, (b) the view of "morals legislation" and (c) the view taken of the appropriateness of examples for consideration of perfectionist principles. Let us consider each in turn.

Autonomy and the Good
Raz's conception of autonomy and its value is perplexing and, at first glance at least, paradoxical. On the one hand, Raz says that personal autonomy is "...a constituent element of the good life,"[4] and he argues that governments must respect the liberty of individuals to make their own choices. This argument involves an endorsement of (a version of) Mill's harm principle. It is tempting to think, then, that Raz holds that there is value in autonomous choosing, even when that which is chosen is, *ex hypothesi*, morally bad or evil. But that is not his view. Rather, he maintains that "...autonomy is valuable only if it is directed at the good (and) it supplies no reason to provide, nor any reason to protect, worthless let alone bad options."[5] Government, rather than turning a blind eye to morality, is charged with the responsibility of "...enabling individuals to pursue valid conceptions of the good and discourag(ing) evil or empty ones."[6]

Thus Raz's endorsement of the value of the autonomous life, which is itself partially responsible for the ascription of the label "liberal" to his theory, does not lead him to endorse a neutralist or anti-perfectionist position with regard to state activity, positions often thought to be constitutive of liberalism. Indeed, he argues that it leads to just the opposite.

It is worth noting that the conceptual tie Raz establishes between autonomy and goodness is *not* established in what one might call the old-fashioned Kantian-Rousseauean way, that is by "moralizing" the concept of autonomy to begin with. Raz is not claiming that one is not "truly" or "genuinely" autonomous if one fails to will and choose the good. Autonomy for Raz is "...essentially about the freedom of persons to choose their own lives."[7] An autonomous life is "...opposed to a life of coerced choices," and is "...discerned not by what there is in it but by how it came to be."[8] He clearly distinguishes this mundane and straightforward usage of the concept of autonomy from the Kantian notion of moral autonomy, wherein autonomy is linked grammatically to willing in accordance with universalizable rules.[9]

How can it be then, that autonomy is a constituent element of the good life and yet at the same time "...valuable only if it is directed at the good."? The solution to this puzzle lies in Raz's understanding and defense of what he terms "moral" or "value pluralism," an idea to be discussed in the next section. For the moment, I want only to have specified the sense in which Raz's conception of the relation between autonomy and the good is likely to make a conventional liberal nervous.

Morals Legislation and the Harm Principle

A conventional liberal view is that respect for individual autonomy is incompatible with legislation enforcing "personal" morality.[10] Mill's harm principle is often taken as the paradigmatic expression of this view. Actions judged not to have harmed others are insulated from the reach of the criminal law, regardless of their moral quality. Denial of this principle of insulation is, on this view, taken to constitute an unwarranted assault upon individual autonomy. The harm principle thus understood excludes morality from the scope of legislation.

Raz defends a "transformed version" of the harm principle.[11] He interprets it not as "...a restraint upon the pursuit of moral goals by the state" but rather as "...a principle about the proper way to enforce morality."[12] This transformed view of the harm principle renders it compatible with Raz's view that "...it is the function of governments to promote morality. That means that governments should promote the moral quality of the life of those whose lives and actions they can effect." The harm principle thus is understood as requiring the state to "...stop(s) at coercion and manipulation only where their use would not promote the ability of people to have a good life but frustrate or diminish it."[13] He (wryly?) notes that "not all the traditional supporters of the harm principle will welcome its vindication in this form."[14]

We shall consider below Raz's reasons for maintaining that harmless immoralities should not be legislated against, a position he shares with the conventional liberal. My aim here is simply to indicate the difference in the underlying premises between Raz and the conventional liberal. As a perfectionist, Raz argues not simply for the permission but for the duty of government to "...act with discrimination to encourage the good and the valuable and to discourage the worthless and the bad."[15] What the conventional liberal refers to as "morals legislation" is obviously not excluded in principle from that sweeping mandate.

No Examples
A third aspect of Raz's theory likely to make conventional liberals nervous is an aspect of his theorizing more than a position taken within that theory, though its legitimation is rooted in a position taken. The position is this. Raz divides political theory into two parts: "political morality" and a "theory of institutions." Political morality is said to "...consist in the principles which should guide political action. It provides the principles on the basis of which the theory of institutions constructs arguments for having political institutions of this character rather than that."[16] In *The Morality of Freedom,* Raz concerns himself exclusively with "political morality," a consequence of which is that he does not discuss the way the principles defended therein are to be "translated" into political institutions. Nor does he discuss any particular policies or issues which would or could be expected to arise through these institutions. This seems innocent enough as a matter of the division of intellectual labor.

A consequence of it, however, is that Raz "...says almost nothing about what makes an option or an individual's conception of the good repugnant or immoral, even though the central thrust of his argument is to establish the government's right, indeed its duty, to extirpate options of this sort."[17] At first glance, this strategy of argument seems hypocritical; Raz's theory demands that governments distinguish, and act upon the distinction, between good and bad ways of life, and yet he himself offers no substantive view in regard to this issue.[18] W.J. Waluchow does take it to be "a serious limitation" of Raz's theory that "it largely forgoes discussion of the concrete implications" it would yield.[19] Yet Jeremy Waldron, critical of Raz in a number of other respects, applauds Raz's abstinence from making concrete ethical judgments. He says that Raz is "...right to ask whether there is anything left in the liberal critique of perfectionism once we set aside the possibility that perfectionism might be deployed to support mistaken standards. As a practical matter that possibility always remains, but it is worth being clear all the same about where exactly the critique is directed. For this reason, perfectionism is better defended without examples."[20]

We shall consider the adequacy of this view later. I take it that it is clear that conventional liberals (and perhaps others?) will not only be made nervous by Raz's refusal to use examples in his theorizing, but will also complain that it constitutes a failure to lay his moral and political cards on the table.

III

Relieving Anxiety: Taking (Some of) the Sting Out of Perfectionism

Raz at one point says of his theory that it "...may sound very rigoristic and paternalistic."[21] I think he means that it may sound very illiberal; Section II sought to explain why this is so. Raz says that while his views may "...conjure images of the state playing big brother forcing or manipulating people to do what it considers good for them against their will," nevertheless, "...nothing could be further from the truth."[22] (Nothing?) I want now to discuss four aspects of his theory which, taken together, may be thought of as aiming at relieving the conventional liberal of his or her anxieties concerning perfectionism.

Moral Pluralism: A Variety of Good Lives
Raz's affirmation of "value pluralism" is the crucial link in the chain of theoretical reasoning designed to show that perfectionism need not yield an illiberal politics. Value pluralism is the view "...that there are many different and incompatible valuable ways of life...many of the routes open to us in our lives are both incompatible and valuable...it is this value multiplicity, this incompatibility of much that is valuable, that I mean by value pluralism."[23]

The effect of value pluralism is to take the sting out of the proposition that the state is bound to concern itself with the moral goodness (or lack thereof) of the lives lived by its subjects. This is so because value pluralism insures that many different ways of life will pass the test of being valuable, or good, ones, and hence we need not fear the spectre of a tyrannical state forcing upon us a single and narrow orthodox form of life. In effect, Raz is asking us to see that it is the monism, rather than the moralism, of (some) perfectionist states which is the genuine object of legitimate liberal fear. Raz's perfectionist state is non-monistic in affirming the diversity of valuable lives. Conventional liberals are thus counselled to relax upon the recognition that there will be a "wide" range of options from which individuals might choose.[24]

The thesis of value pluralism also aims at resolving our original puzzlement over Raz's seemingly paradoxical claim that autonomy was a constituent element of the good life and yet valuable only when directed at the good. How could choice be valuable and yet only be valuable when the good is chosen? Again, Raz asks us to see that this is paradoxical only if we assume moral monism. Given moral pluralism, the exercise of our capacities as autonomous choosers is given room for development and expression without contravening the principle that autonomy is valueless when the bad is chosen. Thus, for example, when Will Kymlicka argues that on a perfectionist view the state would interfere with "...a person's ability to form and revise a conception of the good,"[25] Raz is not without a reply. While granting that this ability is limited in a perfectionist state (that is, it does not extend to a right to choose a bad conception of the good), Raz, besides pointing out that such choice is limited by some standard in any state, can appeal to value pluralism to argue that there is nevertheless adequate space for the exercise of autonomy in forming and revising a conception of the good within the domain of valuable conceptions.

We can see here the sense in which the value of autonomy for Raz is "asymmetrical."[26] The good chosen autonomously is of greater value than if enacted through accident or coercion. However, the bad chosen autonomously is not thereby made valuable; indeed it has a sort of negative value, for in Raz's view the autonomous wrongdoer is worse than the non-autonomous one; "...those who freely choose the immoral, ignoble or worthless we judge more harshly precisely because their choice was free."[27]

Value pluralism thus functions for Raz as "...the bulwark against uniformity, against a society imposing through its government or otherwise a uniform vision of the ideal form of life on its population."[28] The government's fundamental duty is to guarantee "...that an adequate range of diverse and valuable options shall be available to all."[29] Meeting this duty will involve making and enforcing moral judgments about what are and are not "valuable" options, but value pluralism insures that the result of this process will not generate a monist tyranny. Even conventional liberals relieved by this will likely find themselves hoping (praying?) that Razian legislators are well versed in the writings of those who have some experience with the diverse ways of being human.

Political Authority

Raz's account of authority is rich and complex, and I cannot hope to do it exegetical justice here. I want to point to a feature of it which stands as another aspect of Raz's theory which functions to relieve liberal anxiety regarding perfectionist politics.

The relevant feature of Raz's view of authority is succinctly summarized in what he labels the "normal justification" thesis, which is:

> the normal way to establish that a person has authority over another person involves showing that the alleged subject is likely better to comply with reasons which apply to him (other than the alleged authoritative directives) if he accepts the directives of the alleged authority as author-itatively binding and tries to follow them, rather than by trying to follow the reasons which apply to him directly.[30]

This gives rise to Raz's "service conception" of political authority. The (justifiable) state is the servant of its members insofar as it lacks authority *unless* following its directives actually serves to increase the likelihood of reasonable action by the citizen. If that condition is unsatisfied, then authority is lacking. The legitimate state is thus, seen through the lenses of this theory of authority, a relatively benign and beneficent creature, our aid and comfort rather than our oppressor.[31] It's role is to help us act upon the basis of good reasons.

It is through appeal to this service conception of authority that Raz seeks to undermine the force of conventional liberal complaints about perfectionist tyranny. Thus he remarks that "...one needs constant reminders that the fact that the state *considers* anything to be valuable or valueless is no reason for anything. Only its being valuable or valueless is a reason. *If it is likely that the government will not judge such matters correctly, then it has no authority to judge them at all.*"[32]

As was the case with the doctrine of value pluralism, this is at once partially persuasive and gnawingly unsatisfying. One can't help but wonder whether it won't be the government that ends up judging whether that same government's judgment is more likely to be correct.[33] Raz can remind such a wonderer that having the power to decide and deciding what is correct are separate issues, though I am unsure as to how consoled I should be by the thought that if my government should step on me I can point out (to myself? to other theorists?) that it had no authority to do so. On the other hand, this lingering sentiment of dissatisfaction with Raz's refusal to worry sufficiently about the sheer existential power of the state may reflect nothing more substantial than an American's inability to think of authority and the state as anything other than "other," a sentiment which is no doubt responsible for provoking Raz into the irritation which appears (not for the first time) in that "...one needs *constant* reminders..." turn of phrase.

Common Sense and Charitable Readings
A third anxiety relieving aspect closely related to the second is Raz's (perfectly legitimate) plea to us that in evaluating his theory of political morality we ought to interpret it on the assumption that those enacting it have about as much common sense as we do. Mill remarked in *Utilitarianism* that "there is no difficulty in proving any ethical standard whatever to work ill if we suppose universal idiocy to be conjoined with it,"[34] and it is fair of Raz to ask that we read him in such a spirit.

Thus he argues that "...perfectionism is not to be equated with the view that governments should always pursue all moral considerations at all costs. It is the view that whether or not a particular moral objective should be pursued by legal means is a question to be judged on the merit of each case, or class of cases, and not by a general exclusionary rule, as the so-called "neutralists" would have it."[35] Perfectionism can then be seen as "merely a term" indicating that there are only strategic, not principled, inhibitions on governments acting upon "any valid moral reason."[36]

Raz suspects that the results of these strategic inhibitions will look a great deal like the results desired by conventional liberals, and this may well be so. The list of reasons which have traditionally led conventional liberals to fear perfectionism and to seek to exclude the question of the good from politics is very similar to the list of relevant strategic factors a Razian perfectionist legislator would presumably take into account. These would include "...the dangers inherent in the concentration of power in few hands, the dangers of corruption, of bureaucratic distortions and insensitivities, of fallibility of judgement, and uncertainty of purpose, and...the insufficiency and the distortion of the information reaching the central organs of government."[37] Moreover, Raz is fully aware of, and in effect requests that his theory be evaluated upon the recognition that it is aware of, the "weaknesses" and "afflictions" that make actual governments fall short of perfectionist ideals. He closes *The Morality of Freedom* by acknowledging that

...the pursuit of full-blooded perfectionist policies, even of those which are entirely sound and justified, is likely, in many countries if not in all, to backfire by arousing popular resistance leading to civil strife. In such circumstances compromise is the order of the day. There is no abstract doctrine which can delineate what the terms of the compromise should be. All one can say is that it will confine perfectionist measures to matters which command a large measure of social consensus, and it will further restrict the use of coercive and of greatly confining measure and will favor gentler measures favoring one trend or another...[under such circumstances] an attempt by the government to achieve more freedom will achieve less.[38]

Taken together these considerations make perfectionism seem hardly more than common sense. The service conception of authority assures us that states lack authority to enforce unjustified moral ideals, and a charitable view of the conditions of enactment of Raz's principles suggests that prudence, if not principle, will counsel against perfectionist intrusions upon liberty in cases of controversy. Who can complain about what appears to be left over – governmental support for valid moral ideals enjoying consensual social support?

Non-coercive Perfectionist Instruments: Carrots, not Sticks
A fourth anxiety-reducing aspect of Raz's theory is his reminder to us that "...not all perfectionist action is a coercive imposition of a style of life."

> Much of it could be encouraging and facilitating action of the desired kind, or discouraging undesired modes of behaviour. Conferring honours on creative and performing artists, giving grants or loans to people who start community centres, taxing one kind of leisure activity, e.g., hunting, more heavily than others, are all cases in which political action in pursuit of conceptions of the good falls far short of the threatening popular image of imprisoning people who follow their religion, express their views in public, grow long hair, or consume harmless drugs.[39]

To appreciate the force of Raz's point here we need to make clear the distinction between coercive and non-coercive instruments of perfectionist policy and the use to which Raz puts this distinction. The paradigmatic coercive instrument is the criminal law and the power of the state which enforces the sanctions attached thereunto. Raz agrees with the conventional liberal in arguing against the use of the criminal law to pursue perfectionist goals by means of criminalizing and punishing harmless immoralities. As we saw in the previous section, however, his reasoning to this view is formally different than that of the conventional liberal. The conventional liberal understands the harm principle to constitute the principled barrier against such legislation; Raz's opposition is strategic and contingent rather than absolute.[40] Acknowledging that perfectionist principles do not necessarily rule out the criminalization of (what are judged to be) harmless immoralities on moral grounds, he presents the following argument against such criminalization:

> [Coercion]...violates the condition of independence and expresses a relation of domination and an attitude of disrespect for the coerced individual. Second, coercion by criminal penalties is a global and indiscriminate invasion of autonomy. Imprisoning a person prevents him from almost all autonomous pursuits. Other forms of coercion may be less severe, but

they all invade autonomy, and they all, at least in this world, do it in a fairly indiscriminate way. That is, *there is no practical way of ensuring that the coercion will restrict the victim's choice of repugnant options but will not interfere with their other choices.*[41]

Whether this argument is sufficient to underwrite an affirmation of the harm principle is a matter of debate.[42] What does seem clear, however, is that Raz is correct in reminding us not only of the existence of non-coercive (or at least "more mildly coercive") forms of perfectionist action by governments, but also, by means of his examples, of our own intuitive support of many of them.[43] Who, after all, can with a straight face complain if the government distributes citations of honor to citizens who have engaged in exemplary service to the community? (Of course, there will be controversy over particular judgments; but shall we do away with honors for those who help to feed the hungry because we can't agree on whether pro-choice or pro-life people deserve public honors?) Even those who take the preceding question to be a non-rhetorical one will, I assume, grant that there is *some* sort of relevant distinction to be made between the two types of policy instruments Raz distinguishes as coercive and non-coercive. Even if we say that there are elements of coercion attaching to all governmental judgments, if for no other reason than because of the unrivalled means of violence which are in the background of every such act, still it is not the case that all cows are grey – there is a morally relevant and politically important difference between being put in jail and not receiving the benefit of a tax incentive. To the extent that is so, the conventional liberal has here another reason to breathe a little easier about perfectionism. It now appears to amount to governmental support, largely if not exclusively through non-coercive, incentive-based instruments, for valid moral ideals which enjoy widespread consensual social support. With that picture in mind, it's hard not to feel the pull of Raz's theory when he tells us that "...anti-perfectionism in practice would lead not merely to a political stand-off from support for valuable conceptions of the good. It would undermine the chances of survival of many cherished aspects of our culture."[44]

IV

Relieving Anxiety (2): Anti-Anti-Perfectionism

Introduction
The previous two sections have sketched elements of Raz's perfectionist political morality. Another source of support to which he appeals is indirect; it consists of a set of arguments designed to respond to standard objections

to perfectionism raised by conventional liberals. Acknowledging that the concerns underlying these objections are "real and important," Raz nevertheless attempts to show that they do not, properly understood, justify anti-perfectionism. These "anti-anti-perfectionist" arguments, even if successful, could not of course establish the validity of perfectionism. They could, however, result in clearing the argumentative ground in such a way that one might be left more open to and receptive of the appeals of perfectionism. The four anti-perfectionist arguments to which Raz responds can be labelled the "hidden tyranny," "dangerous gamble," "overt tyranny," and "elite moral experts" arguments. Let us consider each in turn.

The "Hidden Tyranny" Argument
According to Raz, "the spring from which anti-perfectionism flows is the feeling that foisting one's conception of the good on people offends their dignity and does not treat them with respect."[45] This "spring" of anti-perfectionism gives rise to a certain view about the role of government in human affairs. This view was given classic expression by Mill in *On Liberty*, in the course of criticizing the belief that the rise of democratic government would itself serve to resolve the problem of governmental oppression of the people, since "the people" or "the will of the people" could not be opposed to itself. Mill argues:

> ...such phrases as "self-government," and "the power of the people over themselves," do not express the true state of the case. The "people" who exercise the power are not always the same people with those over whom it is exercised; and the "self-government" spoken of is not the government of each by himself, but of each by all the rest. The will of the people, moreover, practically means the will of the most numerous or the most active *part* of the people – the majority, or those who succeed in making themselves accepted as the majority; the people, consequently, *may* desire to oppress a part of their number, and precautions are as much needed against this as against any other abuse of power.[46]

This view in turn gives rise to one form of anti-perfectionist argument – the government should not be allowed to act upon considerations of what is morally good for human beings because in fact what will be being acted upon are not such considerations at all, but rather, unavoidably, *what some partial and powerful segment of the community* considers to be what is morally good for human beings. This "hidden tyranny" argument relies on the meaningfulness of the distinction between: (a) good reasons for governmental action which refer to what is good for human beings, and (b) some partial body's view of what constitute good reasons for governmental action which refer to what (that partial body believes) is good for human beings.

This is an intuitively appealing line of argument for anti-perfectionist liberals, and many, including Mill as I understand him, have adopted it. Raz presents a strong argument against it. Accepting the force of his argument will not necessarily lead to the endorsement of perfectionism, but it does, I think, both reveal to anti-perfectionists the weakness of one of their traditional lines of defense, and force them to look elsewhere for support.

The anti-perfectionist argument derives it's plausibility from the idea that all apparent cases of (a) in fact reduce to cases of (b). Raz argues that this is a mistake, resulting from confusing the actions of persons acting as authorities and the actions of persons acting for themselves. Consider Smith, who holds moral view X. As a private person and citizen, Smith advocates the legal enforcement of X. Smith is also a government official who finds herself in a position to act, under color of authority, with regard to X. On Raz's view, the fact that Smith believes there are sound reasons for supporting X is not itself a reason for Smith to act authoritatively in support of X. The *belief* is not a reason for action itself; rather, the appeal is directly to the soundness of the reasons (supporting X) themselves. As Raz puts it, "...it is not merely that authorities refer not to their belief that there are good reasons for their decisions but to the reasons themselves as grounds for action."[47]

This argument is important, for it seems to defeat the "hidden tyranny" argument in the following way. That argument believes that authoritative appeals to good reasons are in effect sheep's clothing which conceal the moral preferences of a natural person or persons. But Raz's argument separates conceptually the two phenomena in a compelling way. Smith acting as authority can never appeal to Smith the natural person's moral beliefs as grounds for a decision; indeed to do so would clearly be recognized as an abdication of Smith's duty as an authority. More importantly, Smith as authority cannot even appeal to Smith *as authority's* belief that there are good reasons supporting X as itself a reason for supporting X; her belief, even in her capacity as authority, is irrelevant. The only relevant and appropriate ground for a decision on her part in support of X is the soundness of the reasons in support of X themselves. We might put it this way: were reasons to speak for and enforce themselves, Smith would be unnecessary – and *that* is the ideal (though unattainable) from which the exercise of authority by natural persons acting as artificial persons is to take its bearings and draw its legitimation. Smith as authority is in a sense a concession to the imperfection of reality. She speaks not her own voice but (imperfectly) the voice of reason, and is necessary only because reason itself is mute.

Now of course Smith will make mistakes. Raz recognizes this, while nevertheless accounting for the binding force of authoritative judgments generally. Thus, "while an authority's belief that a decision is based on sound considerations makes it binding even if it is not in fact sound, the reason for this is that acknowledging the validity of an authority's decision even if it is unsound is in fact more likely to lead to action supported by sound reason than any alternative method of deciding what to do."[48] This is the "normal justification" thesis described above.

Thus the argument of hidden tyranny seems defeated, for it is shown to rest upon a failure to consider carefully the nature of, and justification for, the exercise of authority. Of course, the Smiths of the world may willfully subvert their duties and the procedures which are their source, but that does not show that *authority* is a mask for tyranny, but just the opposite. It shows that the Smiths in question are practicing tyranny by *subverting authority*. And one cannot insist that procedures of authority, to be acceptable, prevent absolutely their own subversion. That is to ask for the impossible, just as it is to insist that authority, in order to be legitimate, never issue in mistaken judgments.

Nevertheless, there is something important in the hidden tyranny argument which remains even after this critique. Granted everything that has been said, still there is the brute existential fact that the procedures of authority are put into motion and have life breathed into them only by what are, in the final analysis, natural persons. Hence there remains the basic and inevitable reality of the imposition of the will of some people upon the wills of others, no matter how much this brute reality is cloaked under the theory of authority. Doubtless this is inevitable, even justifiable, and coterminous with the existence of politics itself; still, it is important, indeed vitally important, that we recognize it as that, rather than deceive ourselves. Moreover, given that point, we have reason to restrain the scope of such activity as much as possible. And that means resisting the assimilation of matters of morality to the long arm of political authority.

The "Dangerous Gamble" Argument

A second source of anti-perfectionism is the recognition that governments are fallible, and will sometimes make mistakes when pursuing perfectionist policies. This gives rise to an argument we can label the "dangerous gamble" one. Raz recognizes the concern that gives rise to the argument, but attempts to deflate the anti-perfectionist significance of it by arguing that a suitably defined perfectionism can, and indeed must, accommodate such problems.

Raz argues that absent some special reason to think moral decisions a category of especially difficult ones, where the chances of error are greater than is the case in non-moral ones, we have no more reason to prohibit all governmental action with regard to morals than we do to prohibit all governmental action on any issue. Moreover, the perfectionist can require of public officials the same caution and attempt to recognize the probabilities and consequences of error in moral matters that all of us would require of such officials as a general duty of office with regard to any and all issues of concern. However stringent and effective that latter duty is, it is also applicable to moral issues, and thence may relieve some of our anti-perfectionist anxiety.

Let's look at Raz's question: is there some special reason to fear failure or the consequences of failure when trying to promote conceptions of the good? We might be tempted to fear failure upon the consideration that moral questions do not admit of right answers, but Raz anticipates such a view and responds in no uncertain terms that this would be to presuppose a "deep skepticism" which in effect undermines any position in political morality, including the anti-perfectionist's, and not just Raz's. Raz aggressively proclaims:

> Nowhere in this book will general moral skepticism be discussed. General moral skepticism claims either that there never is a better moral reason for one action rather than another, or that one can never have good grounds for believing that one action is better supported by moral reason than another. If either of these claims is true then nothing in this book is of any value, nor is there any room for any discussion of the morality of political action.[49]

Suppose, in accordance with the rhetorical spirit of this statement, we label the skeptic's position the position of "wanton irrationality," and provisionally accept Raz's dismissal of it as a non-starter in arguments of political morality. Are there other grounds upon which anti-perfectionist liberals might reasonably resist Raz's view that there are no reasons to fear failure or the consequences of failure when trying to promote conceptions of the good any more than we fear failure or the consequences of failure with regard to other governmental decisions? I think there are, but we have to question certain foundational postulates of Raz's argument rather than the argument itself in order to explicate them.

What postulates, then, are the questionable ones? There are two from which anti-perfectionist liberals may wish to depart. One is that which maintains that the ideal with regard to governmental action is that it meet the test of being in accord with good reason. The other would involve claiming that decisions about the right are less difficult than decisions about the good, and hence it would deny the postulate that all governmental decisions concerning morality, whether they be in regard to principles of right or conceptions of the good, are of the same order of difficulty. Now at first glance, I imagine that most will find the second anti-perfectionist strategy the preferable one, if for no other reason than that the first seems doomed to collapse into the position of wanton irrationality. But I want to suggest that this is not necessarily so, and that in fact the first is the preferable one.

Raz's position depends on setting up the following dichotomy: either (a) one accepts that the criteria of governmental action and policy is being in accordance with good reason or (b) one denies this as the appropriate criteria. The corollary of (a) is Raz's perfectionism; the corollary of (b) is the self-defeating thesis of wanton irrationality, given that neutrality is ruled out as a possibility in the first place. Faced with that menu, the obvious choice is (a) and it's corollary. But is it true that affirming (b) commits one to the thesis of wanton irrationality? To successfully answer "no" to this, we need to specify a sense in which *it is reasonable to reject good reasons* as the criteria of governmental action. In Section V, I attempt to speak in defense of that position.

The "Overt Tyranny" Argument

A third source of anti-perfectionist sentiment is a blunter version of the first, "hidden tyranny," argument. There, the concern was that whatever the intention of legislation, the effect of legislative activity is the imposition of some people's views about the good upon others. Here, the argument is that perfectionism would provide a license allowing people to openly use the government and its organs to impose their favored style of life upon others. Raz says this view rests upon a "confusion" which is both practical and moral.[50] He argues that practically it assumes "...that perfectionist action is aimed by one group at another, attempting to bring it to conform with its habits and way of life."[51] His argument designed to show that this is confused seems especially weak. He points out that this need not necessarily be so, and that perfectionist action could be taken "...in support of social institutions which enjoy unanimous support in the community."[52] Doubtless that is true, but the critic's concern is obviously in regard to those (many) cases where it is not true. Raz also points out in this regard that not all perfectionist action need be coercive, but again it seems a strange response to the anti-perfectionist critic worried about tyranny; his (the critic's) concern is surely with the cases where coercion is involved. I cannot see the force of telling him that some cases won't be like this; what about the ones that are?

The "Elite Moral Experts" Argument

Another criticism Raz considers is that which maintains that "...perfectionism assumes that some people have greater insight into moral truth than others.

But if one assumes that all stand an equal chance of erring in moral matters should we not let all adult persons conduct themselves by their own lights?"[53] Subject to the addition of a clause specifying that that conduct would have to be within bounds which enabled others to have an equal liberty to do so as well, I see nothing obviously weak about this view. Raz's response to it is somewhat peculiar, in that it seems not to respond to it at all, but to raise a different matter. He says that "...whatever else can be said about this argument one point is decisive. Supporting valuable forms of life is a social rather than an individual matter...perfectionist ideals require public action for their viability."[54] The claim that public action is necessary to maintain and provide a variety of valuable forms of life so as to insure the ability of individuals to live autonomously is one of Raz's main arguments in support of perfectionism, and we shall want to consider it more carefully. But I cannot see how it constitutes a response, let alone a "decisive" one, to the anti-perfectionist argument which stems from the view that only the vain and proud are foolish enough to fail to recognize that when it comes to matters moral, we are practically equal in seeing darkly at best.

V

Reason, Will and Nervous Liberalism

Let us turn to a more direct assessment of Raz's theory as thus far explicated. Here I discuss three aspects of Raz's account open to criticism on immanent grounds, then I turn to the larger question of whether Raz succeeds in talking the conventional, anti-perfectionist liberal out of his fears and into an endorsement of perfectionism. I try and explain why he leaves me more, rather than less, afraid of perfectionism.

Perfectionism, Civil Society and the State
One of Raz's arguments in support of perfectionism appeals to the recognition (a) that "...supporting valuable forms of life is a social rather than an individual matter." From (a) he argues to (b), that "...perfectionist ideals require public actions for their validity," and hence that anti-perfectionism in practice would "...undermine the chances of survival of many cherished aspects of our culture."[55]

I accept (a), but find (b) questionable. Taking "social" in (a) to mean "collective" as opposed to "individual", it remains open whether this collective activity is to be located at the level of civil society or at that of the state (or possibly both). Raz closes that issue in stating that the collective action must be "public" for the viability of (valuable) forms of life to be maintained. But is that necessarily so? Conventional liberals sympathetic to (a) might nevertheless argue that such collective activity as is necessary to maintain forms of life can and should be left to occur at the voluntaristic level of civil society. Kymlicka has advanced such an argument, suggesting that rather than seeing the issue as one of perfectionism versus neutrality, it might be better cast as being between "...social perfectionism and state perfectionism – for the flip side of state neutrality is support for the role of perfectionist ideals in civil society."[56]

However, Kymlicka may be robbing Peter to pay Paul in endorsing (and assuming that liberals will endorse) social perfectionism as a means of criticizing state perfectionism. In criticizing state perfectionism, he suggests a number of ways in which the "...threats and inducements of coercive power" entailed by state perfectionism would "...distort rather than improve the process of individual judgment and cultural development."[57] The arguments are, as I see it, strong ones, but Kymlicka admits that the problems which he identifies as telling against state perfectionism "...also arise in the cultural marketplace."[58] The problems referred to here are social prejudice against subordinate groups and the surplus disadvantage placed upon subordinate groups when they are required to (successfully) articulate their claims at the level of law and policy, wherein they must "...immediately aim at persuading the majority" rather than being able to "...gain adherents from the majority slowly, one by one," and wherein they are also forced, as a matter of efficient strategy, to speak about themselves and their practices in a manner "...most palatable to the majority, even if that misdescribes the real meaning and value of the practice, which often arises precisely in opposition to dominant practices."[59]

Kymlicka's arguments may be too powerful for his purposes, for they would seem to tell against social as well as state perfectionism. Where the primary value needing protection is autonomy, coercion in the form of majority opinion at the social level seems hardly less threatening than legal coercion. Even if it is less threatening, and Kymlicka does present a case in support of such a conclusion, we may still wonder whether a liberal might not want to resist Kymlicka's casual (as it seems to me) assertion that the "...flip side of state neutrality is *support* for the role of perfectionist ideals in civil society."[60] It *could* be, though another option, motivated by the same arguments Kymlicka advanced against state perfectionism, would be to affirm a libertarian resistance to perfectionism at either level.

However that may be, it is clear that thinking about perfectionism against the background of the distinction between civil society and the state allows us to see a problematic ambiguity in Raz's theory. Raz says that governments

"...cannot make people have a flourishing autonomous life. That is up to each one to see to himself."[61] Governments can, though, help people flourish "...primarily by guaranteeing that an adequate range of diverse and valuable options shall be available to all."[62] The question arises as to how the menu of options is to be set. We know that Raz allows state action in support of good options and against bad ones. But which good ones? Only those that "already" exist at the level of civil society, or also those that could be brought into existence through state activity? If the former, then the actions of the perfectionist state are constrained by the "prior" workings of civil society, which is, conceptually, the level at which the menu of choices is determined. This "passive" interpretation would seem consistent with Raz's service conception of authority, and also has the advantage, rhetorically, of quieting (some) liberal anxiety about the scope of activity in principle available to a perfectionist state. On this view, the state is merely "tidying up" and reinforcing the decision making which has occurred at the level of civil society. Ironically, the perfectionist state here gains advantage by manifesting an appearance of itself very similar to the traditional images of the neutral, liberal state.

On the other hand, this (relatively) benign state may not be capable of fulfilling the charge put to it by Raz. He does not, after all, say that the state's duty is to reproduce the status quo of civil society, but rather that it is to "...guarantee an adequate range of diverse and valuable options available to all."[63] This raises the question of whether the state can act so as to *create* options necessary to secure "an adequate range" where such a range does not exist (a matter which is itself determined by the state). Raz seems to indicate an affirmative answer to that question when he says that "...governments can help put people in conditions where they are able to have that kind of life [that is, flourishing autonomously] by protecting and promoting the creation of the environment which makes such a life a possibility."[64] "Protecting" can be read as suggesting a state subordinate to civil society; "promoting" is ambiguous, while "the creation of the environment" suggests an activist state which molds civil society in accordance with a definition of what count as good and bad options. This is thus to envision, as a legitimate scenario, cases where the judgments of the perfectionist state regarding good and bad options are enforced, although these judgments are opposed to those held by the citizens at the level of civil society.

This "activist" interpretation of Raz's view seems necessary to allow the state the means of meeting the responsibility of providing or creating an "adequate range" of good options at the level of civil society necessary to sustain autonomy. However, one is thereby forced to wonder about the account of authority which could legitimate such activity; it is obviously not coming from the consent of the governed, since the activity of the state is occasioned precisely by the failures of citizens to achieve an adequate range at the level of civil society. Suppose, for example, that volleyball is a good practice, but that everyone wants to play softball, which is a bad one. What would it mean for the state to "provide" volleyball as an option under such circumstances, that is, in cases where the "good" which is (somehow?) seen clearly by the state is ignored by its citizens? Could such provision be made without violating the liberty of citizens? Perhaps, in the sense that rather than forcing softball players to play volleyball, the perfectionist state could "merely" provide incentives to entice them to "freely" change their practices. But is this less objectionable in principle?

If, on the other hand, to avoid these issues of legitimate authority, we retreat to the passive interpretation of Raz's view of the legitimate scope of state activity, the state can no longer meet the perfectionist charge which Raz has defended as appropriate to it, that of standing in judgment of the good and the bad (not merely *what is held to be* good and bad sociologically) and acting accordingly.

My point is not that Raz leaves this choice hanging, for I think it is clear that he endorses the activist interpretation; it goes hand in hand with his endorsement of the "reason" over the "will" interpretation of the notion of respecting persons, to be discussed in the next section. What I would emphasize is that the degree of latitude provided to the state by the activist view is often obscured in Raz's formulations by the use of "passive" verbs to articulate it. The conjunction of the passive "protecting" with the activist "promoting the creation of" in the quote above is a case in point. Raz's perfectionist *doctrine* requires the activist reading of the legitimate scope of state activity, a fact which, when recognized, is likely to generate anxiety on the part of the conventional liberal. The articulation of this doctrine through the sometime use of passive verbs is a means of relieving that anxiety, but I believe it is ultimately an illusory one.

Reason and Will

In the course of criticizing the theories of liberalism advanced by Rawls and Thomas Nagel, Raz draws a distinction between two ways of interpreting the widely accepted (but very general) notion of a political theory "respecting persons." Raz's question is whether in aiming to respect persons we aim to respect their will or their intellect? To respect will is to argue "that it is sometimes more important for a person to choose freely than to choose correctly, that acting freely is itself an important ingredient of individual well-being." Put more strongly, such a view would maintain that "respecting persons is an imperative binding on us independently of any conception of the good, an imperative that enjoins us to respect the will of others, rather than their intellect."[65] On the other hand, to respect intellect is to respect the *reasonable* choices of individuals, rather than necessarily their brute empirical choices. The notion of "reasonable", of course, admits of various interpretations itself, but I trust the structural difference between the two models of "respecting persons" is evident.

Now each model has an attractive feature, and each an unattractive one. The attractive feature of each is appreciated when it is seen as a response to the unattractive feature of the other. We find ourselves attracted to the will model because of its apparently tolerant and non-judgmental character; everyone's choices are to be respected equally, and no one can ride roughshod over another by using coercion premised on the (alleged) truth of his or her conception of the good. But the intellect model pushes us off our acceptance by raising (at least) one unsettling problem: how is agreement, and hence order, even possible if we insist upon respecting will pure and simple? This is a troubling, seemingly decisive, question. As Raz says, it isn't clear why we should "...reject valid or true principles, the implementation of which may actually be of benefit to all, just because a small sector of the population cannot be convinced of this fact."[66] How is agreement possible if, in effect, each and every brute will is given a veto power over collective choices?

What, then, would solve our problem? To move to the intellect model, of course. Here, we are bound to respect the reasonable choices of others, and that little adjective, however it turns out to be interpreted, will provide the guarantee of consensus. To refuse to agree to rational terms of consensus is to be unreasonable. But just as we are feeling satisfied, the will model unsettles us – by asking whether upon the intellect model it does not turn out that "our duty to act only on political principles to which the reasonable consent is simply the duty to act on well-founded, valid principles. For that is what the reasonable consent to. This eliminates the independent role of consent."[67] We are troubled, then, by the thought that the intellect model of respect, in effect, makes the notion of consent a superfluous one.

We (liberals, at least) seem then to be in a position of not being able to live with the will model, but not being able to live without it. To endorse it is to remove the possibility of consensus, in the name of inclusiveness; to deny it, and affirm instead the intellect model, is to purchase consensus at the price of inclusiveness. What is to be done?

A good deal of philosophical energy has been devoted to seeking the desideratum of a synthetic account integrating the two models in a systematic and normatively compelling way. Raz, however, provocatively suggests that we may have to simply embrace one or the other horn of the dilemma. He writes:

Politics must take people as they come and be accessible to them, capable of commanding their consent without expecting them to change in any radical way. But at the same time, justified political principles may be controversial, and may fail to command actual consent. Nagel and Rawls offer interpretations of this intuition which aim to be both coherent and attractive. Their failure suggests that the underlying idea may be at bottom unstable and incoherent. There may be no middle way between actual (including implied) agreement and rational justification.[68]

Raz has, of course, pursued the path of rational justification through the articulation of a doctrine of perfectionist liberalism. I have come to believe that he is right to doubt the possibility of a synthetic theory integrating the will and intellect models successfully, and thus am sympathetic to the view that liberals must bite the bullet and embrace one or the other model. Ironically, what reading Raz has made me far less convinced of than I once was is that the intellect model is the one worth endorsing.

Raz's theory presupposes conceptions of "good reasons" and "reasonable action" which are epistemologically separate from the practices and discourses of a given social order. This has to be so, otherwise those practices and discourses could not be evaluated from the point of view of reason in a non-circular way. If they could not, in principle, be so evaluated, it would no longer be possible to posit the idea of "good reasons for action" as the rationale of government. If, as Raz claims, a person's fundamental interest lies in "...realizing the sound conception of the good,"[69] and the justification of government lies in its ability to aid this process, then there has to be a way of cashing out the notions of "soundness" and "reason" which reveals them to be uncontaminated by the political and social practices upon which they are to pronounce judgment.

Any socio-political formation will exclude certain identities, forms of life and behaviors from the terms which constitute it as an order. No one, neither Raz nor Rawls nor any other liberal, denies that.[70] What is objectionable about Raz's perfectionism, in my view, is that it acts to consecrate the acts by which the lines of inclusion/exclusion are drawn in the name of a reason which is understood to be non-contingent and non-contestable, a reason which acts, ironically enough in a theory so critical of neutralist liberalism, as a disinterested sovereign power untainted by the politics which it judges.

In so doing, it seems to me to be a discourse which adds unnecessary insult to unavoidable injury. A liberal socio-political formation, like any other, makes possible the realization of some forms of human identity and life at the cost of excluding others. The lines of demarcation which characterize it are, in the last analysis, contingent creations of collective will, not instantiations of transcendental reason. I do not maintain that this means there is nothing more for liberals to say to the people upon whom they impose the terms of liberal order than "more of us than there are of you." There is a great deal for liberals to say by way of explaining their commitment to terms of liberal order and their willingness to exercise power and coercion in order to maintain it in the face of internal challenges. However, one thing I don't think they can legitimately say is that some large and sovereign thing called Reason is underwriting the decision to draw the lines of inclusion/exclusion just here. As I see it, the (overwhelming) temptation to say that is the measure of our weakness, our wish to avoid the responsibility that accompanies acting. The danger of it is that it is an intimation of cruelty, vicariously exercised every time the views of "those people" are dismissed on grounds that they refuse to accept the terms of reasonable discussion, reasonable rules of inference, reasonable rules of evidence, and so on. In my view, Raz's perfectionist liberalism encourages, rather than discourages, our manifest failings in this respect.

From this perspective, Raz's apparently innocuous practice of defending perfectionism without examples appears in a more questionable light. The rationale for the practice, recall, is to avoid entangling the evaluation of perfectionism itself with Raz's (or any other) particular views regarding what modes of life are good and bad. Granted that point, it is nevertheless the case that the avoidance of examples obscures from the observer's consciousness the contentious and arguable position Raz assumes in maintaining that the distinction between good and bad lives is an epistemologically stable, sound and secure one, a distinction based upon a non-contingent Reason uncontaminated by will or power. Raz's defense of this metaphysic relies upon pointing out that "global skeptics" and relativists will believe otherwise; presumably, we all know where *that* path leads.

Perhaps. But someone who isn't bluffed into affirming Raz's confident brand of objectivism by the spectre of being branded "skeptic" or "relativist" might still have doubts about the stability, the firmness, of the epistemic distinction upon which his perfectionist theory is built. And *any* example involving substantive modes of life will exacerbate those doubts, or at least the questions behind them.[71]

Suppose you and I disagree about whether X is a bad mode of life. You say, let's avoid a discussion of X because it will distract us from the discussion of perfectionism in terms of its formal properties as a theory of legitimate state activity. But my point is that the two dimensions are not as distinct from one another as this view supposes. One thing that could (it often does) happen if we discussed X is that as we begin to see X from the perspective of others (and if we begin to see those "others" as "similars"), we will also begin to reflect upon the underlying epistemic question, call it "meta-x", of what it means to talk of "good and bad from the point of view of reason." Such interactions can of course take many paths; one such path involves doubt regarding the sort of epistemic rationalism upon which Raz builds, and hence potentially doubts regarding the adequacy of the perfectionism which is built upon it. The avoidance of examples thus functions so as to divert critical attention away from this potentially destabilizing process, and is thus not as trivial a matter as it first appeared to be.

We may also note in this context the irony contained in the following consideration. Anti-perfectionist liberalism of the type perfected by Rawls is often criticized for being overly abstract and formal, too detached (it is said) from the local meanings and practices of social and political reality. Yet Raz's perfectionism is every bit as formal, abstract and a-political as the neutralist liberalism it criticizes. It is a purely formal perfectionism, a perfectionism without an account of perfection; from this angle of vision, it seems that *neither* position will take its own side in the argument!

Now to be sure, affirmation of the will model of liberalism will generate intractable practical problems. If we strive to include everyone, and everyone is allowed to come just as they are, with the views and ideas they actually have, without those views being sanitized and laundered by the test of "reasonableness," without a plea, then we are not going to be able to articulate a theory which...does what? Which justifies the exercise of power by the state? As Raz says, political theories, like a will account of liberalism, which do not insist upon denying skepticism, "...leave(s) little room for any justification of general policies."[72] Can one not imagine a liberal who would count that a point in favor of his side, not against it? Raz goes on to remark that "Skepticism, whether local or global, holds little promise for any political theorist."[73] That is true, *if* the task of political theorists is to justify the exercise of power by the state. But why should political thinkers feel so compelled? Does the modern state lack bureaucrats as it is?

But that puts it too strongly. Even as we recognize that no synthesis of the will and intellect models is available to us, it does not follow that the alternative stance is one of *affirming one at the expense of the other*. A people who would live freely have reason to realize that each model, and the perspective which it symbolizes, is absolutely necessary to the existence of a regime of freedom. To affirm the intellect model at the expense of the will model is to have become frozen into the perspective of authority and the (entirely legitimate) concern of trying to justify it. It is the frozenness, the immobility of the stance, not the perspective and the concern which defines it, which is the vice here. To affirm the will model at the expense of the intellect model is similarly to have become frozen into the perspective of the subject and the (entirely legitimate) concern of trying to protect it from the fallout arising from the contingencies of even "justified" authority. To become frozen and immobilized here is to have abdicated the responsibility of ruling, to, ironically enough, have come to view authority as itself entirely "other." We cannot affirm one at the expense of the other – and yet no synthesis is possible.

There is no "solution" to this "problem." Perhaps we should say that it is not a "problem" after all, but rather a description of the life-giving antagonism which is constitutive of a free politics. The ancient and venerable trope which intimates this mode of life is "ruling and being ruled in turn." But it is only a trope, not a theory, or a program, or a solution. Because it is only that, and because we yearn so strongly to make it more than that, and because the means by which we attempt such heroic results yield only frozenness and fragmentation, one may say of that beguiling and beautiful trope what one so often has occasion to say of our own efforts to be free: that it is easier said than done.

NOTES

1. An early challenge to Rawls' view, arguing that it had to be at least supplemented by perfectionist considerations, was Vinit Haksar, *Equality, Liberty and Perfectionism* (Oxford: Oxford University Press, 1979).
2. Will Kymlicka, *Contemporary Political Philosophy* (Oxford: Oxford University Press, 1990), pp. 186–7.
3. I say "in effect", *not* "by intention." I find it illuminating to think of certain features of Raz's theory as functioning to relieve liberal anxiety about perfectionism; I do not claim that it was necessarily Raz's personal intention to frame his discourse so as to achieve this aim.
4. Joseph Raz, *The Morality of Freedom* (Oxford: Clarendon Press, 1986), p. 408.
5. *Ibid.*, p. 411.
6. *Ibid.*, p. 133.
7. *Ibid.*, p. 370, n.2.
8. *Ibid.*, p. 371.
9. *Ibid.*, p. 370; see also Robert George, "The Unorthodox Liberalism of Joseph Raz," *Review of Politics*, vol. 53, no. 4 (Fall, 1991), p. 662.
10. For purposes of discussion I am going to refer to this as "the conventional liberal view." That is, of course, a generalization which, like all generalizations, admits of exceptions.
11. Raz, *The Morality of Freedom*, p. 420.
12. *Ibid.*, p. 415.
13. *Ibid.*, p. 426.

14. *Ibid.*
15. Joseph Raz, "Liberalism, Skepticism and Democracy," *Iowa Law Review*, vol. 74, no. 3 (1989), p. 785.
16. Raz, *The Morality of Freedom*, p. 3.
17. Jeremy Waldron, "Autonomy and Perfectionism in Raz's Morality of Freedom," *Southern California Law Review*, vol. 62 (1989), p. 1130.
18. Monogamous marriage does crop up a few times as an illustrative example, but is never overtly defended in principle.
19. W.J. Waluchow, "Critical Notice of Joseph Raz: The Morality of Freedom," *Canadian Journal of Philosophy*, vol. 19, no. 3 (September, 1989), p. 478.
20. Waldron, "Autonomy and Perfectionism in Raz's Morality of Freedom," p. 1130.
21. Raz, *The Morality of Freedom*, p. 412.
22. *Ibid.*
23. Raz, "Liberalism, Skepticism and Democracy," pp. 780–1.
24. The term "wide" is used in Raz, "Liberalism, Skepticism and Democracy," p. 781.
25. Will Kymlicka, *Contemporary Political Philosophy*, p. 33.
26. Heidi M. Hurd, "Justifiably Punishing the Justified," *Michigan Law Review*, vol. 90, no. 8 (August, 1992), p. 2217.
27. Raz, "Liberalism, Skepticism and Democracy," p. 781.
28. *Ibid.*, p. 782.
29. *Ibid.*
30. Raz, *The Morality of Freedom*, p. 53.
31. To say this of the legitimate state is not necessarily to say it of the state per se.
32. Raz, *The Morality of Freedom*, p. 412; emphasis added.
33. See W.J. Waluchow, "Critical Notice," p. 477.
34. John Stuart Mill, *Utilitarianism* (Indianapolis: Hackett Publishing Co., 1979), p. 23.
35. Joseph Raz, "Facing Up: A Reply to Critics," *Southern California Law Review*, vol. 62 (1989), p. 1231.
36. *Ibid.*, p. 1230.
37. Raz, *The Morality of Freedom*, p. 427.
38. *Ibid.*, p. 429.
39. *Ibid.*, p. 161.
40. Robert George takes the opposite view in his "The Unorthodox Liberalism of Joseph Raz," *Review of Politics*, vol. 53, no.4 (Fall, 1991), p. 662. I learned a great deal from George's illuminating discussion, but cannot understand why he views Raz as "...opposing the legal prohibition of victimless immoralities as a matter of moral principle."
41. Raz, *The Morality of Freedom*, p. 419.
42. For the view that it is not, see Wojciech Sadurski, "Joseph Raz on Liberal Neutrality and the Harm Principle," *Oxford Journal of Legal Studies*, vol. 10, no. 1 (1990), pp. 130–3; Raz's defense is at *The Morality of Freedom*, pp. 419–29.
43. On the difficulty of defining "autonomy" and "acts of coercion" independently of one another, see Jeremy Waldron, "Legislation and Moral Neutrality," in R.E. Goodin and A. Reeve, eds, *Liberal Neutrality* (New York: Routledge, 1989), pp. 61–83.
44. Raz, *The Morality of Freedom*, p. 162.
45. *Ibid.*, p. 157.
46. John Stuart Mill, *On Liberty* (Indianapolis: Bobbs-Merrill, 1956), ch. 1, p. 6.

47. Raz, *The Morality of Freedom*, p. 159.
48. *Ibid.*, p. 159.
49. *Ibid.*, p. 160.
50. *Ibid.*, p. 161.
51. *Ibid.*
52. *Ibid.*
53. *Ibid.*, p. 162.
54. *Ibid.*
55. *Ibid.*
56. Kymlicka, *Contemporary Political Philosophy*, p. 219.
57. Will Kymlicka, "Liberal Individualism and Liberal Neutrality," *Ethics*, vol. 99, no. 4 (July, 1989), p. 901; compare with Waldron, "Autonomy and Perfectionism in Raz's Political Theory," pp. 1138–41.
58. Kymlicka, "Liberal Individualism and Liberal Neutrality," p. 901.
59. *Ibid.*
60. Kymlicka, *Contemporary Political Philosophy*, p. 219.
61. Raz, "Liberalism, Skepticism and Democracy," p. 783.
62. *Ibid.*, p. 782.
63. *Ibid.*
64. *Ibid.*, p. 783.
65. Joseph Raz, "Facing Diversity: The Case of Epistemic Abstinence," *Philosophy and Public Affairs*, vol. 19, no. 1 (Winter, 1990), p. 35.
66. *Ibid.*, p. 43.
67. *Ibid.*, p. 46.
68. *Ibid.*
69. *Ibid.*, p. 56.
70. The contemporary theorist who, in my view, takes consequences of this most seriously and thinks it through most deeply is William Connolly. See, for example, "Identity and Difference in Liberalism," in R. Bruce Douglass, Gerald M. Mara and Henry S. Richardson, eds, *Liberalism and the Good* (New York: Routledge, 1990), pp. 65–83.
71. Even the merely illustrative examples Raz does employ unwittingly reveal this. For example, at one point he contrasts the life of a gambler with that of a farmer, in a context which supposes the reader will find it easy to see that all else being equal, the life of the farmer is more valuable than that of the gambler. I am not so sure; Bart Maverick is, on my perfectionistic calculus, ranked higher than any farmer known to me. See Raz, *The Morality of Freedom*, pp. 298–9.
72. Raz, "Liberalism, Skepticism and Democracy," p. 763.
73. *Ibid.*

8   Dworkin on the Foundations of Liberal Equality

Earlier, in Chapter 2, we had occasion to examine in detail the arguments in support of the idea of neutrality about the good advanced by Ronald Dworkin in "Liberalism". In his Tanner Lectures published in 1990, Dworkin offered an account and defense of liberalism significantly different from and more ambitious than that earlier view. In these lectures, Dworkin, like Raz, rejected the idea of a merely political liberalism advanced by Rawls, and set out instead to show that the principles of liberal political order were founded upon a distinctive ethical view (the "challenge model") which spoke directly to the question of the good. This suggests a form of perfectionist liberalism. However, this chapter tries to show that a lingering neutralism undermines Dworkin's attempt to articulate a comprehensive perfectionist liberalism, and that this neutralism also leads Dworkin to treat those who think otherwise than he does in an illiberal, or at least ungenerous, fashion.

I

Ronald Dworkin's Tanner Lectures, "Foundations of Liberal Equality," have hardly elicited comment within the academic political theory community.[1] This is surprising for a number of reasons. First, Dworkin is widely taken to be one of the leading liberal theorists in the English-speaking world, and "Foundations" is a major statement involving reflection upon issues of principle which are at the center of contemporary scholarly debate amongst liberals. Second, "Foundations" introduces a number of ideas and concepts which are new in Dworkin's corpus, and which serve to illuminate and clarify some of his widely discussed earlier works, especially the famous article "Liberalism," which sparked so much argument over the idea of neutrality and its place within liberal political theory.[2] Finally, the lectures are interesting because of the approach they take to the matter of "defending liberalism," an approach which departs in interesting and significant ways from those presently pursued by other leading liberal thinkers, notably John Rawls and Joseph Raz.

Given these facts, I have no ready explanation for the lack of discussion elicited by Dworkin's lectures, except to say that I found them to be frustratingly obscure in a number of respects and, on the whole, quite difficult to follow. To the extent this reaction reflects something other than my failings as a reader, I attribute it to the fact that in his long and intricate discussion Dworkin largely eschews direct engagement with other theorists and their concepts. He chooses instead to construct a conceptual vocabulary of his own which, while obviously relating to these other theorists and ideas, does so in such a way that Dworkin is able to maintain control over the manner in which positions different than his own are conceptualized and defined. One consequence is a neat and orderly progression of dialectical moves leading to the conclusion that a set of claims hesitantly advanced in the beginning are, after all, well founded. Another (unintended) consequence is that the reader often yearns for Dworkin to engage more generously and sympathetically with the positions and theorists with which he disagrees. All the bodies here are buried deeply and cleanly beneath the highly stylized conceptual dichotomies he utilizes as tools of exposition; a considerable degree of excavation is required to purchase enough distance from his conceptual scheme to be able to assess his views clearly and critically.

Contributing to these tasks of excavation and critical assessment is the purpose of this chapter. I want to situate and assess Dworkin's views in relation to those of other liberal theorists concerned, as he is, with the matter of conceptualizing and defending a distinctively liberal political morality.

The assessment is largely critical. Dworkin's version of liberalism founders, I shall argue, because he continues to pursue an aim, what I label the "liberal desideratum" (hereafter "LD"), which other liberal theorists have, in different ways and for different reasons, abandoned. I believe they are correct to have abandoned it, and thus I believe Dworkin mistaken in continuing to pursue it. To the end of explicating the grounds of these judgments, I pursue the following path of exposition. In Section II, I explain what I mean by the liberal desideratum, and also explicate the key conceptual dichotomies Dworkin utilizes in pursuing his argument. In Section III, I consider the difference between Dworkin's, Rawls' and Raz's approach to articulating and defending liberalism. Finally, in Section IV, I seek to demonstrate the sense in which I claim that Dworkin pursues LD and the reasons which render this quest fruitless.

II

The Liberal Desideratum

The LD is to give an account of liberal order which shows it to be both inclusive of and fair toward all ways of life which themselves are willing to abide by the terms of fairness. I do not attribute LD to any particular theorist, though I believe the pursuit of it was characteristic of much liberal theorizing in the 1970s, that is in the period just before "communitarianism" replaced "Marxism" as the prevalent language of criticism by means of which the dominant liberal discourse was pressed and criticized in the academy. The pursuit of LD may be seen, it seems to me, in (the early) Rawls' *A Theory of Justice*, in Dworkin's "Liberalism," in Ackerman's *Social Justice and the Liberal State*, and in Part III, "Utopia", of Nozick's *Anarchy, State and Utopia*. However, one consequence of nearly a decade of critical communitarian discourse has been the widespread abandonment of the pursuit of LD, or at least the abandonment of the overt pursuit of a robust form of it.[3]

LD continues nevertheless, I believe, to be held as an accurate description of the aims, and often achievements, of liberalism by many "lay" liberals, both inside and outside the academy. The appeal of LD is clear and simple: if fulfilled, it follows that a liberal political order is qualitatively different from all the various forms of non-liberal political order, for only liberalism avoids imposing a conception of the good upon individuals and hence only liberalism genuinely respects human freedom and the diversity of human nature. This is to view liberalism not as one amongst a number of modes of collective life, each different but none transcendently superior, but to see it rather as a unique form of political order structurally unlike all the rest, allowing freedom of life-pursuits rather than prescribing such pursuits through the affirmation of some conception of the good. It is to see it as a "social union of social unions," or as a "framework for communities" rather than a community, or as, in an older version, a "rational and homogeneous state."[4] If LD were achievable and achieved, it would seem almost irrational not to be a liberal. Anyone who doubts the persistence of the desire for LD may reflect upon whether he or she knows many liberals who believe that.

Note that LD as an aim makes sense only on the assumption that the criteria of "fairness" are independent of the terms of liberal order themselves; otherwise the argument in support of those terms appealing to fairness would be circular. One factor underlying the abandonment of the pursuit of LD has been an increasing degree of skepticism about the possibility of such independence.

Dworkin's Conceptual Tools

In "Foundations," Dworkin utilizes a number of conceptual terms of art. A brief explanation of the most important of these follows.

Continuity versus Discontinuity
These terms denote alternative strategies for reconciling the (sometimes) competing demands of two "perspectives" on life, the personal and the

political.[5] The personal perspective is taken in "...making decisions about [our] own life and conduct, in deciding, for example, what kind of job to take, or whom to marry, or what help they owe a colleague, or whether to bend some rule on behalf of a friend, or whether their lives are going badly or well."[6]

Dworkin casually dismisses political theories which maintain that, because the conflict between the perspectives is "genuine and insurmountable," one of the perspectives must be reformulated in terms of the other so as to dissolve the tension.[7] He instead outlines two strategies of reconciliation between the perspectives. The strategy of discontinuity "...argues that the two perspectives are compatible because the second, political, perspective, is in a special but important sense *artificial*, a social construction whose purpose is exactly to provide a perspective that no one need regard as the application of his full ethical convictions to political decisions, so that people of diverse and conflicting personal perspectives can occupy it together."[8]

The strategy of continuity, on the other hand, seeks to connect "ethics" with politics directly, by articulating a "liberal ethics," that is, an account of the good life, and then arguing that this ethical account is the philosophical foundation of political liberalism.[9] On this view, "...ethics and politics are intertwined so that some of the most far-reaching questions about the character of the good life are political questions, too."[10]

Impact versus Challenge Model of the Good

These terms denote alternative models of the good life, and thus stand as the options available to one who has chosen to pursue the strategy of continuity, for that strategy necessitates a (liberal) ethics upon which to build a (liberal) politics, or in more familiar language, an account of the good from which to derive principles of right. The strategy of discontinuity, on the other hand, attempts to drive a sharp wedge between the good and the right.

The impact model is defined as holding "...that the value of a good life consists in its product, that is, in its consequences for the rest of the world."[11] The challenge model "...argues that the value of a good life lies in the inherent value of a skillful performance of living."[12] Dworkin gives the sense of the key contrast in remarking that "...the challenge account finds ethical value in the performance of living rather than in the independent value of some product a life leaves behind.... The value of a life successful on these [challenge] standards does not consist in the objective value of its impact on the world...but in the skillful, in most cases intuitively skillful, managing of a challenge. A good life, on this view, has the kind of value a brilliant dive has and retains when the ripples have died away."[13]

I read this as a transposition of contrasts familiar at the political level onto the personal level. Hence we might think of the impact model as "consequentialist" and "teleological," the challenge model as "procedural" and "deontological." In Nozick's vernacular, the challenge model is an "historical" account of ethics, the impact model an "end-state" account. Dworkin adopts different attitudes regarding the sharpness of the contrast between the models at different places in the text. At times he is moderate, saying he hopes only to have shown that the challenge model must "...have at least an important place in any overall ethics," and acknowledging that each model captures some of our intuitions about ethics.[14] At other times, he contrasts the models sharply, speaks of their "incompatibility," and champions the challenge model by (purporting to be) revealing things like how the impact model makes "...many popular views...seem silly and self-indulgent."[15] I think much the same could be said about the two models of ethics that can be said about the correlative contrasts at the political level: that only an ideologue or a philosopher in the grip of an ideology would be unable to rest content with acknowledging that any sane person would acknowledge the force of both procedures and consequences in these matters. Dworkin will not leave it at that, insisting that "...our ethical intuitions will remain divided and inconclusive until we settle on one or the other, or for some more comprehensive model that includes and orders both, if that is possible."[16] I confess to not being made quite as nervous by the prospect of division and inconclusiveness in theoretical ethics as Dworkin seems to be; indeed it is (what I sense to be) a rather demanding will to order bent upon purging the last ounce of ambiguity informing Dworkin's exposition that seems to me the more unsettling phenomenon.

Critical versus Volitional Well-being

These concepts denote alternative aspects of the kind of goodness a good life is said to have. As Dworkin defines it, "...someone's volitional well-being is improved, and for just that reason, when he has or achieves what in fact he wants. His critical well-being is improved by his having or achieving what he *should* want, that is, the achievements or experiences that it would make his life a worse one *not* to want."[17] Volitional and critical "interests" are defined accordingly as interests the satisfaction of which leads to the particular type of well-being.

Dworkin remarks in passing that this distinction is not simply a restatement of the familiar contrast between subjective and objective well-being (wants/needs, preferences/rights, apparent/real interests), but like Bernard Williams I find it difficult to locate the relevant differences. Williams indirectly, but sharply, comments upon the consequences of Dworkin's penchant for coining his own conceptual currency in remarking that "...despite the misleading implications which Dworkin rightly points out, I still think there is something to be said for the Hegelian terminology of 'real' interests. 'Real' arouses the suspicion of liberals, while 'critical' placates them, but it is useful to recall those suspicions, particularly as a reminder that someone has to interpret these interests."[18]

Parameters and Limitations
These concepts denote a distinction between alternative ways of conceptualizing the circumstances out of which ethical action takes place upon the part of an agent. "Parameters" is the concept Dworkin is most concerned to explicate, for it is closely linked to the defense of the challenge model of the good. But it can be understood only in contrast with the (somewhat peculiar) meaning he gives to the notion of "limitations."

Dworkin asserts that on any plausible version of the impact model of the good, "...all the circumstances of any person's actual life act as limitations on the quality of life he can have."[19] He gives the following illustration. "Mortality, for example, is a very important limit: most people could create more [value] if they lived longer. Talent, wealth, personality, language, technology, and culture provide other limits, and their force as limits will be much greater for some people, and in some time and places, than others."[20] On the other hand, if (doubtless to avoid the crudity of the view just stated) we occupy the perspective of the challenge model, Dworkin asserts that "...we must treat some of the circumstances in which a person lives differently, as parameters that help define what a good performance of living would be for him."[21] He gives this illustration of a "parameter." "The fact that I am a member of the American political community is not a limitation on my ability to lead a good life I could describe in isolation from that connection. It rather states a condition of a good life for me: it is a life appropriate to someone whose situation includes that connection."[22]

Dworkin's caricature of the "impact model" and its prescribed view of "limitations" are difficult to take seriously. I doubt one could dig up the crudest utilitarian and find quite the cast of mind conveyed in the remark regarding mortality. Certainly there is no reason for supposing that proponents of some version of the impact model must be so simple-minded that they could not, like proponents of the challenge model, mark the difference between "limitations" and "parameters." However that may be, let us return to the exposition.

"Parameters" are thus circumstances which are conceptualized as constituents of an agent's ethical identity (at least for a particular point in time), as providing the ground from which options can meaningfully be considered and choices sensibly made. To extend Dworkin's example for illustration, in thinking about whether to participate in a rally against American policy in the Middle East to be held in Trafalgar Square, one thing framing Dworkin's view of the choices open to him might well be his understanding of what would constitute appropriate ethical behavior for an American citizen (rather than, say, a "human being" or a "British citizen") in such circumstances.

I have no criticism to make of Dworkin's notion of a "parameter", though I would note two features of his explication of it. First, it is a particularly vivid, and therefore annoying, instance of a case where the complexity of and controversy surrounding the "matter" being discussed is ignored through the usage of an idiosyncratic vocabulary. The "matters" Dworkin is "really" discussing in raising the distinction between limitations and parameters include: the concept of the self operative in liberal theory, the question of whether identity is understood as created, discovered, and so on, the question of the account of choice in relation to identity over time. At the forefront of debate over liberal theory, these are matters of great complexity and significance. They have received careful and elaborate consideration in the writings of, among others, Sandel, Kymlicka, MacIntyre, Taylor and Parfit. Now it would be silly to insist that Dworkin should do a "literature review." But how seriously can we be expected to take a discussion which disposes of these issues through an invented dichotomy, one side of which articulates a position so foolish that only a straw man would maintain it?

III

Retreating from LD

Why have liberals increasingly come to abandon the (overt) pursuit of a (robust) form of LD? Doubtless many factors are at work here, but I propose to briefly discuss one for purposes of illustration. The retreat from LD can be seen clearly if we note that the idea of the "autonomous life" has come to be seen by liberals as a particular, substantive conception of the good life competing with others rather than as a meta-view which merely provides the point of access for choice amongst the competing substantive views. This acknowledgment is expressed clearly, for example, in the attitude Rawls has adopted toward Kant and Mill in his later writings. Kant and Mill are there said to have rooted their conceptions of political liberalism in comprehensive moral doctrines which take "autonomy" and "individuality" respectively as accounts of the good which politics serves. (They are, then, both perfectionists and practioners of what Dworkin termed the strategy of "continuity.") According to Rawls, in so doing they unnecessarily circumscribe and limit the degree to which liberal *political* doctrine opens itself to being affirmed by those who might reject the Kantian and/or Millean conceptions of the good life,[23] conceptions which Rawls at one time went so far as to refer to as "sectarian doctrine(s)."[24]

What is noteworthy here is the acceptance by Rawls of the claim that liberal theory in its historically most compelling forms has been the expression of a comprehensive conception of what constitutes a good life for man. Once this is granted, the continued pursuit of LD seems futile. As Rawls puts it:

> No society can include within itself all forms of life. We may indeed lament the limited space, as it were, of social worlds, and of ours in particular; and we may regret some of the inevitable effects of our culture and social structure.... As Berlin has long maintained, there is no social world without loss.[25]

In the face of this recognition, LD is gone, though obviously not forgotten. Indeed, I hypothesize that Rawls' attribution of "lamentation" and "regret" to (especially) "us" in this passage is an indicator of the seductive power of that ideal over the liberal mind; why we should lament or regret the non-existence of something (a universally inclusive mode of social life) which could not, of necessity, exist is otherwise inexplicable.

Two quite different responses have developed to this state of affairs. One is the articulation of liberalism as a "merely" political doctrine, the other the articulation of liberalism as a perfectionist doctrine. Rawls is the best known exponent of the former strategy, while Joseph Raz's *The Morality of Freedom* is an exemplar of the second.[26] Interestingly, Dworkin takes issue with each of these strategies, and a consideration of his disagreements with Rawls and Raz will help show the degree to which he remains committed to the pursuit of LD. Rawls' views can be described as non-comprehensive and non-perfectionist. Raz's views are comprehensive and perfectionist. Dworkin is distinctive in arguing for a liberalism which is at once comprehensive (the strategy of "continuity") and yet non-perfectionist. I believe his position is inconsistent, and that liberalism is forced in either the direction of political minimalism or perfectionism. We must first, however, explain briefly the rock and the hard place betwixt which (I claim) Dworkin is caught.

Rawls' and Raz's Response to the Abandonment of LD

Rawls has explicitly adopted what Dworkin calls the strategy of discontinuity for articulating and defending liberalism. Liberalism is, for Rawls, limited in the scope of its concern and application. It is, he argues, best understood as a political doctrine, not a philosophy of life generally.[27]

The ground of political liberalism is to be sought in what Rawls calls an "overlapping consensus" rather than in what Dworkin calls an "ethics," that is, a comprehensive conception of the good life. The overlapping consensus of support for political liberalism would be comprised of (adherents of) various comprehensive doctrines of the good, but it would be derived from none of them. Each would find its own way to supporting political liberalism. Rawls employs the metaphor of a "...module, an essential constituent part, that fits into and can be supported by various reasonable comprehensive doctrines that endure in the society regulated by it," to describe the idea of an overlapping consensus.[28]

Rawls intends his conception of liberal doctrine to be understood as being not only non-comprehensive but also non-perfectionist. Although he allows the liberal state to support the *political* virtues of character which are necessary for the reproduction of the regime, he wishes to distinguish this from the perfectionist sanctioning of state support for some preferred way of life generally. On Rawls' terms, the liberal state can acknowledge as virtues and support the nurturance of, for example, "civility and tolerance," but only insofar as these can be shown to be constitutive virtues of a liberal public person. They cannot be recognized or supported as virtues of personal character, though it may happen that they are defined as such according to some particular comprehensive conception of the good.[29] Numerous questions can be raised about this view, but for the moment I want simply to accept Rawls' self-description of it to bring out the contrasts with Dworkin. Clearly Rawls departs from Dworkin's judgment that liberal political principles "...will be stronger if (they) can also be seen as drawn from ethical convictions."[30] Indeed he departs sharply, for his view is just the opposite, that (political) liberalism is greatly weakened when linked to a particular conception of the good.

Dworkin does criticize Rawls' position, though his criticisms avoid directly engaging the reasons which lead Rawls to move to his "minimalist" position. The move to conceptualizing liberalism as political/non-comprehensive was motivated by Rawls' belief that fair and stable terms of cooperation in highly pluralistic societies could not be obtained through appeal to consensus on any comprehensive conception of the good. Only the "oppressive use of state power" could generate such "consensus."[31] The aim of inclusion thus motivates the move to reformulating liberalism as a political doctrine applicable to the public sphere only. The same aim motivates the quest for a non-perfectionist version of political liberalism, one based upon an overlapping consensus rather than an appeal to an account of the good.

Raz's response to the abandonment of LD is quite different from that of Rawls, though interestingly it proceeds from a very similar point of view in some respects.[32] Aside from the similarity of searching for a way of redescribing liberalism such that it needn't presuppose LD as an end, Raz seems to agree with Rawls that the articulation of a perfectionist liberalism must also be to articulate a comprehensive moral view which includes politics as one of its fields of application. Of course, Raz opts to explicitly and overtly defend such a view, while Rawls ardently avoids it; but both agree that these are the two viable alternatives. Table 8.1 may help clarify this point.

Table 8.1: Varieties of Liberal Self-description

	PERFECTIONIST	NON-PERFECTIONIST
COMPREHENSIVE	IV. Raz	I. Dworkin
POLITICAL ONLY	III. (a-political religions?)	II. Rawls

Raz and Rawls treat quadrants II and IV as the only viable ones, or to put it another way, they treat the two dimensions of the table here as pretty much one dimension. For Rawls, a "comprehensive" moral view is, in a sense, simply a perfectionist view about the good life for man identified in terms of its scope of application rather than in terms of its substance; but scope and substance are parts of the same general whole. As I read Rawls, he does not entertain the idea of a comprehensive, yet non-perfectionist, account of liberalism. Similarly, Raz takes perfectionism to be the view that the state is allowed, indeed required, to act (under specified conditions, to be sure) upon the basis of judgments regarding good and bad modes of life.[33] That is to think of "perfectionism" in such a way that it is bound up with the affirmation of what Rawls terms a "comprehensive" moral ideal.

In any case, Raz's affirmation of perfectionist liberalism proceeds from the abandonment of LD. This may be seen in the fact that while he speaks of "autonomy" as "...a constituent element of the good life,"[34] he nevertheless acknowledges that "autonomy is, to be sure, inconsistent with various alternative forms of valuable lives."[35] And he overtly denies the argument, often found in liberal attempts to achieve LD, that an autonomy-supporting culture does not affect the nature, but only the number, of the opportunities provided to individuals. Raz argues that, to the contrary, "...an autonomy-supporting culture offers its members opportunities which cannot be had in a non-autonomous environment, and lacks most of the opportunities available in the latter."[36] That, I take it, is to acknowledge that political liberalism and the "autonomy-supporting" culture it is both creator and creature of cannot achieve the universality of scope with regard to ways of life characteristic of LD. But whereas Rawls would recommend separating the defense of liberalism from any connection to autonomy understood as an ideal of personal character, Raz argues for affirming the linkage. The aim of activity by the liberal state, for Raz, is not neutrality with regard to conceptions of the good, but rather the enhancement of the goodness of the lives of its citizens.

I make no attempt here to comparatively evaluate the minimalist and perfectionist paths pursued by Rawls and Raz, though I hope the contrast between their responses is tolerably clear. Let us label it a contrast between *inclusion* and *vigor* as characteristic aims of their respective theories. The aims are themselves competitive ones; Rawls purchases inclusion through the appeal of an overlapping consensus only by detaching political liberalism from ethics, and thus the purchase is at the cost of the substantive vigor of his liberalism. Raz purchases vigor through the affirmation of perfectionism and the critique of neutrality, but at the cost of affirming the principled legitimacy of state activity based upon moral judgments about the goodness or badness of its citizen's life choices, which is to say at the cost of inclusion. Different people will weigh and evaluate these costs differently. What I note here is the trade-off which seems to be required between the aims.

Dworkin, however, denies that a trade-off is necessary. He believes it possible to tie political liberalism to a comprehensive moral view about the good life (the "strategy of continuity"), thus achieving a more vigorous liberalism than that of Rawls, while nevertheless avoiding perfectionism and the paternalistic politics that are thought to accompany it, thus achieving a more inclusive liberalism than that of Raz.

IV

There are three key aspects of Dworkin's argument in support of these views. They are (1) his understanding of the structure of the challenge model of ethics, (2) his conception of "ethical integrity," and (3) his distinction between first- and third-person aspects of a person's ethical views.

The Structure of Dworkin's Models of Ethics

Dworkin is aware that affirmation of the strategy of continuity as a means of expressing liberalism will raise concerns about the cost of exclusion. He frames the "problem" this way:

> Since liberalism is tolerant, and in some sense neutral among different conceptions people have about how to lead their lives, a liberal ethic must

be abstract. It cannot consist in some detailed description of the good life that is controversial within the political community, like the popular view that a life of power flowing from economic success is eminently satisfying and the opposite view that such a life is insensitive and mean. A liberal ethics must have a structural and philosophical rather than substantive character. It must consist in propositions like those I described in the Introduction, supporting a performance rather than a product conception of ethical value, for example, *which do not rule out any substantive, detailed conception of a good life likely to be popular in our political community.* A liberal ethics must have more than that negative virtue, however. It must be sufficiently muscular to form a distinctive liberal ethics, so that anyone embracing the views it deploys would be more likely also to embrace liberal politics.[37]

This passage vividly conveys Dworkin's unwillingness to abandon the pursuit of LD. To minimalist liberals who worry about inclusion, Dworkin offers the prospect of a liberal account of the good which will tolerate all conceptions of the good (or at least those "likely to be popular"); the liberal theory of the good here is conceived as a meta-theory (structural, not substantive) which can accommodate an array of different substantive conceptions.

Whether this will placate the concerns of minimalists is another question. One gnawingly unsettling aspect of the account is the "likely to be popular" rider attached to the clause specifying the scope of toleration. Dworkin doesn't explain the rationale of the qualification. Given the long-standing existence of the notion that "tolerance is only tested in *un*popular cases," this omission seems odd.

A second concern would be over determining the degree to which the meta-theory of the good characteristic of liberalism influences the substance, and thereby limits the array, of the conceptions of the good which make up the "menu" of concrete options open to individuals. To the degree this is so, the inclusiveness of Dworkin's formulation is compromised. This, of course, supposes that there *is* a connection between the "meta-theory" and the "menu" which remains even after the overt attempt to drive a wedge between the two characteristic of LD pursuing strategies like Dworkin's here. I would agree with Raz that it is implausible to deny such a connection. That Dworkin should avoid recognition of this connection is odd, given his trenchant criticisms of the views of Thomas Scanlon and Thomas Nagel earlier in these lectures. There, Dworkin argues that appeals to "reasonableness" as an impartial criteria for objectively distinguishing substantive ethical views from one another fail to achieve their aim, because our (competing) conceptions of "reasonableness" are not independent of these ethical views themselves, but affected by them.[38] Yet when he discusses his own challenge model of ethics, he seems less prone to notice the implicit connection between form and content which he had glimpsed clearly when criticizing Scanlon and Nagel. The passage cited just previously speaks of a liberal ethic having a "structural...*rather than* substantive character," signifying a sharp distinction between form and content.

A third concern would be over the manner in which the meta-theory functions, not in relation to substantive conceptions of the good "under it", as it were, but in relation to other meta-theories "beside it." Obviously, the pursuit of such alternatives is going to be severely limited, if not rendered impossible, by the liberal meta-theory. This will raise questions about inclusiveness, and perhaps that is one reason Dworkin hardly mentions such a possibility. I say "hardly" because, as we shall see below, such alternative modes of life do make a brief appearance in Dworkin's narrative, though they are dressed up in the garb of fanaticism and irrationalism. Perhaps there is a happy congruence between the categories of "unpopular in our society" modes of life and "fanatical" modes of life. Perhaps not.

In distinguishing form from content with regard to models of ethics, Dworkin may be robbing Peter to pay Paul. To the extent the concerns outlined above can be answered in ways congenial to minimalists, the concerns of perfectionists will only be heightened. And Dworkin *has* promised to pay them too, through the promise of a "muscular" liberal ethic which has more than just the negative virtue of non-exclusion. But if the liberal ethic really is such that it is abstract enough to satisfy the minimalist's concerns, perfectionists will wonder if it is not vacuous. And if it is not vacuous, must it not exclude? Dworkin claims to avoid this dilemma because we can distinguish between "...the philosophical level of ethics, where liberalism takes sides, and more substantive levels, where the side it takes at the philosophical level dictates neutrality."[39] But the distinction between form/content upon which these moves turn is not itself a given, but a position already partly constitutive of a liberal view. As Brian Barry remarks, "If the principle of neutrality were itself neutral between different belief systems and conceptions of the good, we would be home and dry. But this is not so. The principle of neutrality does indeed put them all on the same footing, *but to accept that this is how things ought to be organized it is necessary to have an outlook that is, in broad terms, liberal.* "[40]

The Concept of "Ethical Integrity"

The concept of "ethical integrity" serves an important function in Dworkin's theory. It attempts to steer a middle path between (what are perceived as) the unacceptable alternatives of straightforwardly subjective and objective accounts of ethical value, and purports to yield at once (a) a non-relative account of value which nevertheless (b) is such that morally paternalistic practices upon the part of the state are ruled out. It is another device by which Dworkin seeks to satisfy the demands of what are often thought to be competing perspectives.

Ethical integrity is "...the condition someone achieves who is able to live out of the conviction that his life, in its central features, is an appropriate one for him, that no other life he might live would be a plainly better response to the parameters of his ethical situation rightly judged."[41] A crucial consequence of "giving priority" to ethical integrity is that it results in the stipulation "...that a life that never achieves that kind of integrity cannot be critically better for someone to lead than a life that does."[42] Thus it follows that moral paternalism, that is state action which coerces in the name of the good, can only be irrational and counter-productive; as Dworkin puts it, "...nothing can improve the critical value of a life unless it is seen as an improvement by the person whose life it is."[43]

Dworkin believes that the challenge model of ethics and the notion of ethical integrity which attends it correspond to and imaginatively capture and express many of our fundamental intuitions about ethics. I confess that I find the doctrine of ethical integrity deeply counter-intuitive, and can't help speculating that the significance Dworkin attributes to it is less a function of its intrinsic plausibility than of its pivotal function of, in a single stroke, avoiding both skepticism about value and paternalism. Like most contemporary liberal theorists, Dworkin is anxious that his defense of liberal political principles advocating a spirit of tolerance and generosity toward alternative modes of life not be mistaken for assuming skepticism about the rationality of the distinction between good and bad modes of life, or, heaven forbid, the even more threatening spectre of "moral relativism."[44] Dworkin thus points out to his readers that "recognizing the priority of ethical integrity does not make ethics subjective in the first person, that is, for someone considering how he himself should live." He insists that integrity, rather than licensing the subject to stamp his or her present beliefs with the label of "good," "requires me to reflect from time to time on whether I do find the life I am living satisfactory, and to take doubts and twinges to heart. It also requires me to open my mind to the advice and example of others...."[45] It is not explained why "integrity" requires these things. Of course, one could say that activities such as these are definitionally constitutive of the idea of "ethical integrity," but Dworkin can't afford to say that, for it would be to win a hollow victory for the challenge model of ethics and the liberalism derived from it. Yet I think he does say as much, for all intents and purposes, when he remarks that "...ethical integrity is not a different demand, in the first person, from the demand of ethics itself. I must want to live a good life, and not merely one I think good, to satisfy either."[46] The second sentence cloaks the audacity of the first. The first, by tying "ethics" generally to integrity, results in the conclusion that the challenge model of ethics is superior to the impact model because, given that "integrity" is part of the challenge but not the impact model, the challenge model is the only genuine ethical theory. That is what I meant above by referring to a hollow victory.

Having expressed his anti-relativism, Dworkin defends the other flank of the notion of integrity by arguing that paternalism, or at least the forms of paternalism worth worrying about, cannot be justified on his account. There are three categories of paternalism which Dworkin discusses; I'll label these (i) mild and acceptable, (ii) strong and unacceptable and (iii) deep and unacceptable.

Mild and acceptable paternalism consists of legal requirements "...forcing people to take precautions that are reasonable within their own structure of preferences."[47] Dworkin is brief and casual in his remarks concerning the legitimacy of such action, but the core idea seems to be that paternalism in the service of volitional, rather than critical, interests is unproblematic. He gives the example of seat belt laws, remarking that "...the state makes people wear seat belts in order to keep them from harm it assumes they already want to avoid."[48] Later, he declares that such forms of "superficial paternalism" are "easily defended."[49] My libertarian sympathies are limited, but they do extend to the point of finding fault with Dworkin's somewhat cavalier assumptions about what is obviously sensible with respect to this form of paternalism. The degree of legitimacy of the state "assuming what (people) already want to avoid" is, at the very least, an arguable matter. Moreover, there is, to my nose, an odor of excess disciplinary concern arising from the idea of the state helping people to be more efficient pursuers of the satisfaction of their preferences. Thus, even granting that a form of paternalist policy (x) would in fact increase the degree to which I could achieve the satisfaction of my own freely chosen preferences, I do not think it follows that (x) is thence easily or obviously justified. I may, with (in my view) justification, prefer a lesser "amount" of satisfaction of my preferences if that is the price of maintaining the liberty to frivolously fritter away my time in the face of the threat to that liberty posed by a kindly state bent upon enabling me ("empowering me"?) to act more efficiently.[50]

Strong and unacceptable paternalism is aimed not at volitional but at critical interests, and is the view "...that the state has a right or even an obligation to make people's lives better in the *critical* sense, not only against their will, that is, but against their conviction."[51] Dworkin argues that while the impact model of ethics accepts the theoretical basis of such critical paternalism, the challenge model and its notion of integrity deny it. This is because the idea of integrity denies that "...a person's life can be improved just by forcing him into some act or abstinence he thinks valueless."[52] The doctrine of integrity maintains that "...the right motive or sense is necessary to the right performance."[53] It would follow, then, that critical paternalism is necessarily self-defeating. The doctrine of integrity functions here to allow Dworkin to maintain a commitment to an objective, non-relative account of the value of alternative modes of life while at the same time blocking any justification of critical paternalism which could be grounded in such an account.

Deep paternalism is somewhat different from strong paternalism. As defined by Dworkin, it is "...the suggestion that people should be protected from choosing wasteful or bad lives not by flat prohibitions of the criminal law but by educational decisions and devices that remove bad options from people's view and imagination."[54] Readers familiar with the contemporary literature will recognize this as (part of) the position on paternalism taken by Joseph Raz. The argument that paternalism is self-defeating, used to rebut strong paternalism, will not work here, since deep (or "cultural") paternalism need not directly coerce or legally force individual behavior.[55] Moreover, when deep paternalism is coupled with (as it is in the case of Raz) a defense of moral pluralism, that is, the thesis "...that there are many different and incompatible valuable ways of life,"[56] then paternalism leaves a range of choices open to the agent rather than coercing to a single one. Deep paternalism aims at pruning the menu of choices open to agents, removing bad ones but leaving a plurality of good ones. Thus it is not the will of the agent, but rather the objects of that will's choice, that are affected by such paternalism. Raz's view, defended at great length (and with a great deal more subtlety than I am able to convey here), is that while autonomy is itself a component of the good life for us, it does not automatically convey value on the objects of choice when exercised. In other words, a bad or evil mode of life does not become other than that simply because someone autonomously chooses to live it. According to Raz, autonomy supplies "...no reason to provide, nor any reason to protect, worthless let alone bad options."[57] It is the duty of government, on his view, to enable individuals to "...pursue valid conceptions of the good and discourage evil or empty ones."[58]

Dworkin's response is twofold. First, he argues that paternalist pruning of options is unacceptable on the challenge model because "...a challenge cannot be more interesting, or in any other way a more valuable challenge to face, when it has been narrowed, simplified, and bowderlized by others in advance, and that is as much true when we are ignorant of what they have done as when we are all too aware of it."[59] This argument is inconclusive as it is. Deep paternalism would, in an obvious and mundane sense, "narrow" and "simplify" the choices open to an agent: it would reduce the quantity of such choices.[60] It is an open question, however, as to whether one's choices are "narrowed" or "simplified" in a *morally significant* sense simply because the sheer number of them is decreased. Indeed, choosing amongst alternative, yet irreconcilable, goods is often taken to be a paradigmatic expression of complexity and difficulty, even to the point of tragedy.

Dworkin's second response to deep paternalism is difficult to evaluate because it is difficult to be sure of its meaning. He considers the view that a challenge might be thought more valuable if the chances of selecting a truly good life are improved, as *ex hypothesi* they would be under a successful policy of deep paternalist pruning of options. He responds that this misunderstands the challenge model "profoundly" because it "confuses parameters and limitations."[61] Here is his reply in full:

> It [deep paternalism] assumes that we have some standard of what a good life is that *transcends* the question of what circumstances are appropriate for people deciding how to live, and so can be used in answering that question, by stipulating that the best circumstances are those most likely to produce the really correct answer. On the challenge view, living well is responding appropriately to circumstances rightly judged, and that means the direction of the argument must go in the other way. We must have some *independent* ground for thinking it is better for people to choose in ignorance of lives other people disapprove; we cannot, without begging the question, argue that people will lead better lives if their choices are narrowed. Once that point is grasped, any temptation toward conceptual [sic] paternalism must disappear.[62]

The rhetorical tone of this passage, especially the concluding sentence, suggests that it constitutes an argument providing support for the challenge model of ethics. Yet so far as I can see it is simply a restatement of the difference between the challenge model and the alternative, impact, model. Consider "the point" referred to in the final sentence which, when "grasped," is said to dispel any "temptation" toward deep paternalism. What is this "point," exactly? Referring to the two previous sentences, we see that it is that the challenge model denies what is called a "transcendent" standard of the good life, while the alternative view affirms it. Read carefully, one can see that nothing in the passage even speaks to the issue of which of these two views is correct; the passage merely states the difference between them. Yet when Dworkin refers back to this passage in his summary of this section a few pages later, he writes: "The challenge model *undermines* conceptual paternalism, finally, because that form of paternalism assumes an independent, transcendent picture of ethical value the [challenge] model begins by rejecting."[63] That is a wonderfully revealing sentence. That the challenge model rejects what the alternative accepts is obvious; how that can constitute the activity of "undermining" the alternative model is less so.

The doctrine of ethical integrity is intended to show that strong and deep paternalism are unacceptable, by showing that they are, properly understood, self-defeating. That would be an extraordinarily fortunate conclusion for a liberal of Dworkin's stripe to be able to reach; it would save him or her the trouble of having to choose, and defend the choice, between freedom and virtue. I think this "happy coincidence" quality of the doctrine is itself enough to justify deep suspicion of its validity; in any case, I have tried to show in this section that Dworkin's actual arguments fall short of allaying such doubts, let alone persuading one of the soundness of the challenge model and the doctrine of ethical integrity.

First-person and Third-person Ethics

A third conceptual device by means of which Dworkin pursues LD is the distinction between "first- and-third person" dimensions of an agent's ethical views. The distinction functions so as to enable Dworkin to claim a sense of universality for his liberal ethic even as he grants its partiality. Hence while he acknowledges that the acceptance of the challenge model of ethics would require some people (that is, non-liberals!) to change their third-person ethical views (that is, views about what others should do), he nevertheless claims that the model could be "...generally accepted without people having to abandon *what I believe* is important to them."[64] I leave it to the reader to speculate as to whether those (millions of people) who do not accept the priority of first-person over third-person ethical demands will be comforted at the thought that if they would accept a view premised on that priority they would not have to abandon anything which Ronald Dworkin thinks important to them.

The challenge model would require a shift in the third-person dimension of some people's ethical views because it would require that coercive paternalism in the name of the good be rejected, and some people do not now reject such paternalism. This is to recognize the partiality of liberalism; as Dworkin puts it, liberalism based upon the challenge model is "...not neutral about third-person ethics. It insists, for example, on the proposition I just cited: that no one can improve another's life by forcing him to behave differently, against his will and his convictions."[65] This seeming admission is simultaneously withdrawn, however, when one, according to Dworkin, recognizes nevertheless that "...almost anyone could occupy the position of an ethical liberal without abandoning the heart of his ethical convictions understood in the first person."[66]

The problem with this is that the first-/third-person distinction cannot serve to buttress the appeal of the liberal ethic because it is itself an expression of that ethic, not independent of it. The point is not that third-person views should take priority over first-person views. It is rather that the very conceptualization which allows a person's "ethical views" to be disaggregated into first- and third-person components is already one which bespeaks a liberal point of view. The claim that no one loses anything of significance in accepting the first-/third-person split and the concomitant priority of the first person begs the question. Certainly, anyone who denies the split and that prioritization *would* lose something of significance – his ethical identity as he understands it.

The (to my taste) somewhat unsavory imperial and assimilating flavor of Dworkin's conception of liberalism is seen most vividly when he comments upon (what he sees as) the broad and "ecumenic" appeal of the challenge model of ethics. In an unintentionally ironic passage, he remarks that "...the enduring power of liberalism suggests that the challenge model, or at least central aspects of it, already has a grip on the ethical imagination of a great many people, and reflection should increase its appeal to others."[67] A political theory, says Dworkin, should carry "...consensual promise: we should be able to present it to enlightened democratic politics with some prospects of success."[68] Since, it is argued, people can be more readily expected to change their third-person rather than their first-person views, liberalism is said to fulfill this test of consensual promise. The inclusiveness of this justifiably "optimistic view" is limited only by the recalcitrance of those who would apparently fall outside the bounds of the "enlightened" populace alluded to above, those who comprise the "almost" segment of the populace of which "almost anyone" could be an ethical liberal without abandoning anything of significance. Who are these resisters who, inexplicably, refuse the evident attractions of liberalism? Dworkin tells us in no uncertain terms: "...the fanatic who thinks God will punish him, for eternity, unless he kills us. We must not turn our backs to him, or to his luggage, but he cannot be part of our liberal community."[69] That is an image of non-liberalism well suited to one who maintains what looks like a rather zealous faith in its own right in the liberal desideratum; the terms of liberal order apparently exclude only religiously zealous murderers. Whether it is their disposition toward murder or toward religion which is their greater vice is hard to say.

V

Conclusion

None of the conceptual innovations discussed above seem to me capable of establishing the appeal of the challenge model of ethics. Hence I think Dworkin's continued pursuit of LD is mistaken, and that the choice between Rawlsian minimalism (or something like it) and Razian perfectionism (or something like it) is unavoidable for the liberal.

Of course, one can understand a liberal's desire not to leave it at that, and hence one can understand the appeal of Dworkin's project. Rawls and Raz each attempt to theoretically stop at slippery points on slopes which point toward more unsettling destinations. Beyond Rawls' notion of an overlapping consensus of support for a merely political liberalism lies a less inspiring (though perhaps more realistic) vision of liberal politics as a Hobbesian modus vivendi amongst competing interests and factions. Beyond Raz's defense of autonomy as a constituent component of the good life lies the spectre of an illiberal perfectionism more robust than a liberal might care to stomach.[70] Needless to say, a version of liberal theory which could fulfill LD is a far more attractive prospect than either of those. One might even say that, regarded as a narrative for the purpose of engendering good liberal citizenship, Dworkin's rhetoric in the service of LD is an act of civic patriotism if not a piece of sound philosophy. Even so, it is, it seems to me, an essentially quixotic act, for it is a bit late in the day to suppose that the Protestantism of "ethical integrity" and like notions is sufficient to satisfy and tame the polyglot of demands made in the name of identity so characteristic of contemporary politics. The praise of diversity attendant to liberalism since the mid-nineteenth century appears to be coming home to roost, and the sound of groups scorning the offer of implicitly homogenizing practices like those embodying the first-/third-person split ("...we are going to be who we are...") is likely to haunt liberal ears for the foreseeable future.

NOTES

1. Ronald Dworkin, "Foundations of Liberal Equality," in Grethe B. Peterson, ed., *The Tanner Lectures on Human Values*, vol. 11 (Salt Lake City: University of Utah Press, 1990), pp. 1–119; important companion pieces are Ronald Dworkin, "What is Equality? Part 3: The Place of Liberty," *Iowa Law Review*, vol. 73, no. 1 (1987), pp. 1–54; Ronald Dworkin, "What is Equality? Part 4: Political Equality," *University of San Francisco Law Review*, vol. 22, no. 1 (Fall, 1987),

pp. 1–30; and Ronald Dworkin, "Liberal Community," *California Law Review*, vol. 77, no. 3 (May, 1989), pp. 479–504. The latter piece is responded to by Philip Selznick, "Dworkin's Unfinished Task," and Bernard Williams, "Dworkin on Community and Critical Interests," in the same issue, pp. 505–20. Aside from these, there is a brief critical discussion in Richard J. Arneson, "Liberal Democratic Community," in John W. Chapman and Ian Shapiro, eds, *Democratic Community: Nomos XXXV* (New York: New York University Press, 1993), pp. 197–202. Even briefer, though interesting, remarks of commentary can be found in Ronald Beiner, *What's the Matter With Liberalism?* (Berkeley: University of California Press, 1992), p. 71, and John Rawls, *Political Liberalism* (New York: Columbia University Press, 1993), p. 211.

2. Ronald Dworkin, "Liberalism," in Stuart Hampshire, ed., *Public and Private Morality* (Cambridge: Cambridge University Press, 1978), pp. 113–43.

3. One may wonder at the failure to mention other critical discourses in this context, especially those of feminism and post-modernism. I agree that a serious engagement with either would go a long way toward moderating the passion for LD. The statement in the text, mentioning only communitarians, should be read as an empirical hypothesis regarding the discourses that liberals read, listen to and take seriously. I might wish that hypothesis were false, but I do not think it is.

4. The allusions are to, respectively, Rawls, Nozick and Hegel.

5. Dworkin, "Foundations of Liberal Equality," p. 12.

6. *Ibid*. None of these decisions seem "essentially" or "naturally" personal to me, and obviously marriage and job assignment have been regulated in many societies.

7. *Ibid.*, p. 16.

8. *Ibid.*, p. 17.

9. I am here following Dworkin in using "ethics" to denote the subject matter of living well individually, as distinct from "politics" which denotes issues of collective concern.

10. Dworkin, "Foundations of Liberal Equality," p. 21.

11. *Ibid.*, pp. 53–4.

12. *Ibid.*, p. 54.

13. *Ibid.*, pp. 7–8.

14. *Ibid.*, p. 88; see also p. 53 in this regard.

15. *Ibid.*, p. 57.

16. *Ibid.*, p. 53.

17. *Ibid.*, p. 43.

18. Williams, "Dworkin on Community and Critical Interests," p. 515.

19. Dworkin, "Foundations of Liberal Equality," p. 66.

20. *Ibid.*, p. 67.

21. *Ibid.*

22. *Ibid.*, p. 68.

23. Rawls, *Political Liberalism*, p. 37.

24. See John Rawls, "Justice as Fairness: Political not Metaphysical," *Philosophy and Public Affairs*, vol. 14, no. 3 (Summer, 1985), p. 246. This language has been removed from the text of *Political Liberalism*.

25. Rawls, *Political Liberalism*, p. 197.

26. Other "minimalist" works would include Judith Shklar, "The Liberalism of Fear," in Nancy Rosenblum, ed., *Liberalism and the Moral Life* (Cambridge, Mass.: Harvard University Press, 1991), pp. 21–38, and Charles Larmore, "Political Liberalism," *Political Theory*, vol. 18, no. 3 (August, 1990), pp. 339–60. Other "perfectionist" works would include William Galston, *Liberal Purposes* (Cambridge: Cambridge University Press, 1991), and Stephen Macedo, *Liberal Virtues* (Oxford: Clarendon Press, 1990).
27. Rawls, *Political Liberalism*, p. 175.
28. *Ibid.*, p. 12.
29. *Ibid.*, p. 194.
30. Dworkin, "Foundations of Liberal Equality," p. 13.
31. Rawls, *Political Liberalism*, p. 37.
32. Discussions of Raz's perfectionist liberal theory include: Robert George, "The Unorthodox Liberalism of Joseph Raz," *Review of Politics*, vol. 53, no. 4 (Fall, 1991), pp. 652–71; Margaret Moore, "Liberalism and the Ideal of the Good Life," *Review of Politics*, vol. 53, no. 4 (Fall, 1991), pp. 672–90; Jeremy Waldron, "Autonomy and Perfectionism in Raz's Morality of Freedom," *Southern California Law Review*, vol. 62 (1989), pp. 1130–53; Wojciech Sadurski, "Joseph Raz on Liberal Neutrality and the Harm Principle," *Oxford Journal of Legal Studies*, vol. 10, no. 1 (1990), pp. 130–3; W.J. Waluchow, "Critical Notice of Joseph Raz: The Morality of Freedom," *Canadian Journal of Philosophy*, vol. 19, no. 3 (September, 1989), pp. 476–9.
33. See Joseph Raz, *The Morality of Freedom* (Oxford: Oxford University Press, 1986), especially pp. 110–62 and 401–30.
34. *Ibid.*, p. 390.
35. *Ibid.*, p. 395.
36. *Ibid.*, p. 392.
37. Dworkin, "Foundations of Liberal Equality," pp. 20–1; emphasis added.
38. *Ibid.*, pp. 25–32.
39. *Ibid.*, p. 42.
40. Brian Barry, "How Not to Defend Liberal Institutions," in B. Douglass, G. Mara and H. Richardson, eds, *Liberalism and the Good* (New York: Routledge, 1990), pp. 50–1; emphasis added.
41. Dworkin, "Foundations of Liberal Equality," p. 80.
42. *Ibid.*
43. *Ibid.*, p. 85.
44. This anxiety is usually explained as a consequence of the realization that, as a matter of logic, defenses of liberalism based upon skepticism about the good or relativism are self-defeating. I harbor the suspicion that the more relevant factor at work here is the rhetorical success of the cultural right in the United States over the past decade or so, which has frightened many liberals into confessing publicly their commitment to and belief in the objectivity of morals, along with other good things.
45. Dworkin, "Foundations of Liberal Equality," p. 80.
46. *Ibid.*, p. 81.
47. *Ibid.*, p. 85.
48. *Ibid.*, p. 77.
49. *Ibid.*, p. 85.

50. One could reply: but then *that* is your preference, and hence there's no reason in principle why that could not be accommodated in the considerations concerning the justifiability of (*x*).
51. Dworkin, "Foundations of Liberal Equality," p. 77.
52. *Ibid.*, p. 78.
53. *Ibid.*
54. *Ibid.*, p. 83.
55. See Joseph Raz, *The Morality of Freedom* (Oxford: Clarendon Press, 1986), pp. 157–62.
56. Joseph Raz, "Liberalism, Skepticism and Democracy," *Iowa Law Review*, vol. 74, no. 3 (1989), p. 780.
57. Raz, *The Morality of Freedom*, p. 411.
58. *Ibid.*, p. 133.
59. Dworkin, "Foundations of Liberal Equality," p. 84.
60. Or at least I will grant this for the sake of argument. Actually, it could be the case that removing certain options actually serves to increase the range of quantitative options open to an agent, that is, effectively preventing people from choosing to be drug addicts can have the effect of making more, not less, options open to them.
61. Dworkin, "Foundations of Liberal Equality," p. 84.
62. *Ibid.*, pp. 84–5; I believe the "conceptual" in the final sentence is a typographical error, and that "cultural" was intended. "Cultural" is the adjective used earlier in the text to describe the type of paternalism Dworkin is here arguing against (what I have labelled "deep"), and "conceptual" as an adjective describing a type of paternalism appears nowhere else in the text.
63. Dworkin, "Foundations of Liberal Equality," p. 86.
64. *Ibid.*, p. 112; emphasis added.
65. *Ibid.*, p. 117.
66. *Ibid.*, p. 113.
67. *Ibid.*
68. *Ibid.*
69. *Ibid.*
70. See the suggestive remarks in this vein in Robert George, "The Unorthodox Liberalism of Joseph Raz," *Review of Politics*, vol. 53, no. 4 (Fall, 1991), pp. 652–71.

9   Vulgar Liberalism

Contemporary liberal discourse is dominated by the competition between political (Rawls) and perfectionist (Raz, Dworkin) models. The ignored third party to this conversation is that of what Rawls calls the "modus vivendi" view, or what I refer to here as vulgar liberalism.[1] Both political and perfectionist liberals, as well as critics of liberalism, take it as more or less obvious that this model is deeply deficient. This chapter tries to show that this is not so, and that there is a good deal to be said in defense of "merely" vulgar liberalism.

But is "a good deal" enough? That is more difficult to say. It may well be the case that only those claimed by and devoted to something other than liberalism could be enthusiastic about the appeal of this minimalist type of political liberalism. But that would itself be a telling fact, at least in light of the professed attempt by the ecumenical political liberals to propose terms of political association with broad appeal to more people than simply those who already affirm liberalism as a comprehensive philosophy of life. Vulgar liberalism is less liberal but more political than political liberalism – and therefore more likely to approach the ecumenical end sought by political liberalism itself.

I

During the 1970s, Anglo-American discussion regarding the meaning and justification of a liberal socio-political order centered around the theme of rights versus utility as a possible theoretical foundation for such an order. The signal moment here was Rawls' monumental work, *A Theory of Justice*, and the responses elicited by it. The 1980s saw a turn away from this conflict in terms of the main lines of debate characterizing discussion about liberalism. The signal event here was the communitarian critique of liberalism, one result of which was the increasing degree to which liberals began self-consciously to speak directly to the issue of "defending liberalism." Very broadly, we witnessed a shift from liberals arguing with each other about rights versus utility to liberals exploring alternative ways of rationally defending the faith in the face of challenges from "outside."

At present, we can identify three primary "strategies of liberal self-defense" that have emerged from the dialogue with the communitarians. As these defenses constitute at the same time different understandings of what,

185

in essence, a liberal socio-political order is (that is, they are at once justificatory and descriptive conceptions), I shall refer to them as "models" of a liberal order. They are (1) the modus vivendi model, (2) the neutrality model and (3) the ideal-based model.

I will elaborate and specify these models more carefully. To anticipate, I want to propose that contemporary liberalism would benefit from a deeper recognition of and appreciation for the value of Model 1, the modus vivendi model. This "vulgar" model of liberalism, historically associated with the name of Hobbes, has come to be treated by later liberals as an embarrassment, in ways similar to the manner in which western Marxists have sought to distance themselves from their "vulgar" cousins. I refer here to the complaint by liberals that it is a mistake to suppose that the primary Hobbesian value of civil peace exhausts the set of ideals from which liberals can draw in the attempt to defend their faith.

Critics of liberalism, finding Hobbesian values to be "minimal," "low," "base," "uninspiring," or fit only for "possessive individualists," attack liberalism upon the basis of such judgments. Many liberals have, wittingly or unwittingly, accepted the force of this criticism insofar as they have embarked upon the task of articulating and defending a version of liberalism premised upon the pursuit and/or achievement of loftier and more inspiring ideals, for example self-development, self-realization or autonomy.

This is, I think, a mistake on the part of liberals, who weaken the ultimate adequacy of the liberalism to which they are committed by implicitly accepting the critics' negative portrayal of Hobbes and "vulgar" liberalism. Poorly equipped to underwrite the successful pursuit of "nobler than Hobbesian" ideals, liberal political theory is left vulnerable to decisive criticisms, especially from the left, once it is recast too exclusively in terms of those ideals. My view is that liberals ought to recognize this and cease feeling guilty about it. Hobbesian liberalism is defensible in its own right; liberals ought to let him out of the closet and affirm him as their own. There is less than meets the eye to the new wave of "perfectionist" and "ideal-based" versions of liberalism, and more to be said for "vulgar" liberalism than might first seem apparent.

In Section II, I outline the main features of the neutrality and ideal-based models of liberalism. The absence of the modus vivendi model from this discussion is a reflection of more than an authorial intention to set up the punchline. With a very few notable exceptions, the modus vivendi model lacks contemporary champions, and has come to be treated as something of a straw man. To the extent this is so, the lack of attention it receives in Section II mirrors the distribution of discourse in contemporary political theory generally. Section III begins the attempt to redress this imbalance, by redescribing the neutrality and ideal-based models through the lenses of the modus vivendi model.[2] Though critical of the leading contemporary versions of liberalism, the discussion therein remains within the confines of a framework of understanding which conceptualizes the three models as alternatives to one another. Transcending those confines would entail conceptualizing the three models of liberalism as essentially related parts of a greater whole rather than as alternative whole accounts of liberalism in and of themselves.[3] For the moment, however, I shall rest content with adducing considerations which can lead one to sympathize with Jean Hampton's (somewhat exasperated?) declaration that "I am one philosopher who does not think that calling a methodology 'Hobbesian' is an argument against it."[4]

II

The Reigning Models of Liberal Self-defense

The enterprise of employing "neutrality" as a sort of master concept for elaborating the focal meaning of liberal political theory in a contemporary context was first carried out thoroughly and self-consciously in Ronald Dworkin's important essay, "Liberalism," and in Bruce Ackerman's *Social Justice and the Liberal State*.[5] In a recent review essay, William Galston has provided a nice summary of the aims, achievements and meaning of this endeavor. He summarizes:

> Neutrality of procedure consists in a special constraint on reasons that can be invoked to justify public policy. It stands in roughly the same relation to political deliberation as do rules of evidence to trial advocacy. Specifically, a reason is not publicly valid if it appeals to, or rests upon, the presumed superiority of any particular conception of the good life. A policy is illegitimate if such a conception is an ineliminable element of its proposed justification.[6]

Now while these first efforts at redescribing liberalism in terms of neutrality did indeed reinvigorate the faith, they quickly came under widespread and, in my view, decisive criticism, much of it from self-described liberals. Without purporting to do justice to the intricacy of these arguments, we can nevertheless summarize by saying that the critics' view came down to this: the doctrine of state neutrality with regard to individual conceptions of the good is not itself a neutral position. Rather than *avoiding* the contentious and apparently interminable debate over the issue of the nature of the good life and the appropriate relation between individual and state, liberal neutrality was charged with *constituting* a position within that debate. The rhetorical tenor of such arguments tended to contrast (what was seen as) the somewhat naive and pollyannish perspective of the neutrality theorists with the more robust and self-confident character of ideal-based liberalisms. Where neutrality theories seemed to resemble too closely the apocryphal liberal unable to take his own side in an argument, the ideal-based theories connoted a liberal character willing and proud to take its stand and fight – or at least argue.

Thus, for example, William Galston argued:

No form of political life can be justified without some view of what is good for individuals. In practice, liberal theorists covertly employ theories of the good. But their insistence that they do not reduces the rigor of their theories and leaves the liberal polity unnecessarily vulnerable to criticism.[7]

Similarly, Brian Barry maintains that trying to sell liberalism to non-liberals on the basis of neutrality amounts to fiddling amongst the flames:

If the principle of neutrality were itself neutral between different belief systems and conceptions of the good, we would be home and dry. But that is not so. The principle of neutrality does indeed put them all on the same footing, but to accept that this is how things ought to be organized it is necessary to have an outlook that is, in broad terms, liberal.[8]

The essence of an ideal-based model of liberalism, then, is the specification of a theory of the good life generally as the foundation of a political theory specifying the proper (and improper) activities of the state. To use Dworkin's terms, such a model entails the view that there is *continuity* between the domain of "ethics" (theories of the good life) and that of "politics" (theories of proper state activity).[9] In a moment, we shall consider the case for the alternative strategy of *discontinuity*. It is important to realize, however, that there can be as many ideal-based models of liberalism as there are theories of the good life.

Hence in the contemporary literature there are a number of different versions of the ideal-based model. Joseph Raz has defended a "perfectionist" account of liberal political morality based upon the promotion of individual autonomy which seeks to justify a level of positive state activity significantly beyond the more limited conception of state activity envisioned by neutrality theorists.[10] William Galston, in a series of important articles, has accepted the idea of a continuous link between individual virtue and the liberal polity, sought to specify and defend the components of a specifically liberal theory of virtuous character, and argued for the legitimacy of a program of "civic education" aimed at developing and maintaining such a character.[11] Ronald Dworkin has worked out, with great subtlety, a distinction between what he calls the "challenge model" and the "impact model" of what constitutes a good life, and argued that acceptance of the challenge model serves as the foundation for a liberal theory of politics.[12] Yet another example of an ideal-based model of liberalism has recently been articulated by Will Kymlicka, arguing that the defensibility of a liberal political order follows from "our essential interest in leading a life that is good." Kymlicka uses the conceptual notion of living a life "from the inside" as the basis upon which to elaborate a theory of the good which is treated as the foundation of a defense of a liberal political order.[13]

I make no attempt here to assess the soundness of these accounts. It suffices for present purposes to have a grasp of their structure, the way in which they each pursue the strategy of continuity.

The leading competitor to the ideal-based model is now what might be referred to as the "second generation" of neutrality theories. Two detailed versions are those of Charles Larmore and John Rawls, and we shall take these to serve as exemplars of the model.[14] It is first necessary to clarify the sense in which these theories constitute versions of the neutrality model, given that each has abandoned the more grandiose claims of foundational neutrality which characterized the "first-generation" theories of Ackerman and Dworkin.

While both Rawls and Larmore continue to employ a conception of state neutrality regarding individually held conceptions of the good in the elaboration of their theories, neither claims that this neutrality can encompass the complete range of conceptions of the good, nor does either claim that state neutrality is itself a "neutral value" needing no defense.[15] Thus each recognizes, far more overtly than was the case in first-generation neutrality models, the necessary limits of liberal state "neutrality," and speaks of a "wide range" of allowable conceptions rather than of a complete range.[16] Rawls identifies two ways in which liberal principles of right may function so as to exclude the effective practical pursuit of some conceptions of the good. Some conceptions of the good will be in "direct conflict" with the principles of right, and some will simply "...fail to gain adherents under the political and social conditions of a just constitutional regime."[17]

In line with this circumscribed conception of neutrality, these second-generation models shift the focus of theoretical attention from the issue of "neutrality versus non-neutrality" to that of "political" conceptions of justice versus "metaphysical" conceptions. The latter term refers simply to theories of justice which pursue the strategy of continuity between ethics and politics, that is, to ideal-based models. Political conceptions of justice, on the other hand, are defined by two key features: (i) non-reliance on any "comprehensive moral ideal" (that is, conception of the good) for foundational support and (ii) a sharply drawn separation between the public and private spheres of socio-political life. Thus while at the private level individuals are thought of as "thick" persons with constitutive commitments to particular substantive conceptions of the good about which they may well disagree, as citizens at the public level they are represented as "thin" persons who, abstracting from their particular conceptions of the good, seek the terms of an "overlapping consensus" of principles of right by which they may live as free and equal persons with their various compatriots. The terms of the principles of right are understood as being constituted *without* any reference to the particular conceptions of the good held by the individuals who will live in accordance with these principles; hence the crucial difference between this model and the ideal-based one.[18]

Each model defines itself against the background of the other. From the point of view of the neutrality model, the ideal-based model represents a failure to appreciate fully the range and depth of disagreement regarding the good characteristic of modern cosmopolitan societies, or what Rawls refers to as "the fact of pluralism."[19] As Larmore frames it, "In modern times we have come to recognize a multiplicity of ways in which a fulfilled life can be lived, without any perceptible hierarchy among them. And we have also been forced to acknowledge that even where we do believe that we have discerned the superiority of some ways of life to others, reasonable people may often not share our view."[20] Both Rawls and Larmore include within their understanding of the idea of conceptions of the good life highly formalized conceptions which refer to the way in which a life is lived rather than the particular substance of that life in terms of concrete ends pursued. For example, both use the Kantian notion of the autonomous life and John Stuart Mill's notion of "individuality" as examples of familiar foundations for liberal justice which would be rejected on the neutrality model. Larmore describes the liberalisms of Kant and Mill as "...simply another part of the problem," while Rawls refers to them as "sectarian doctrines."[21] Thus the ideals of the good life utilized by the contemporary ideal-based model theorists discussed above would, despite their highly formal character, be unacceptable foundations for a liberal theory of justice from the point of view of Rawls and Larmore.

On the other hand, from the point of view of the ideal-based model, the neutrality model represents an internally incoherent theoretical formulation which, when properly understood, can be seen to fail at making good its own claims in one of two ways. Either a conception of the good (or "comprehensive moral ideal") is implicitly and unwittingly invoked along the way and traded upon in the formulation of the principles of justice, or, if it is allowed that no such moral foundation is invoked, we are, it is claimed, left with no theory of *justice* or *right* at all, but rather with a prudential peace treaty amongst warring factions, the terms of which carry no force as morally obligatory duties. In the first instance, the neutrality model is said to be only a naive version of the ideal-based model after all; in the second, the spectre of Hobbes is raised and the neutrality model is said to be not a model of political *justice* at all, but a "mere" modus vivendi. Either way, the upshot of the criticism is to advocate conscious pursuit of the strategy of continuity through employment of the ideal-based model as a means of defending liberalism.

Considered as a two-sided argument, my view is that the ideal-based theorists have so far gotten the best of the neutrality theorists, though I make no claim to show that here. I hope only to have made tolerably clear the essential basis of dispute between them. As contemporary debate within liberal political theory is largely taken up, in one way or another, with the dispute between these two models, it is worth noting that a view shared by them is the hostility to what is variously called the "Hobbesian" or "prudential" or "modus vivendi" model of political justice – vulgar liberalism.

That hostility is something that itself needs explaining; in the course of attempting that, I want to try and describe the two dominant models not as they appear in the eyes of their adherents or through the lenses of the opposed dominant model, but as they appear from the point of view within the model of vulgar liberalism. Doubtless such a perspective will only provide a partial and incomplete angle of vision; is the fact that it is so often ignored justification enough for at least having a look?

III

The View From Below

The modus vivendi model of liberalism is the creation of its critics, and it was created for the purpose of allowing them to explain what they are not. It is primarily the neutrality theorists who have concerned themselves with it, for obvious reasons. No one is going to mistake an ideal-based version of liberalism for a "mere" modus vivendi account, since a conception of the good is explicitly posited as the foundation of such accounts. But things are not as clear with regard to the neutrality models. When Rawls renounces "metaphysical" accounts of justice and argues for a "political" conception which aims at securing stability through the achievement of an "overlapping consensus," he appears to be engaged in the, broadly speaking, Hobbesian enterprise of pragmatically looking for ways to insure civil peace and order among those who disagree.

He insists, however, that this appearance is deceiving, and goes to great length to distinguish his idea of a political account of justice from a modus vivendi one.[22] Larmore also distances his theory from such a reading:

We may think of political liberalism as the effort to occupy a point between two extremes. One extreme lies in basing political neutrality, as Kant and Mill did, on individualist ideals claiming to shape our overall conception of the good life, and not just our role as citizens. The other extreme consists in basing political neutrality on solely strategic considerations. In this view, individuals who have different ideals of the good life, but are roughly equal in power, may strike a bargain, according to which political principles to be established will not favor any of these rival ideals. This approach is basically a Hobbesian one, since it aims to ground a moral principle (neutrality) on nonmoral, purely prudential motives.[23]

This passage catches nicely the aversion amongst contemporary liberals to being mistaken for a Hobbesian: such a view is thought not to be "moral," but merely "prudential." Rawls and Larmore each stress that their neutrality theories are not merely pragmatic or prudential. Thus Rawls:

The idea of an overlapping consensus may seem essentially Hobbesian. But against this, two remarks: first, justice as fairness is a moral conception: it has conceptions of the person and society, and concepts of right and fairness, as well as principles of justice with their complement of the virtues through which those principles are embodied in human character and regulate political and social life.... Second, in such a consensus each of the comprehensive philosophical, religious, and moral doctrines accepts justice as fairness in its own way; that is, each comprehensive doctrine, from within its own point of view, is led to accept the public reasons of justice specified by justice as fairness.[24]

I do not fully understand the force of these remarks, and harbor the suspicion that (what seems to me to be) their ad hoc quality arises primarily from the perceived need to make sure one is not mistaken for a Hobbesian rather than from any intrinsic features of the theory itself. Consider the first claim; that Rawls' conception of political justice (hereafter "JAF" for ease of reference) is moral and not Hobbesian/prudential because it utilizes moral concepts. It is of course true that JAF does utilize such concepts, but I cannot see the significance; Hobbes, after all, also gives an account which utilizes the concepts of "right," "justice," and so forth, and the nineteen "Lawes of Nature" adumbrated in Chapters 14 and 15 of *Leviathan* comprise, in effect, an account of virtuous liberal character which compares favorably in terms of depth and specificity with any such account developed by a contemporary liberal theorist.[25] The only argument I can see for refusing to grant Hobbes' account status as a moral account in the sense under discussion here would be one which insisted that because his moral theory is not sharply separated from the theory of power and human passion with which it is (admittedly) bound up, it cannot "properly" be termed moral, and must be seen as an account which "reduces" morality to prudence. But that argument will seem obviously compelling only to someone who has already accepted the Kantian version of the dualism between "morality" and "prudence." Where the Kantian sees "reductionism" when looking at Hobbes, a Hobbesian sees "inflationism" when looking at Kant.

Consider the second claim, that JAF is "moral" in the sense that each of those plural "comprehensive" doctrines of the good, which can accept the terms of the overlapping consensus on principles of right it provides, does so "in its own way...from within its own point of view."[26] The idea here seems to be that the terms of right are accepted because at least some element of the comprehensive moral view (which element is therefore itself "moral") matches or links up with (some parts of? the whole of?) the terms of right. I read this to be a point about *motivation*; the terms of right are accepted, *ex hypothesi*, apart from any calculation of strategic advantage or disadvantage, and hence the appellation "moral."

I have two doubts about the success of this argument. First, if I am right to read it as an argument about the motivations of *agents holding* various comprehensive moral conceptions rather than as an argument about the terms of the comprehensive moral conceptions themselves, then the issue is an empirical and contingent one and cannot be decided by theoretical argument. Consider Jones, who holds comprehensive moral conception X, which, we assume, does contain elements which match or link up with the terms of right in whatever way is sufficient to satisfy Rawls' requirements here;[27] whether Jones' motivation for accepting the terms of liberal right stems from a "moral" appreciation of this linkage and a consequent decision to act in accord with that recognition, or whether it stems from a prudent appreciation of, let's say, the minority power position of Jones and her fellow travelers within the given society, remains an open question.

Second, suppose my reading in terms of motivation is wrong, and we instead take Rawls' point to be one regarding the analytical degree of linkage between the terms of the comprehensive moral conception itself and the terms of liberal right. Then the "argument" for the greater practicality of this "political" conception of justice (relative to ideal-based conceptions) becomes no argument at all, but rather a *description* of analytical linkage or the lack thereof.[28] Moreover, if this second reading were that which constituted the public understanding of justice in a society, it would create perverse incentives for adherents of comprehensive moral ideals which would not fall within the terms of the liberal overlapping consensus to artificially and deceptively "inflate" the terms of their ideal so as to include just enough "liberal material" to establish the necessary degree of linkage to be included. Again, the issue of whether they (or anyone) "really believes and acts upon" these moral components or whether they merely pay lip service to them is ultimately an empirical one.[29] Hobbesian liberals will not worry too much about this. While greatly concerned with stability, they will focus upon behavior rather than attitudes, and upon the coercive power of the liberal state as a means of creating material incentives not to violate the terms of justice rather than upon the existence of "moral" wills disdaining such activity.

Apart from the matter of distinguishing the nature of their neutrality model theories from a Hobbesian modus vivendi model, both Rawls and Larmore also claim a certain practical advantage for their theories over the modus vivendi model. Consideration of this claim will allow us to mount more overtly the fundamentals of a Hobbesian response.

Larmore argues that the Hobbesian approach "...seems inherently unstable, since it is hostage to the shifting distribution of power: Individuals will lose their reason to uphold the agreement if their relative power or bargaining strength increases significantly."[30] Rawls likewise suggests that on the Hobbesian, modus vivendi model, stability comes to depend upon "...happenstance and a balance of relative forces."[31]

In choosing to join the argument with Hobbesians on the particular issue of stability, it seems to me that Larmore and Rawls embark upon an enterprise with about as much prospect of success as that of arguing scripture with the devil. Let us grant that on a Hobbesian model, (i) adherence to principles of justice is necessarily underwritten by a rough balance of power between adherents, (ii) in the absence of such material preconditions, adherence to justice is conceptualized as doubtful at best, impossible at worst, and (iii) even in the presence of such conditions, adherence to justice is conceptualized as fragile and something less than guaranteed. Thus the attainment of political stability/threat of instability is understood not so much as a "problem" which can be "solved" to a greater or lesser degree, but as an inherent condition of political life which can be "coped with" better or worse.[32] Therefore a Hobbesian liberal will grant, up to a point, Rawls' and Larmore's point that stability on his/her model rests upon "a balance of relative forces." But only up to a point; for it is not true on a Hobbesian model, as Larmore claims, that "Individuals will lose their reason to uphold the agreement if their relative power or bargaining strength increases significantly," or as Rawls claims, that stability depends on "happenstance." A rough balance of power provides a necessary motivation for the hypothetical decision to accept the authority of the liberal state, but the existence of such a state brings into being other sources of motivation for adherence; most obviously the threat of punishment for disobedience, but also the actual experience of the benefits of "commodious living" made possible by a system of social and civil order. Now it is true that should the imbalance of power become so great that one group is able to monopolize ownership of the state itself, anything resembling a liberal form of stability would be lost; but it is not true that rough equality of social power is the *only* resource for stability to which a Hobbesian liberal can appeal. My point is that Rawls' and Larmore's formulations tend to overestimate the prospects of instability on a Hobbesian, modus vivendi model of liberalism, because they underestimate the sources of motivation for adherence on such a model.

Apart from this, I think they overestimate the sources of stability provided by their neutrality models of justice. I think this happens because each tends to underestimate the coercive role of the state in their respective accounts of liberal justice and its attendant stability.[33] Stability is seen, on their model, as arising from consensus at the level of *beliefs of citizens*; Rawls, for example, thinks of stability as resting primarily upon the existence of a wide and inclusive overlapping consensus constituted of various pieces of people's *beliefs about the good*. Given such a consensus, stability is postulated as following. The state reflects the terms of that social consensus; benignly insuring it, perhaps, but not creating or building it.

But the link between belief on the one hand and motivation and behavior on the other is simply assumed. It is that assumption which underlies the claim that the neutrality-based model of "political" justice is practically superior to the modus vivendi model because it underwrites stability more securely. This argument hinges on the underlying notion that whereas the modus vivendi model generates only prudential motivations for adherence, the neutrality model generates "moral" motivations, which are, it is postulated, impervious to the distribution of power.

I have one observation about and one objection to the arguments here. First, there is the question of whether there is any such thing as a distinctly moral motivation different in nature from a non-moral or prudential motivation; here again we run up against the issue which divides Kantians from empiricists. I do not purport to judge that debate here, but simply point out that the Kantian position on it (and the further assumption that the moral will is of greater force than the prudential will) underlies the claims advanced by Rawls and Larmore in the name of stability.

Second, and more importantly, even if we grant Rawls and Larmore both those points, I cannot see that either actually gives an account of moral *motivation*, though each seems to assume himself to have done so. That is what I mean by saying the link between belief and motivation is simply assumed on their account; they give an account of belief, but treat it as if it were an account of motivation. With regard to Rawls, for example, what is actually argued is the existence of a descriptive link or match between elements of individual's conceptions of the good and elements of the public conception of justice. But what is not explained is why the existence of that analytical link provides the individual with a motivation (moral or otherwise, for that matter) to adhere to the public conception. For example: suppose my conception of the good is to live the life prescribed by Methodism. Part of this ideal, let us say, is that of showing respect and concern for all others equally, even if they disagree with me. I find that this corresponds to the duty of tolerance as inscribed by liberal justice and embodied in the law of my liberal state. I thus find that my ideal of the good can fit within the overlapping consensus of my liberal state. Still: *how does any of this have anything to do with my motivation for acting in accordance with the laws of that state?* What is the link between a coincidence of beliefs and motivation to act? Why even assume that my motivations to action, whatever they truly are, bear any connection at all to my "conception of the good"?[34] Perhaps I am a sinner in spite of the fact that my conception of the good is saintly – such a condition is not unknown amongst humankind.

Note as well that Rawls' and Larmore's stability arguments assume not simply a link, but an extremely powerful one, between moral belief and motivation, one sufficient to override the force of whatever non-moral motivations move us. In the absence of an explanation of the assumed link between (moral) belief and motivated behavior, I cannot see why there is any reason to accept the argument of Rawls and Larmore that their neutrality accounts are superior to a modus vivendi account of justice in terms of stability.

I can envision two lines of response which might be invoked here. One would be to claim that principles of right are one thing, sources of actual behavior another; does my argument not confuse the "is" with the "ought"? Second, it can be pointed out that Rawls explicitly acknowledges that his theory presupposes upon the part of persons (a) a "sense of Justice" and (b) the desire to act in accordance with it. Hence my objections are beside the point, since the matters I have claimed to be left unaccounted for on his account are actually encompassed within (a) and (b).

My response to the first claim is that in invoking the criteria of "practicality" and "stability" for purposes of assessing the political accounts of justice developed by Rawls and Larmore, and hence in making the issue of motivation a central one, I am simply responding to the invitation they offer, for each, in setting out to bypass "metaphysical" claims, asks us to evaluate in terms of these practical criteria. In response to the second claim, I would remark that for any political theory to simply posit a "sense of justice" and the desire to act in accordance with it would be to ask *something* of its audience; for a political theory which claims as one of its great virtues its practical, non-metaphysical, character, it seems to me to ask an awful lot.

Through the Hobbesian lens, the neutrality model's claim to take seriously the practical problem of ensuring stability in the face of the "fact of pluralism" in the modern world appears unwarranted. A Hobbesian would only wish that we should be so lucky as to face no greater problem than that from which Rawls and Larmore begin. Let me explain.

The "fact of pluralism" for them is constituted by two key conditions; one is the existence in modern constitutional democracies of a diversity of views about what constitutes the good life.[35] These views are referred to as "conceptions of the good," or "comprehensive moral ideals." Second, there is the claim that no such view could be made the foundation of the public conception of justice without employing the "oppressive use of state power."[36] Hence the task of avoiding any ideal-based account of liberal justice.

I suggest that this is quite a sanitized understanding of the degree to which pluralistic conflict threatens social and political stability. The picture connoted by formulations such as "disputes about the nature of the good life" and "alternative conceptions of the good" is a relatively benign and pacific one, and I think that point holds even if it is granted for the sake of argument that the Hobbesian account of the state of nature, which constitutes a very different conceptualization of the "fact of pluralism," is an extreme one. To conceive of the central threat to the stability of a liberal, constitutional order as disagreement about the nature of the good life is to think of liberal political life as if it were analogous to a philosophical debate amongst friends. With our attention focused upon the fact that they disagree about the concrete answer to the question of the good life, it is easy to overlook just how much social order is implicitly being assumed when we suppose that *that* question is the root of conflict and the threat to stability. This is not a picture of people fighting over wealth, or power, or race, or ethnicity, or selfishness, or greed, or vainglory, or – well, just about anything people actually fight over in the real world. It is in fact a picture which resembles more than anything else the, relatively speaking, genteel disagreements amongst contemporary political philosophers about the viability of liberal political theory! Is it really the case that the continued stability of existing liberal regimes is in any way whatsoever dependent upon a professor of political philosophy's ability to define the terms of an overlapping consensus amongst alternative conceptions of the good life? I want to be careful to avoid a possible misunderstanding of my point here. I do *not* wish to align myself with those who complain that the concerns of contemporary political philosophers are not "political" enough, that they are "alienated" from actual political life. I am content to have political philosophers talk about whatever they like, and if they want to talk about strategies of justification, or epistemological aspects of liberal theories, or any of the other "abstract" issues which so infuriate those critics who would wish them to be more "engaged," so be it. My complaint is rather that Rawls and Larmore have themselves fallen prey to the pleading for making political theory practical and useful, with what seem to me unfortunate results. One of those is the very rarefied picture of political conflict described above. If a political theory does choose to concern itself with the subjects of political conflict and stability (a very different thing than concerning itself with actually contributing to stability and the avoidance of conflict), then surely it has got to recognize that what is going on "out there" is not well captured by the idea of "disagreement about the good life." Perhaps to call it instead a "war of all against all" is to go too far in the opposite direction; but it still seems to me closer to capturing the truth of the matter.

Moreover, I suggest that the Hobbesian proposition that a rough equality of power is a necessary precondition for a stable liberal order is a highly plausible one, and that Rawls and Larmore are too hasty in their dismissal of it.[37] They maintain that stability on the modus vivendi account is always fragile because a shift in the distribution of power would give that group which, let us say, gained a great deal of it an incentive to "rewrite" the terms of the social contract so as to benefit itself. I grant that a Hobbesian modus vivendi model of liberal justice would provide no guarantee against this occurrence; what I fail to see is (a) how any other model does provide such a guarantee and (b) why there is reason to believe that the fallen world in which we live is not actually like this. Rawls' and Larmore's point is that if people had a moral rather than a prudential motivation to adhere to the terms of liberal justice, they would not rewrite the terms of justice in their favor even if they came to possess the degree of power which would make it possible for them to do so. I grant that that is true, but it is simply true by definition, that is, *if* people act on the basis of what is right rather than on the basis of what serves their interests, *then* they will not take advantage of others even when they could get away with it.[38] Still, it is difficult to see how an overlap between elements of a person's full conception of the good and elements of the terms of public justice provides reason to think people will actually be so motivated.

Certainly such behavior is much to be desired, but a Hobbesian model of liberal justice will not count too heavily on it when assessing the means of stability, on the suspicion that it presumes "...a generosity too rarely found to be presumed on, especially in the pursuers of Wealth, Command, or sensuall Pleasure; which are the greatest part of mankind."[39] A Hobbesian strategy for maintaining the rough equality of power necessary to underwrite liberal justice would be twofold. On one hand, the state itself would manipulate the conditions giving rise to the distribution of power in society so as to attempt to maintain the requisite balance of power. On the other hand, the problem is that of securing protection for social groups against the agency of the state itself, for it too represents a potential dominating power; this points in the direction of the familiar liberal palliatives of separating powers and checks and balances. It is true that these directives point in contradictory directions, but that result is simply in the nature of the beast; the political art of maintaining a balance between liberty and order is just that.

Now of course this sketch of a Hobbesian model of *liberal* justice is not exactly equivalent to the account of justice Hobbes himself actually gave. The second strategy identified above, that of securing protection against the agency of the state, is notoriously that which Hobbes has been criticized for ignoring ever since Locke pointed out that in doing so he (Hobbes) was in effect supposing "...that men are so foolish, that they take care to avoid what mischiefs may be done them by pole-cats, or foxes; but are content, nay, think it safety, to be devoured by lions."[40] My plea must thus be for some latitude in employing the notion of a Hobbesian model of liberal justice (as opposed to Hobbes' model of justice per se). I appeal to the spirit, not always the letter, of Hobbes' particular views. In doing so, I follow the generous (and in my view right-minded) example of Rawls himself, who fortunately provides an excellent and succinct definition of the Hobbesian model of liberal justice. Identifying Montesquieu, Hume, and Madison as Hobbesian in spirit in the sense employed here, he writes: "Occasionally I refer to the Hobbesian strand in liberalism, by which I mean the idea that ordered liberty is best achieved by skilful constitutional design framed to guide self- (family-) and group-interests to work for social purposes by the use of various devices such as balance of powers and the like."[41] This definition allows us to frame the issue of defending liberalism in a way which joins the central issue directly. Rather than arguing over whether Hobbes (or anyone else) is a liberal or not according to (what must of necessity be) a stipulative definition, we can, as Rawls does and as I wish to do here, join the issue of whether the Hobbesian spirit of seeking and relying upon a rough equality of power as the linchpin of a liberal order is superior or inferior to the two rival approaches.[42]

While Rawls maintains that his model of liberalism is directed to the practical task of "mediating society's deepest conflicts"[43] and trying to "conceive how social unity can be both possible and stable...in a society marked by deep divisions between opposing and incommensurable

conceptions of the good,"[44] a Hobbesian liberal will surmise that if citizens
are civilized to the point that the deepest sources of conflict amongst them
are their arguments about the nature of the good life, then all in all things
are going pretty well. Similarly, Larmore's neutrality model, by his own
account, rests upon the hypothesis that citizens are committed to the twin
values of "rational dialogue" and "equal respect."[45] The former supposes a
willingness upon the part of citizens who disagree about the good to abstract
from disputed propositions and search for common ground so as to continue
the conversation; the latter supposes a willingness upon the part of the
powerful to continue to converse with those who are "strange and weak."[46]
A Hobbesian liberal will think that the latter invocation of value is the
practical problem of insuring a rough equality of power being wished away,
while the former tends to downplay the fact that there will always be those
willing to just fight about it instead. What distinguishes the Hobbesian
liberal from the neutrality model liberal here is not so much that the Hobbesian
does not share the hope that people should accept the terms of liberal justice
and obey them for "moral" reasons, but rather that s/he does not ground the
faith in such hopes, and instead looks for those "auxiliary precautions" that
might supply "the defect of better motives."[47]

It will be complained that "auxiliary" precautions quickly become more
than that, that the development of better motives is precluded by the (implicit)
sanctioning of the legitimacy of lesser ones which a Hobbesian approach
embodies. There is force to that complaint; what defines a Hobbesian liberal
is not that he denies that, but rather that he discounts it in light of what he
sees as the potential price of misplaced hopes. Or to put it in the terms of a
contemporary policy dispute embodying this difference in views: the
Hobbesian approach is to distribute condoms rather than preach abstinence.
There is a price to either choice.

What of ideal-based models of liberalism viewed from below? Insofar as
they represent, relative to neutrality models, a liberalism secure enough
with itself to openly proclaim, profess and enforce the components of the
creed which are constitutive of itself, rather than cloak these under the gentle
rubric of neutrality, I think a Hobbesian has cause to look favorably upon
them. On the other hand, the Hobbesian will view the neutrality model's
concern with the attainment of the mundane good of stability as salutary
relative to the tendency of ideal-based liberalisms to generate scorn for it.
Hobbesians take the measure of civil polity by the yardstick of the *summum
malum*, and on that instrument the mark labelled "civil peace" is not preceded
by the adjective "mere." When liberalism is conceived according to the
image of some conception of the *summum bonum*, there is a tendency to forget

that that mark is not a given in human affairs but an (always incomplete) achievement of human artifice. Amnesia regarding the fragility of human order can create a space which the love of ideals (and idols) fills to overflowing. Where great expectations are both generated and unfulfilled, guilt is often the consequence, part of which manifests itself as an aversion to "mere" Hobbesian liberalism. There are, to be sure, goods greater than civil peace and personal security; but here, a Hobbesian liberal will join neutrality theorists in doubting, if not fearing, that these should be made the stuff of politics.

A liberal order cannot even nearly fulfill the longings of the heart and soul which move us; but a Hobbesian liberal will see no reason either to say things which suggest it can or to feel particularly remorseful about not saying them. She will not begrudge those who search for or find "autonomy," "individuality," "liberation," or even their "own true self;" but given the "warped wood"[48] of which the liberal ship is constructed, she will think it worth a great deal simply to see it sail – even if many of the passengers, (relatively) warm and (somewhat) dry above the raging waves and endless depths, do not. Perhaps she will even come to imagine some far shore where there might be rest for the weary. Perhaps not.

NOTES

1. John Gray has recently written a number of essays giving eloquent voice to this idea under the label of "pluralism." See especially *Enlightenment's Wake* (Oxford: Oxford University Press, 1995).
2. These lenses are the same ones Hobbes attempted to provide in *Leviathan*, and which are spoken of explicitly in Chapter 18: "For all men are by nature provided of notable multiplying glasses, (that is their Passions and Self-love,) through which, every little payment appeareth a great grievance; but are destitute of those prospective glasses, (namely Morall and Civill Science,) to see a farre off the miseries that hang over them, and cannot without such payments be avoyded;" Thomas Hobbes, *Leviathan*, ed. C.B. Macpherson (Harmondsworth: Penguin Classics, 1968), p. 239. Similar lenses serve Judith Shklar in her sympathetic portrayal of "the liberalism of fear," the point of view from which one "...may, thus, be less inclined to celebrate the blessings of liberty than to consider the dangers of tyranny and war that threaten it;" Judith Shklar, "The Liberalism of Fear," in Nancy Rosenblum, ed., *Liberalism and the Moral Life* (Cambridge, Mass.: Harvard University Press, 1989), p. 27; see also George Kateb, "Hobbes and the Irrationality of Politics," *Political Theory*, vol. 17, no. 3 (August, 1989), pp. 355–91.

3. Such an approach is sketched in Thomas Spragens, *Reason and Democracy* (Durham, N.C.: Duke University Press, 1990), p. 254.

4. Jean Hampton, "Should Political Philosophy be Done Without Metaphysics?," *Ethics*, vol. 99, no. 4 (July, 1989), p. 807.

5. Ronald Dworkin, "Liberalism," in Stuart Hampshire, ed., *Public and Private Morality* (Cambridge: Cambridge University Press, 1978), pp. 113–43; Bruce Ackerman, *Social Justice and the Liberal State* (New Haven, CT: Yale University Press, 1980); for a discussion of Rawls in terms of his relation to the "neutrality enterprise," see Joseph Raz, *The Morality of Freedom* (Oxford: Clarendon Press, 1986), pp. 117–34.

6. William Galston, "On Liberalism," *Polity*, vol. 23, no. 2 (Winter, 1990), pp. 320–1.

7. William Galston, "Defending Liberalism," *American Political Science Review*, vol. 76, no. 3 (September, 1982), p. 621.

8. Brian Barry, "How Not to Defend Liberal Institutions," *British Journal of Political Science*, vol. 20, pt. 1 (January, 1990), p. 8.

9. Ronald Dworkin, "Foundations of Liberal Equality," in Grethe B. Peterson, ed., *The Tanner Lectures on Human Values*, vol. 11, 1990 (Salt Lake City: University of Utah Press, 1990), p. 6.

10. Joseph Raz, *The Morality of Freedom*, especially pp. 369–430.

11. William Galston, "Liberal Virtues," *American Political Science Review*, vol. 82, no. 4 (December, 1988), pp. 1277–91; "Public Morality and Religion in the Liberal State," *PS*, vol. 19, no. 3 (Fall, 1986), pp. 807–24; "Civic Education in the Liberal State," in Nancy Rosenblum, ed., *Liberalism and the Moral Life* (Cambridge, Mass.: Harvard University Press, 1989), pp. 89–102.

12. Dworkin, "Foundations of Liberal Equality."

13. Will Kymlicka, *Liberalism, Community, and Culture* (Oxford: Clarendon Press, 1989), pp. 12–13.

14. Charles Larmore, *Patterns of Moral Complexity* (Cambridge: Cambridge University Press, 1987); Charles Larmore, "Political Liberalism," *Political Theory*, vol. 18, no. 3 (August, 1990), pp. 339–60; John Rawls, "Justice as Fairness: Political not Metaphysical," *Philosophy and Public Affairs*, vol. 14, no. 3 (Summer, 1985), pp. 223–51; John Rawls, "The Idea of an Overlapping Consensus," *Oxford Journal of Legal Studies*, vol. 7, no. 1 (Spring, 1987), pp. 1–27; John Rawls, "The Priority of Right and Ideas of the Good," *Philosophy and Public Affairs*, vol. 17, no. 4 (Fall, 1988), pp. 251–76. For a discussion see Margaret Moore, "Justice for Our Times," *Canadian Journal of Political Science*, vol. 23, no. 3 (September, 1990), pp. 459–82.

15. Thus Larmore, in *Patterns of Moral Complexity*, p. 44: "Its (the liberal state's) neutrality is not meant to be one of *outcome*, but rather one of *procedure*. That is, political neutrality consists in a constraint on what factors can be invoked to justify a political decision."

16. Rawls, "The Priority of Right and Ideas of the Good," p. 258; Larmore, *Patterns of Moral Complexity*, p. 60.

17. Rawls, "The Priority of Right and Ideas of the Good," p. 265; compare with Larmore, *Patterns of Moral Complexity*, p. 43.

18. The formulation in the text follows Rawls; compare with Larmore, *Patterns of Moral Complexity*, p. 45.

19. See John Rawls, "The Idea of an Overlapping Consensus," pp. 3–5.

20. Larmore, *Patterns of Moral Complexity*, p. 43; compare with Rawls, "The Idea of an Overlapping Consensus," p. 4.
21. Larmore, "Political Liberalism," pp. 343, 345; Rawls, "Justice as Fairness: Political not Metaphysical," p. 246.
22. See Rawls, "The Priority of Right and Ideas of the Good," pp. 274–5; "Justice as Fairness: Political not Metaphysical," pp. 278–80; "The Idea of an Overlapping Consensus," pp. 9–12.
23. Larmore, "Political Liberalism," p. 346; compare with the very similar formulation announcing an intention to "steer a course between the Hobbesian strand in liberalism and a liberalism founded on a comprehensive moral doctrine," in Rawls, "The Idea of an Overlapping Consensus," p. 23. In his earlier book, *Patterns of Moral Complexity*, Larmore referred to his preferred account of justice *as* a "modus vivendi" theory. In this article, he uses the term "political liberalism" to describe it, and points out that all along his view has been close to that of Rawls (see pp. 358–9). In short, what Larmore referred to as a "modus vivendi" account in the book is *not* what Rawls meant by the term, and Larmore has changed the label in order to avoid confusion.
24. Rawls, "Justice as Fairness: Political not Metaphysical," p. 247. Compare with Larmore, "Political Liberalism," p. 346.
25. For example, the tenth law of nature, which teaches that "...at the entrance into conditions of Peace, no man require to reserve to himselfe any Right, which he is not content should be reserved to every one of the rest.... The observers of this law, are those we call MODEST, and the breakers Arrogant men;" (ch. 15, p. 212). This format is followed throughout; the Laws of Nature amount to an account of the virtues and vices of character attendant to those persons who "acknowledge one another for his Equall by Nature," – that is, to liberal persons.
26. Rawls, "Justice as Fairness: Political not Metaphysical," p. 247.
27. I note that no such account of what *degree* of "matching" or "linking up" is necessary to constitute "moral" adherence to the overlapping consensus is provided by Rawls or Larmore. As I read them, the degree assumed amounts to, in effect, whatever is necessary to achieve the appellation "moral", that is, whatever is necessary to be described as non-Hobbesian.

    Now this is no small issue. If the "degree condition" were defined along the (Kantian) lines of proceeding from a noumenal will untainted by phenomenal desire, the claim of these theorists to be working out a conception of justice more "political" and "practical" than that of the ideal-based theorists would be rendered highly questionable; if, on the other hand, the definition of the "degree condition" is relaxed to allow for such considerations, it is hard to see why Hobbes has to be pushed out of the picture.
28. It is this consideration which leads me to think that the "motivation" reading of the argument must be the preferred one on the terms of Rawls' and Larmore's theories.
29. I grant, though, that in the long run this may actually work out to be the opposite of a perverse incentive; that to which the parents pay lip service may become that which the children believe. "Modern pluralistic regimes have typically come into being, it is increasingly recognized, not because of some preexisting wide consensus on 'basic values,' but rather because various groups that had been at each other's throats for a prolonged period had to recognize their mutual inability to achieve dominance. Tolerance and acceptance of pluralism resulted

eventually from a standoff between bitterly hostile opposing groups;" Albert O. Hirschman, *The Rhetoric of Reaction: Perversity, Futility, Jeopardy* (Cambridge, Mass.: Harvard University Press, 1991), p. 168.

30. Larmore, "Political Liberalism," p. 346.

31. Rawls, "The Idea of an Overlapping Consensus," p. 11.

32. For critical discussion of the view that "solving problems" is the appropriate task of political theory, see Tracy Strong, *The Idea of Political Theory* (Notre Dame: University of Notre Dame Press, 1990), pp. 110–15.

33. My remarks here were stimulated by the discussion in Jean Hampton, "Should Political Philosophy be Done Without Metaphysics?," pp. 799–807.

34. It could be objected here that my reading of the idea of a "conception of the good" is misguided, and that this term is best understood as simply describing whatever ends in life a person actually does pursue. On that reading, there could be no gap between belief and motivation/action, by definition; we define a person's "conception of the good" in terms of their actual behavior. However: if that reading is employed to meet my objection here, then one would consequently no longer be able to invoke the claim that the overlapping consensus is moral rather than prudential because it is comprised of elements of individuals' (moral) "conceptions of the good."

35. For Rawls, see "The Idea of an Overlapping Consensus," pp. 3–8; for Larmore, *Patterns of Moral Complexity*, pp. 42–50.

36. Rawls, "The Idea of an Overlapping Consensus," p. 4; it is the second feature which distinguishes the neutrality model from the ideal-based model.

37. Do I understand Hobbes as claiming (1) that rough equality of power is a necessary precondition for justice or (2) that humans are in fact so equal that we can use that equality for the establishment of political justice? The famous passage on equality opening Chapter 13 of *Leviathan* can be, and has been, read in both ways; my own understanding is closer to (1). I think Hobbes treats rough equality of power as a task to be achieved socially rather than as a natural or ontological fact. I think he also knew that one way of achieving it socially would be to rhetorically present it as if it were a natural or ontological fact. I think this is what he does in Chapter 13. Note that the defense of the postulate of natural human equality therein closes on a note of wry wit: "For there is not ordinarily a greater signe of the equall distribution of any thing, than that every man is contented with his share."

38. The reader may find it hard to believe that my portrayal of their position can be fair here. But consider carefully the exact language of the following statement by Rawls designed to show how his account of justice as an overlapping consensus is superior to a modus vivendi account in terms of insuring stability (the passage alludes to a hypothetical example of an overlapping consensus amongst three comprehensive moral ideals which Rawls uses for purposes of illustration):

> The preceding two aspects (moral object and moral grounds) of an overlapping consensus connect with a third aspect, that of stability: that is, those who affirm the various views supporting the political conception *will not* withdraw their support of it should the relative strength of their view in society increase and eventually become dominant. *So long as the three views are affirmed and not revised, the political conception will still be supported regardless of shifts in*

the distribution of political power. We might say: each view supports the political conception for its own sake, or on its own merits; and the test for this is whether the consensus is stable with respect to changes in the distribution of power among views. This feature of stability highlights a basic contrast between an overlapping consensus and a modus vivendi, the stability of which does depend on happenstance and a balance of relative forces. (Rawls, "The Idea of an Overlapping Consensus," p. 11; emphasis added)

It is easy to be carried along by the drift of the language here, but I believe the entire paragraph is tautological, as is evidenced by careful attention to the passages underlined.

39. Hobbes, *Leviathan*, ch. 14, p. 200.
40. John Locke, *Second Treatise of Government*, ed. C.B. Macpherson (Indianapolis: Hackett Publishing Company, 1980 (1690)), ch. 7, par. 93, p. 50.
41. Rawls, "The Idea of an Overlapping Consensus," p. 2.
42. To forestall a possible misunderstanding, let me point out that the "minimalist" version of liberal theory being expressed here should not be confused with, or taken to be an endorsement of, Nozick's or other libertarian, rights-based, forms of anti-welfare state "liberal minimalism." Hobbes' state is not a night-watchman whose essential, and only legitimate, function is the protection of (supposed) pre-political property rights. Indeed, Hobbes' political theory is, as I understand it, perfectly consistent with state activity in the form of redistributing wealth and power. Libertarians, Locke being the most famous, have always recognized, and of course complained about, that aspect of Hobbes' views. I differ from them in counting it as one of his virtues as a thinker. Hobbes' "minimalism" is about the ends which one can expect a liberal order to achieve; it is not a minimalism about the means, in the form of the extent of state activity, which can be employed in attaining those ends. Thus what I am calling "Hobbesian liberalism" is not the same as libertarian liberalism.
43. Rawls, "The Idea of an Overlapping Consensus," p. 24.
44. Rawls, "Justice as Fairness: Political not Metaphysical," p. 251.
45. Larmore, *Patterns of Moral Complexity*, pp. 58–62.
46. *Ibid.*, p. 60.
47. James Madison, "Federalist #51," in C. Rossiter, ed., *The Federalist Papers* (New York: New American Library, 1960), p. 322.
48. Kant, speaking of human nature; "Idea for a Universal History with a Cosmopolitan Purpose," in Hans Reiss, ed., *Kant's Political Writings* (Cambridge: Cambridge University Press, 1970), p. 46.

Index

207